# THE
# IMITATION
# OF CHRIST

# THE
# IMITATION
## OF CHRIST

# THOMAS àKEMPIS

**Bridge-Logos**
Alachua, Florida 32615  USA

# Bridge-Logos

Alachua, Florida 32615 USA

*The Imitation Of Christ*
by Thomas à Kempis

Rewritten and updated by Harold J. Chadwick

Copyright 1999 by Bridge-Logos Publishers

Library of Congress Catalog Card Number: 98-074679
International Standard Book Number: 978-0-88270-766-2

Printed in the United States of America.

# Contents

## Book One
### Advice Useful For a Spiritual Life

## Book Two
### Advice About Internal Things

## Book Three
### Internal Consolation

## Book Four
### Exhortation to Receive Holy Communion

# FOREWORD

This is a marvelous book!

It is filled with scripturally-based maxims and spiritual concepts that will lead any honest seeker as deep into the inward life with Christ as it is possible for a human being to go. Some have said that with the exception of the Bible this is the most helpful spiritual book ever written. Not long ago it was being printed every day of every year somewhere in the world.

In recent years, however, the popularity of *The Imitation of Christ* has waned, due perhaps not only to the secular nature of this age, but also to the vocal and written changes in our modern English language that have made it more difficult to understand the spiritual maxims and concepts it contains. As we have moved further away from familiarity with its words and sentence structures, the valuable maxims and concepts it contains have become increasingly cloudy and vague.

That is the reason why we have revised and rewritten *The Imitation of Christ*, and issued it in a plainly written and easy to understand Pure Gold Classic version. Valuable maxims and concepts that are in themselves sometimes difficult to understand, should not be written in words and sentences that are difficult to understand. When this is done, the double struggle of reading and understanding can so frustrate and dishearten the most determined reader that the book is laid aside to gather dust. The most valuable writing in the world is of no value if it is too difficult to read and understand. And this is a most valuable book!

This Pure Gold Classic version of *The Imitation of Christ* is not a book for Kempis' purists. It is a book for those with open and seeking hearts, for those who desire to know and follow Christ deeper than they ever have before, and for those who are more interested in the help and guidance of its marvelous spiritual maxims and concepts than in the preservation of Kempis's choice of language.

When Kempis wrote his material he addressed it to men in a male-dominated age, and most purists insist that it remain male-oriented even though we are hopefully passing beyond that time of men's illusions of superiority. One current version states that women have had no trouble understanding Kempis's writing down through the centuries, and all modern women readers have to do is adjust their thinking sufficiently to apply the material to themselves. But surely Kempis himself would not have thought that way if he were writing today, and surely God does not think that way either. So for this Pure Gold Classic version, Kempis's material was rewritten to be gender-neutral. The only places where the words "man" or "men" is used is in Scripture quotations, and a time or two when Kempis tells a story about a man.

Kempis also addressed most of his material to monks in monasteries—not a vocation and location that applies to most readers of *The Imitation of Christ* today. For that reason his material was rewritten as much as possible to apply to anyone of any vocation and location.

It has been said that Kempis used and alluded to between 850 and 1000 Scriptures verses, but most versions of *The Imitation of Christ* do not provide the scriptural references to those versions. In this Pure Gold Version, we have included over 1000 Scripture references and notes. These appear at the end of each chapter

Many of the Endnotes contain multiple Scripture references, and where the reference is to a book in the Apocrypha, the verse has been included, since most Protestant Bibles do not contain the Apocrypha. Also, throughout *The Imitation of Christ*, words have been added to the text in brackets [ ] to clarify the text or add additional thought to it.

At the beginning of *Imitation* we have also added a selection of devotional excerpts from the entire text, both as a sampling of what is contained throughout the book, and as a mini-book of devotional meditations within the book. The excerpts are referenced to the main text by Book (Kempis divided *Imitation* into four Books), chapter, section, and subsection.

While reading *The Imitation of Christ*, it should be kept in mind that Thomas à Kempis was a Roman Catholic monk writing to Roman Catholic monks in pre-Reformation times, and so his material contains many references to the doctrines of that church—doctrines that at times are contrary to Protestant doctrines. But most of the material in this truly great book is applicable to all faiths, for it mainly deals with our relationship to Christ and how to increase and deepen that relationship until it is a true wonder upon the earth. For this reason, wherever it was possible without doing a great disservice to Brother Kempis's Roman Catholic doctrines, his material was revised to embrace all Christians—and hopefully offend the beliefs of none. I pray it was done successfully.

Having lived with a 16th century edition of *The Imitation of Christ* for nearly six months, reading and rereading each word and sentence several times, comparing the text to more recent versions, checking the meanings of hundreds of words in my computer dictionary, checking every Bible reference for accuracy, searching several versions of the Bible whenever there seemed to be a non-referenced Bible quotation or an allusion to Bible text, checking every Apocrypha reference, and then revising and rewriting each sentence several times until I was certain this modern language version was as close to Kempis's meaning as it could be, I think I developed a strong sense of the heart of that good and godly man. The more I did, the more I worked from his heart to my heart—and I pray to your heart.

One final word. This book should not be read like a novel or a magazine, scanned quickly or read in large amounts at one time. It contains marvelous inspirational and motivational maxims and concepts that should be read as you would read the Book of Proverbs—slowly, carefully, and meditatively.

*First*, read a small portion—no more than a numbered section, and preferably only a paragraph or a sentence. *Second*, meditate upon what you have read—think deeply about it, turn it over and over in your mind. (There are some who say they don't know how to meditate, but if you know how to worry, you know how to meditate. Worry is simply negative meditation, so do the opposite of that when you read from this book.) *Third*, pause and be still for a while and sense the nearness of God in what you have read. (In the Book of Psalms that is what is meant by the word *Selah*.) *Fourth*, resolve to amend your inward attitudes and outward actions in the light of what you have read and your new understanding.

If you will do that, this book will change your life for the better. It has mine.

Harold J. Chadwick

# THOMAS à KEMPIS

Thomas à Kempis (1379/80 – 1471) is remembered for one literary work: *The Imitation of Christ*. He probably wrote the four books (sections) that comprise it sometime between 1420 and 1427–since the first hand-written manuscripts appeared around 1427.

By 1450 over 250 hand-written copies had been made. In 1472 the first printed edition was made using Johannes Gutenberg's new method of printing with moveable type. From that point on the book spread rapidly across the European continent. A French edition was printed in Paris in 1481 and an Italian edition in Italy in 1483–followed by 50 more Italian editions before the end of the 16th century.

By the end of the 19th century, 300 editions had been printed in Italian, 350 in German, 600 in Latin, several hundred in French, and hundreds more in English. By 1779 there were at least 1800 editions and translations. There is no telling today how many times the book has been translated and edited or how many versions there have been.

The first English version of *The Imitation of Christ* was translated from Latin in 1460 by an unknown translator who left out the fourth book. This was a hand-written manuscript. In 1502, William Atkinson, a Cambridge scholar, produced the first printed English version, but also left out the fourth book. Then Lady Margaret Beaufort, mother of King Henry VII, translated the fourth book from a French version in 1503. Her work was combined with Atkinson's, and the resulting complete book was reprinted many times in the early 16th century. Over the years since then, Thomas à Kempis's book has been translated and printed in over fifty languages.

Among the translators was John Wesley (1703-1791), founder of Methodism, who was so certain the book was the best summary of a disciplined Christian life that he translated it for his followers. It is doubtful if there is any great Christian leader, past or present, Roman Catholic or Protestant, who has not read *The Imitation of Christ.*

At the beginning of this century, it was said that *The Imitation of Christ* was being printed somewhere in the world every day. This is no longer true in this day of hyper-active Christianity and increasing secularism in the Church, both of which are contrary to the internal life of Christ and the quiet times of contemplation and reflection that it demands. Yet there are signs here and there of an inward stirring of many of God's people, a growing hunger to know the Christ-within the way the ancient saints knew Him, and to draw apart from today's religious noise and clamor to quietly meditate upon Christ and experience the joy and wonder of that inward peace that He promised all who would believe in Him: "Peace I leave with you; my peace I give you" (John 14:27). It is to show the way to that peace that Thomas à Kempis wrote this book.

Thomas à Kempis was born Thomas Hamerken about 1380 in the walled city of Kempen near Cologne, Germany. It is from his birthplace that his later name was taken: Thomas of Kempen, or as it is used in the Latin version, Thomas à Kempis. As a youth he studied in his mother's school for children. Then in 1392 he traveled by himself—some say he walked—eighty miles to the town of Deventer in the Netherlands (Low Countries, which also includes Belgium and Luxembourg), where he hoped to join a small religious community founded by Gerard Groote and now directed by Master Florentius Radewijns. His older brother, Jan, had made the trip several years earlier.

The community order—the Brethren of the Common Life—was noted for its Latin studies and the copying and illustrating of manuscripts. Even at this early age Thomas longed for an education and the quiet life of reading and study. In his latter years he often declared, "I sought for rest but never found it, except in a little corner with a little book."

The Brethren of the Common Life was founded by Gerard Groote to counter the lukewarmness that had developed in the faith of the Roman Catholics in the Low Countries. He wanted to revitalize the faith that the Dutch formerly had, and so his movement took on the name "New Devotion" (*Devotio moderna*). It was not an attempt to change Roman Catholic doctrine, but to renew faith in it's doctrines and in the hearts of Catholics in that region.

After Groote's death in 1385, Florentius Radewijns became head of the Brethren community in Deventer. He also continued as a canon in the local church, and continued to live in the religious community with other clerics and several laymen. Their purpose was to instill the principles of the "New Devotion" in the people with whom they worked.

The Brethren lived peaceful lives, never publicly protested against anything, never responded to public uprisings or demonstrations of any kind, and never were inflammatory as some of the reformers were, such as Martin Luther. They preached love, obedience, and humility, occupied themselves with compassionate good works, fed the hungry, sheltered the homeless, and cared for the sick. They encouraged public reforms by secular people, while they worked for reforms within the church and monastic orders. They were committed to good education and established Brotherhood schools all over Germany and the Low Countries.

Unlike the "begging friars" who were so common in those days, the Brethren worked at regular trades and supported their community with their income. Noted for their skills at copying and illustrating manuscripts, they were often hired as copyists or artistic illuminators of manuscripts, both religious and secular. The money they earned went into a common fund for the order. Although they practiced the contemplative life, in practical, everyday, affairs, the Brethren of the Common Life stressed charitable Christian service.

When Thomas arrived at Deventer in 1392, he learned that his brother, Jan, was no longer there, but had left to join the Brethren of the Common Life, and since 1390 had been a canon at their monastery in Windesheim, which was about twenty miles north of Deventer. So Thomas traveled there, and after meeting Jan, told him of his desire to study. Jan suggested that he go to Master Florentius Radewijns in Deventer and wrote a letter for him to present to Florentius.

So Thomas returned to Deventer and presented himself and his brother's letter to Master Florentius, who accepted him into the community. Although Thomas had no money and could not pay for his room and board, the kindly Radewijns, perhaps somehow glimpsing in the young Thomas what he was destined to become, said he could stay in the community without charge until a suitable residence was found for him in the city—the community facilities were not large enough to house both the Brethren and school students. Florentius arranged for Thomas to attend the academy of Jan Boehm, and provided the school books and paid the fee for Thomas to continue his education. He also found him residence at the home of a pious woman in Deventer. A few years later, however, he was able to return to the community and live there.

Of his time with the Brethren, Thomas wrote: "All I earned I gave to the community; the rest I needed [for books and fees] was given by Florentius. Here I learned to read and write the Holy Scriptures and books on moral subjects, but it was chiefly through the sweet conversation of the Brethren that I was inspired yet more strongly to despise the world."

Thomas completed his studies in 1399, seven years after he arrived in Deventer. Earlier that year, his brother, Jan, had been elected to the priorship of the recently founded Brethren monastery of Mount St. Agnes, at Agnetenberg, beyond the walls of the city of Zwolle. At Florentius' suggestion, Thomas visited his brother there and requested admission into that community. Having become familiar with the spirituality of the Brethren of the Common Life through Florentius's community, he was eager to join with them in their way of life. He was accepted into the community immediately.

From the beginning, Thomas—who was now known as Thomas à Kempis, or Thomas of Kempen—devoted himself to participating in the life of the Brethren. He shared their hours of prayer and work, and learned not only how to copy liturgical and devotional books, but also manuscripts that the community needed for their own library or to sell.

In 1406, on the feast of Corpus Christi, which is a feast in honor of the Eucharist that is celebrated on the first Thursday after Trinity Sunday, Thomas was accepted into the congregation of the Canons Regular of St. Augustine and received its white habit.

In 1408, he took their three vows of religion—poverty, chastity, and obedience.

Then in 1413, at the age of 33, he was ordained a priest. Twelve years later he was made sub-prior of the monastery, and was given the responsibility of training the novices. For a while he also served as treasurer (procurator), but apparently had little liking or talent for that position, and was soon relieved of it by his superiors. Except for a three-year exile, Thomas spent his entire religious life at Mount St. Agnes.

Until his death on July 25, 1471 at the age of ninety-two, Thomas gave his life to acts of devotion, copying manuscripts, writing letters, hymns, and biographies, counseling others, and creating his enduring work *The Imitation of Christ*. Several dozen other devotional works also flowed from his pen, including: *Prayers and Meditations on the Life of Christ, The Soul's Soliloquy, The Garden of Roses, On Solitude and Silence, The Elevation of the Mind,* and *On the Three Tabernacles*. He also made a copy of the entire Bible in five volumes—the work spanned a period of 14 years from 1425 to 1439, and is still preserved in the library at Darmstadt, a city of southwest Germany southeast of Frankfurt

In the Chronicle of Mount St. Agnes it is written about Thomas à Kempis' death, "having completed on the feast of St. James the Greater, the 92nd year of his age, the 63rd of his religious life, and the 58th of his priesthood."

His body was interred on the monastery grounds, but 200 years after the Reformation, the monastery having been long destroyed, his remains were transferred to Zwolle, where they still reside in the Church of St. Michael. In 1897 a monument was erected over them, with an inscription in Latin that translates: "To the honor, not the memory, of Thomas à Kempis, whose name is more enduring than any monument."

*The reliquary with the relics of Thomas à Kempis.*

*Monument on Mount Saint Agnes in Zwolle. "Here Thomas à Kempis lived in the service of the Lord and wrote* The Imitation of Christ.

# DEVOTIONAL MEDITATIONS FROM THE IMITATION OF CHRIST

If you want to fully and feelingly understand the words of Christ, you must endeavor to conform your life wholly to the life of Christ. (Book One, 1:2c)

I had rather *feel* compunction than know its definition. (Book One, 1:3c)

It is vanity [meaningless] to wish for a long life, and to be careless about living a good and useful life. (Book One, 1:4d)

It is vanity [meaningless] to be concerned with only this present life, and not to consider those things that are to come. (Book One, 1:4e)

If you know yourself well you will become lowly in your own sight and not delight in the praises of others. (Book One, 2:1c)

Many words do not satisfy the soul, but a good life comforts the mind, and a pure conscience inspires confidence in God. (Book One, 2:2d)

If you think you have great understanding and knowledge, understand also that there are many things that you know nothing about. (Book One, 2:3c)

The highest and most profitable learning is true knowledge and understanding of ourselves. (Book One, 2:4a)

The more you are at harmony within yourself and become inwardly simple, the more you will understand higher things without effort, for you will receive intellectual light from above. (Book One, 3:3a)

A humble knowledge of yourself is a surer way to God than an involved intellectual search after learning. (Book One, 3:4b)

Those who are little in themselves and do not care about being given honor are truly great. (Book One, 3:6f)

It is also great wisdom not to believe everything that you hear, and not to immediately tell others what you have heard or believe. (Book One, 4:2b)

The more humble we are in ourselves, and the more subject we are to God, the more prudent we will be in all our affairs, and the more we will enjoy peace and quiet in our hearts. (Book One, 4:2e)

Each word of the Scriptures must be read with the same spirit in which it was written. (Book One, 5:1b)

If you desire to benefit from the Scriptures, read with humility, simplicity, and faithfulness—never with a desire to become known as a Bible scholar. (Book One, 5:2d)

Whenever we desire anything excessively, we become restless within ourselves. (Book One, 6:1a)

Those who indulge in their sensual desires are soon burdened by a guilty conscience because they yielded to their passions, which did not bring them the peace they were trying to obtain. (Book One 6:2a)

Do what you are able to do, and God will help your good effort. (Book One, 7:1d)

If there is any good in you, believe that there is much more in others, so that you will stay humble in yourself. (Book One, 7:3c)

The humble enjoy continual peace, but the hearts of proud people are disturbed by envy and frequent hostility. (Book One, 7:3e)

We think sometimes that we please others by our presence, but instead we offend them with those bad qualities that they discover in us. (Book One, 8:2c)

I have often heard that it is safer to listen and accept counsel than it is to give it. (Book One, 9:3a)

Why do we so willingly speak and talk one with another, when we seldom stop speaking before we have hurt our conscience? (Book One, 10:1d)

Evil habits and neglect of our own spiritual progress cause us to speak too freely in thoughtless ways. (Book One, 10:2d)

We are too much led by our passions, and too concerned about temporary things. (Book One, 11:2c)

Our [spiritual] fervor and progress should increase daily, but now it is regarded as something great if we retain even some part of our first zeal. (Book One, 11:5c)

When good people are afflicted, tempted, or troubled with evil thoughts, then they understand better the great need they have of God, realizing that without Him they can do nothing that is good. (Book One, 12:2b)

All saints passed through many tribulations and temptations, and are benefited because of that. (Book One, 13:2b)

It is no great thing if we are devout and fervent when we are not afflicted, but if during adversity we bear ourselves patiently, there is hope then of great progress in grace. (Book One, 13:8b)

An old habit is not easy to break, and none of us are willing to be guided further than we can understand. (Book One, 14:3a)

Without love, external works are of no profit, but whatever is done out of love, no matter how little or contemptible it is in the sight of the world, becomes wholly fruitful. (Book One, 15:1c)

Endeavor to be patient in enduring the failures and weaknesses of others, no matter what kind they are, for you yourself have many failings that must be endured by others. (Book One, 16:2b)

Times of adversity best reveal how much righteousness or strength we have. (Book One, 16:4b)

The lives of good religious people should be adorned with all moral excellence and righteousness, so that they will inwardly be the same as they seem outwardly. (Book One, 19:1a)

If those who firmly purpose often fail, what will those do who seldom purpose anything or purpose with little resolution? (Book One, 19:2b)

No one rules securely except those who are willing to be ruled. (Book One, 20:2g)

It is better for you to live privately and take care of yourself than it is to neglect your soul even though you could work wonders in the world. (Book One, 20:6d)

A happy going out often brings an unhappy going home, and a joyful evening often makes a sad morning. (Book One, 20:7c)

Keep your eyes on yourself first, and be especially sure to admonish yourself before you admonish any of your close friends. (Book One, 21:3b)

If you would often think of your death instead of your living long, there is no question but that you would be more zealous to improve [spiritually]. (Book One, 21:5a)

Our happiness does not consist in having an abundance of temporal goods, for a moderate amount is enough for us. (Book One, 22:2c)

One moment you resolve to be more careful how you act, and a short while later you behave as though you had never had any such purpose at all. (Book One, 22:6c)

You should arrange yourself and all your thoughts and actions as if today you were going to die. (Book One, 23:1e)

Be assured that you cannot have two paradises—it is impossible to enjoy excessive pleasures in this world and reign with Christ in the next world. (Book One, 24:6k)

Be careful and strenuous to avoid those things in yourself that frequently displease you in others. (Book One, 25:4d)

Remember, in the same way that you watch what others do, others watch what you do. (Book One, 25:5c)

You will always rejoice in the evening if you spend your day profitably. (Book One, 25:10g)

When you have Christ you are rich and have all you need. He will be your faithful helper in all things and provide all your future needs so that you will not need to rely upon others. (Book Two, 1:2d)

Those that take your part today will be against you tomorrow, and often they change directions like the wind. (Book Two, 1:3b)

Put all your trust in God, let Him be your fear and your love, and He will answer for you and will do what is best for you. (Book Two, 1:3c)

If Christ was willing to suffer and be despised, how do you dare to complain about anyone? (Book Two, 1:5b)

Those who are well organized and settled within themselves are not bothered by the strange and perverse behavior of others. (Book Two, 1:7e)

If you can suffer in silence, you will without doubt see that the Lord will help you. (Book Two, 2:1d)

Do not think that you have made any [spiritual] progress unless you feel that you are inferior to all others. (Book Two, 2:2e)

Keep yourself in peace first, and then you will be able to bring peace to others. (Book Two, 3:1a)

You know well how to excuse and color your own deeds, but you are not willing to accept the excuses of others. (Book Two, 3:2a)

There are two things that lift a person up from earthly things: simplicity and purity. (Book Two, 4:1a)

We often do wrong, and then do something even worse by excusing ourselves. (Book Two, 5:1d)

A soul that loves God despises all things that are inferior to God. (Book Two, 5:3e)

Have a good conscience and you will always have joy. (Book Two, 6:1b)

The glory that is given and received from people is short-lived. (Book Two, 6:2b)

You are not more holy when you are praised, or more worthless when you are disparaged. (Book Two, 6:3b)

Love Jesus and keep Him for your friend, for when all others go away He will not forsake you or allow you to perish in the end. (Book Two, 7:1e)

The poorest person is the one who lives without Jesus, and the richest person is the one who is in favor with Jesus. (Book Two, 8:2f)

Love everything for Jesus' sake, but Jesus for Himself. (Book Two, 8:4a)

The greatest saints before God are the least in their own judgments; and the more saintly they are, the more humble they are within themselves. (Book Two, 10:4b)

Many love Jesus, so long as adversities do not happen to them. (Book Two, 11:1g)

Rarely is anyone found who is so spiritual as to be stripped of love of all earthly things. (Book Two, 11:4a)

No one can relate to the suffering of Christ as much as the person who has suffered like Him. (Book Two, 12:4d)

Prepare yourself to endure many adversities and various kinds of trouble in this difficult life, for that is the way it will be with you wherever you are, and you will find it that way no matter where you hide yourself. (Book Two, 12:10b)

Our worthiness and the development of our spiritual condition does not lie in many delights and comforts, but rather in enduring through great afflictions and tribulations. (Book Two, 12:14e)

Blessed are the ears that eagerly listen for the breath of the divine whisper, and do not pay attention to the many whisperings of this world. (Book Three, 1:1c)

The world promises things that are temporary and inferior, and it is served with great eagerness—I [God] promise things most high and eternal, and yet the hearts of people are not receptive. (Book Three, 3:2c)

Fear nothing, blame nothing, flee nothing as much as your faults and sins, which should be more displeasing to you than losing earthly goods. (Book Three, 4:3d)

Love is a great thing, yes, and thoroughly good—by itself it makes everything light that is heavy, and endures evenly everything that is uneven. (Book Three, 5:3a)

Nothing is sweeter than love, nothing more courageous, nothing higher, nothing wider, nothing more pleasant, nothing fuller or better in heaven and earth, for love is of God and can rest only in God, who is above all created things. (Book Three, 5:3f)

Love is swift, sincere, affectionate, pleasant, amiable, courageous, patient, faithful, prudent, long-suffering, and never seeks its own. (Book Three, 5:7a)

It is better and safer for you to conceal the grace of devotion, not to exalt yourself or speak or think much about it, but rather to despise yourself and fear that it has been given to someone unworthy of it. (Book Three, 7:1a)

It is better to have little understanding and a small amount of good sense with humility, than to have great treasures of learning with conceited self-complacency. (Book Three, 7:3c)

Not every inclination that seems good should be followed immediately, nor should every contrary feeling be rejected immediately. (Book Three, 11:2b)

The lesser of two evils should always be chosen. (Book Three, 12:2b)

Because you still love yourself excessively, you are afraid to submit yourself completely to the will of others. (Book Three, 13:2a)

Not all the world can make those proud whom the truth has made subject to itself, and those who have set their entire hope in God cannot be moved by the praises of others. (Book Three, 14:4d)

You cannot be satisfied with any temporal goods because you were not created to enjoy them. (Book Three, 16:1g)

The more you willingly accept suffering, the wiser you act and the greater is the reward you will receive—and if you have diligently prepared yourself in mind and habit to accept suffering, the more easily you will endure it. (Book Three, 19:2a)

The world is often blamed for being deceitful and foolish, and yet no one easily parts with it because the desires of the flesh are too powerful. (Book Three, 20:4d)

Those who consider themselves the most wicked of all people, and judge themselves to be the most unworthy, are the most fit to receive the greater blessings. (Book Three, 22:2d)

Do not judge the words or actions of others rashly, and do not involve yourself in things that are not your concern—by doing this you will scarcely or seldom be disturbed. (Book Three, 25:1g)

If you come to the place of complete contempt for yourself, then you will enjoy as much peace as you are capable of having in this earthly life. (Book Three, 25:3f)

Understand that love of yourself hurts you more than anything in the world. (Book Three, 27:1b)

If you look for this or that, or want to be here or there, so you can better enjoy your own pleasure and benefit, you will never be at rest or free from troubled thoughts, for there will be something lacking in everything, and in every place there will be someone to afflict you. (Book Three, 27:2c)

Do not let your peace depend on the words of people, for whether they speak well or ill of you does not make you a different person. (Book Three, 28:2a)

It is useless and unprofitable to be either disturbed or pleased about future events, which perhaps will never happen. (Book Three, 30:2f)

When you think that almost everything is lost, often your greatest reward is close at hand. (Book Three, 30:3f)

Unless we are lifted up in spirit, freed from all creatures, and wholly united to God, whatever we know and have are of no great importance. (Book Three, 31:2b)

It is of great hindrance that we rest in [spiritual] signs and things perceived by the senses, and have little concern about perfectly humbling ourselves. (Book Three, 31:3b)

Nature looks at the outward things of a person, grace looks at the inward things. (Book Three, 31:5c)

Keep this short and perfect word: "Give up everything and you will find everything." (Book Three, 32:1d)

Most people talk a great deal, and therefore little trust should be placed in them. (Book Three, 36:1c)

Fear God, and you will not be frightened by people. (Book Three, 6:3b)

You must rule and control your actions, not let them rule and control you—as if you were a slave or a hireling. (Book Three, 38:1b)

True [spiritual] progress consists in denying yourself, and those who have so denied themselves live in great freedom and security. (Book Three, 39:3a)

The further you withdraw from human consolation, the nearer you come to God. (Book Three, 42:1f)

Never read the Word so you can appear more knowledgeable or wiser. Study it to learn of your sins and how to discipline yourself, for this will benefit you more than knowing the answers to many difficult questions. (Book Three, 43:1c-d)

It is more beneficial to turn your eyes away from unpleasant things, and to leave every person to their own opinion, rather than be caught in quarrelsome conversations. (Book Three, 44:1c)

Many have been known for their virtue and have been hurt by being too hastily commended for it. (Book Three, 45:6a)

Because you are afraid of being despised, you will not accept reproof for your faults and you try to hide in excuses. (Book Three, 46:1f)

Behold, if everything that could be maliciously invented was said against you, how much would it hurt you if you let it pass and gave it no more consideration than you would a blade of grass? Could those words remove as much as one hair from your head? (Book Three, 46:2d)

It is often your duty [to God] to do what you would rather not do, and to leave undone what you wish to do. (Book Three, Part 3, 49:4e)

How is a person ever better by being considered great by people? The deceitful flatter the deceitful, the proud exalt the proud, the blind commend the blind, the weak magnify the weak—and in so doing, each person deceives the other and increases their shame while foolishly praising them. (Book Three, 50:8b-c)

Everyone indeed desires what is good, and assumes there is some good in their words and deeds—therefore, because of the assumption of good, many are deceived. (Book Three, 54:1b)

Woe to those who disdain to humble themselves willingly with the little children, for the low gate of the kingdom of heaven will not allow them to enter. (Book Three, 58:10a)

Whatever You would give Me [Christ] besides yourself is of no value to Me, for I seek you and not your gifts. (Book Four, 8:1d)

God often gives in one short moment what He denied for a long time—sometimes He gives at the end what He deferred granting at the beginning of your prayer. (Book Four, 15:1c)

Sometimes it is not a weighty matter that obstructs and hides grace from us, but a small matter—that is, if anything can be called small that hinders such great good. (Book Four, 15:2d)

Anyone ... who lifts up their intention to God with a simple heart, keeps clear of all immoderate liking or disliking of created things, will be the most fit to receive grace and will be qualified for the gift of true devotion. (Book Four, 15:3b)

It is a blessed simplicity when a person leaves the difficult way of questions and disputes and goes forward in the plain and firm path of God's commandments. (Book Four, 18:2a)

Faith is required of you, and a sincere life, not lofty understanding or deep inquiry into the mysteries of God. (Book Four, 18:2c)

Submit yourself to God and humble your understanding to faith, and the light of knowledge will be given you to the degree that is profitable and necessary for you. (Book Four, 18:2e)

God walks with the simple, reveals Himself to the humble, gives understanding to the little ones, opens the perception of pure minds, and hides [His] grace from the curious and proud. (Book Four, 18:4c)

Human reason is weak and can be deceived, but true faith cannot be deceived. (Book Four, 18:4d)

God, who is eternal and incomprehensible, and of infinite power, does great and unsearchable things in heaven and on earth, and there is no tracing out [visible sign] of His marvelous works. (Book Four, 18:5c)

If all the works of God were such that they could easily be understood by human reason, they could not justly be called marvelous or inexpressible. (Book Four, 18:5d)

## BOOK ONE

# ADVICE USEFUL FOR A SPIRITUAL LIFE

## 1
### IMITATING CHRIST AND DESPISING ALL THE WORTHLESS THINGS OF THE WORLD

"He who follows Me, walks not in darkness,"[1] says the Lord. These are the words of Christ by which we are told that we should imitate His life and manners[2] if we want to be truly enlightened and delivered from all blindness of heart.

Let our chief endeavor, therefore, be to meditate upon the life of Jesus Christ.

2. The doctrine of Christ exceeds all the doctrines of the saints, and the one that has His Spirit will find in it a hidden manna.[3]

There are, however, many who often hear the gospel of Christ and are little affected by it because they lack the Spirit of Christ.[4]

But if you want to fully and feelingly understand the words of Christ, you must endeavor to conform your life wholly to the life of Christ.

3. What good will it do you to debate the Trinity [see note[5]] wisely if you lack humility and are thereby displeasing to the Trinity?

It is not understanding that makes a person holy, it is a virtuous life that makes one dear to God.

I had rather *feel* compunction than know its definition.

If you knew the whole Bible by heart, and the sayings of all the philosophers, what would all that profit you without the love of God[6] and without grace?[7]

"Vanity of vanities . . . all is vanity" [see note[8]], except to love God and serve him only.

This is the highest wisdom—to disdain the world and hurry toward the kingdom of heaven.

4. It is vanity, therefore, to seek after perishing riches and to trust in them.

It is also vanity to seek after honors and to desire to climb to high positions.

It is vanity to follow the desires of the flesh, and to labor for those things for which you will later be severely judged.

It is vanity to wish for a long life, and to be careless about living a good and useful life.

It is vanity to be concerned with only this present life, and not to consider those things that are to come.

It is vanity to love things that speedily pass away, and not to hurry in the direction where everlasting joy abides.

5. Think often about the proverb, "The eye is not satisfied with seeing, nor the ear filled with hearing."[9]

Make an effort, therefore, to remove your heart from the love of visible things, and to turn yourself to those things that are invisible.[10]

For those who follow their evil passions stain their consciences and lose the favor of God.

1   John 8:12
2   1 Corinthians 11:1
3   Colossians 1:27
4   2 Corinthians 3:17
5   The doctrine of the union of three divine persons, the Father, Son, and Holy Spirit, in one God.
6   1 Corinthians 13:2
7   Ephesians 2:8
8   Ecclesiastes 1:2—The NIV translates this verse: "Meaningless! Meaningless!" says the Teacher. "Utterly meaningless! Everything is meaningless." The word *vanity* also refers to something that is vain, futile, useless, frivolous, or worthless.
9   Ecclesiastes 1:8
10  Hebrews 11:27

# 2

## THINK HUMBLY OF YOURSELF

All naturally desire knowledge,[1] but what good is knowledge without the fear of God?

Surely humble peasants [see note[2]] who serve God are better than proud philosophers who strive to understand the ways of the universe and neglect their own souls.

If you know yourself well you will become lowly in your own sight and not delight in the praises of others.

If I understood all things in the world and had not love, what help would that be to me in the sight of God who will judge the things that I do?[3]

2. Stay away from any unreasonable desire for knowledge, for in it there is great distraction and deception.

Scholarly people like to appear scholarly to others, and to be thought of as being wise.[4]

There are many things that you can know that are of little profit to your soul, and you are very unwise if you concentrate on anything other than those things that benefit your salvation.

Many words do not satisfy the soul, but a good life comforts the mind, and a pure conscience inspires confidence in God.

3. The more you know and the better you understand, the more severely you will be judged, unless your life is also holy.

Do not praise yourself, therefore, because of any knowledge or talent you may have, but rather let the knowledge and talent make you humble and careful.

If you think you have great understanding and knowledge, understand also that there are many things that you know nothing about.

Do not appear to be very wise, but rather admit your own ignorance.[5]

Why prefer yourself before others, since there are many who are more knowledgeable and skillful in the Scriptures than you are?

If you want to know or learn anything profitably, then desire to be unknown and to be little esteemed by others.

4. The highest and most profitable learning is true knowledge and understanding of ourselves.

It is great wisdom and perfection to esteem ourselves as nothing, and to always think well and highly of others.

If you see another person sin openly, or commit a serious crime, you should not think as yourself as better, for you do not know how long you will be able to remain in good circumstances.

We are all frail,[6] but you should think of no one as being frailer than yourself.

1 Ecclesiastes 1:13
2 In Kempis's day, a peasant was a member of a class of small farmers, farm tenants, sharecroppers, and laborers on the land—and often considered to be an uncouth, crude, or ill-bred person.
3 1 Corinthians 13:3
4 1 Corinthians 8:1
5 Romans 12:16
6 Genesis 8:21

# 3

## THE DOCTRINE OF TRUTH

Happy is the person who is taught by truth alone, not by figure and words that pass away, but as truth is in itself.

We are often deceived by our own opinions and senses, and so we discern little by them.

What good is it to dispute greatly about secret things that are hard to understand, when we will not be reproved on the day of judgment for things that we are ignorant about?

It is foolish to neglect the things that are beneficial and necessary to us, and give our minds to things that arouse our interest and damage us—we have eyes but cannot see.[1]

2. And what have we to do with *genus* and *species*? [2] He to whom the Eternal Word speaks is delivered from a world of unnecessary thoughts.

From that Eternal Word are all things, and all things speak of Him—and He is the Beginning, Who also speaks to us.

Without that Word no one understands or judges rightly.

The person to whom all things are Him, who reduces all things to Him, and who sees all things in Him, enjoys a quiet mind and remains at peace in God.[3]

*O God, who art the truth, make me one with Thee in everlasting love.*

*It is often tedious to me to read and hear many things: in Thee is all that I would have and can desire.*

*Let all theologians hold their peace, let all creatures be silent in Thy sight, speak Thou alone unto me.*

3. The more you are at harmony within yourself and become inwardly simple, the more you will understand higher things without effort, for you will receive intellectual light from above.[4]

A pure, sincere, and calm spirit is not distracted by doing many things, because it works all things to the honor of God—and since it is inwardly still and quiet, it does not seek to satisfy itself in anything it does.

What, indeed, hinders and troubles you more than the undisciplined desires of your own heart?

Good and godly people arrange within themselves ahead of time those things that they must do;

Not being moved in keeping with the desires of an evil disposition, but in keeping with the guidance of right reason.

Who struggles more than those who strive to overcome themselves?

This should be our endeavor: to conquer ourselves, and daily to grow stronger and to make a further growth in holiness.

4. Every perfection in this life has some imperfection mixed with it, and none of our knowledge is without some darkness.

A humble knowledge of yourself is a surer way to God than an involved intellectual search after learning;

Yet learning is not to be condemned, and the mere knowledge of something is not to be disliked. Learning is good in itself and ordained by God, but a good conscience and a virtuous life should always be preferred before it.

However, because many endeavor to get knowledge rather than live well, they are often deceived and get no or very little benefits.

5. If we put as much effort into rooting out our vices and implanting virtues as we do in trying to solve questions, there would not be so much hurt caused, or such disgraceful incidences in the world, or so much moral looseness practiced in religious organizations.

Truly, at the day of judgment we will not be examined for what we have read, but for what we have done;[5] not for how well we have spoken, but for how virtuously we have lived.

Tell me now, where are all those theologians and teachers that you knew so well when they were alive and famous for their knowledge?

Others have now taken their places and perhaps scarcely ever think about them. While they were alive they seemed to be important people, but now they are seldom mentioned.

6. Oh, how quickly the glory of the world passes away![6]

Oh, that their life had been in keeping with their knowledge!—then their study and reading would have been worthwhile.

There are many who perish because they care more about fruitless knowledge[7] in this world then they do about serving God.

And because they choose to be great rather than humble, they therefore become futile in their thoughts.[8]

Those who are great in love are truly great

Those who are little in themselves and do not care about being given honor are truly great.[9]

Those who count all earthly things as dung so that they may gain Christ are truly wise.[10]

Those who do the will of God and forsake their own wills are truly learned.

1 Psalm 115:5
2 Kempis may have been referring to matters of biology, or disputes about the outward appearance or form of the Eucharistic elements that is retained after their consecration. For long before his time the doctrine that the bread actually turned into the flesh of Christ was strongly disputed. See John 6:50-57; John 6:60-66.
3 Philippians 4:7
4 Matthew 11:25, Luke 10:21
5 Matthew 25:14-46
6 Ecclesiastes 2:11
7 Titus 1:10
8 Romans 1:21
9 Matthew 8:4, 23:11
10 Philippians 3:8

# 4

## Wisdom and Forethought in Our Actions

We must not listen to every saying or suggestion,[1] but with caution and patience we should ponder everything in keeping with the will of God.

But alas!—it is our weakness that we often rather believe and speak evil of others than believe and speak good.

Those that are perfect do not easily believe everything that a person tells them, for they know that human frailty is prone to evil[2] and likely to be defective when the person speaks.[3]

2. It is great wisdom not to hurry in your course of actions,[4] and not to be obstinate about your own opinions;

It is also great wisdom not to believe everything that you hear, and not to immediately tell others[5] what you have heard or believe.

Consult with the person who is wise and conscientious, and seek the advice of those who are better than yourself rather than depending on your own resources.[6]

Living a good life makes us wise before God,[7] and gives us experiences in many things.[8]

The more humble we are in ourselves, and the more subject we are to God, the more prudent we will be in all our affairs, and the more we will enjoy peace and quiet in our hearts.

1  1 John 4:1
2  Genesis 8:21
3  James 3:2
4  Proverbs 19:2
5  Proverbs 17:9
6  Proverbs 12:15
7  Proverbs 15:33
8  Ecclesiastes 1:16

# 5
## THE READING OF THE HOLY SCRIPTURES

Truth, not eloquence, is to be sought for in reading the holy Scriptures.

Each word of the Scriptures must be read with the same spirit in which it was written.[1]

We should search the Scriptures for those things that will give us spiritual benefits rather than superior speech.

We should read plain and devout books as willingly as high sounding and profound ones.

Do not be offended by the authority of the writer, whether a person of great or small learning, but let the love of pure truth encourage you to read.[2]

Do not search for who spoke this or that, but focus on what was said.

2. People pass away, but the truth of the Lord remains forever.[3]

God speaks to us in different ways, without respect of those through whom He speaks.[4]

Our own curiosity often hinders us when we read the Scriptures, causing us to waste time examining and discussing things that we should simply read and pass over without undue attention.

If you desire to benefit from the Scriptures, read with humility, simplicity, and faithfulness—never with a desire to become known as a Bible scholar.

Inquire willingly and listen without speaking to the words of holy men and women, and do not dislike the parables of the elders, for the stories are not told without good reasons.[5]

1 Romans 15:4
2 1 Corinthians 2:4

3 Psalm 117:2, Luke 21:33
4 Romans 2:11, 10:12; Colossians 3:11
5 Proverbs 1:6, Ecclesiastes 12:9

# 6
## Immoderate Desires

Whenever we desire anything excessively, we become those who are not yet perfectly dead to themselves, are quickly tempted and overcome in small and unimportant things.

The weak in spirit, and those that are still somewhat carnal and find pleasure in sensual things, can hardly stay away completely from earthly desires:

Therefore they are depressed when they abstain from such things, and easily become angry when anyone reproves them.

2. Those who indulge in their sensual [see note[1]] desires are soon burdened by a guilty conscience because they yielded to their passions, which did not bring them the peace they were trying to obtain.

True peace of heart, therefore, is gotten by resisting our passions, not by obeying them.

There is no peace in the heart of a carnal person, nor in the person that is addicted to outward things, but there is peace in the heart of a spiritual and devout person.

1   Relating to or affecting any of the senses or a sense organ;
    sensory. Not referring to sexuality as it does so much today.

33

## 7
### FLEEING FROM FRUITLESS HOPE AND PRIDE

He is vain who puts his trust in people [see note[1]], or in any created thing.

Do not be ashamed to serve others for the love of Jesus Christ, or to be thought of as a poor person.

Do not be overconfident in yourself, but place your trust in God.[2]

Do what you are able to do, and God will help your good effort.

Trust not in your own wisdom,[3] nor in the cleverness of anyone; but rather in the grace of God, Who helps the humble, and humbles those that are proud.

2. Do not glory in wealth if you have it, nor in friends who are powerful; but in God who gives all things, and Who desires above all to give you Himself.

Do not praise yourself because of any personal attractiveness of form or face, which may be marred and destroyed by a little sickness.

Take no pleasure in your natural talents or intelligence, lest [for fear that] you may thereby displease God, to Whom belongs whatever natural abilities that you have.

3. Do not think of yourself as better than others,[4] lest perhaps in the sight of God, who knows what is in everyone, you be accounted worse than they.

Do not be proud of your good works,[5] for the judgment of God is far different from the judgment of people, and what pleases them often offends Him.

If there is any good in you, believe that there is much more in others, so that you will stay humble within yourself.

It is not harmful to you to consider yourself less than all others, but it is very harmful to you to think that you are better than anyone else.

The humble enjoy continual peace, but the hearts of proud people are disturbed by envy and frequent hostility.

1   Jeremiah 17:5—In most of our current Bible versions, the
    word "vain" in this quotation is translated as "cursed." But
    as used in the text it probably means "foolish."
2   Psalm 31:1
3   Jeremiah 9:23
4   Exodus 3:11
5   Job 9:20

# 8
## TOO MUCH FAMILIARITY IS TO BE AVOIDED

Do not open your heart to everyone, but discuss your personal affairs with those who are wise and fear God.[1]

Do not exchange your thoughts and feelings with the very young and with strangers.[2]

Do not flatter the rich, and do not be eager to be associated with renowned people.

Keep company with the humble and simple ones, with the devout and virtuous, and talk with them of those things that encourage emotional, mental, or spiritual improvement.[3] Do not be overly intimate with any person, but, in general, commend all good people to God.

Desire to be intimate with God alone, and avoid intimate relationships with others.

2. We must have love toward all, but familiarity with others is not beneficial.

Sometimes it happens that we esteem someone who is unknown to us because of the good report that others have given to us, but when we do meet we discover that the person is somewhat unpleasant.

We think sometimes that we please others by our presence, but instead we offend them with those bad qualities that they discover in us.

1 Ecclesiastes 8:12
2 Proverbs 5:10
3 1 Thessalonians 5:11

# 9

## OBEDIENCE AND SUBJECTION

It is a great thing to live in obedience, to be under a superior, and not to be our own judges.

It is much safer to obey than to govern.

Many live under obedience out of necessity rather than out of love. Those who do are discontented and easily distressed. They will never obtain peace of mind until they willingly and heartily put themselves under obedience for the love of God.

Go wherever you want to, you will find no peace of mind except in humble obedience to the rule of a superior. Imagining that a change of places will bring happiness has deceived many.

2. It is a truth that everyone of us is willing to do that which pleases us the most, and we are most likely to esteem those who agree with us;

But if God is among us, we must sometimes give up our own opinion for the sake of peace.

Who among us is wise enough to fully understand all things?

Do not, therefore, be too confident in your own opinion, but be willing to listen to the advice of others.

If what you think is good and yet you put it aside for God and follow the opinion of another, it will be beneficial to you.

3. I have often heard that it is safer to listen and accept counsel than it is to give it.

It may also happen that even though one's opinion may be good,  refusal to yield to others when reason or a special cause requires it is a sign of pride and stubbornness.

# 10
## Avoiding Excessive Words

Avoid the din and commotion of the world as much as you can,[1] for discussing worldly affairs and problems is a great hindrance [to spiritual life], even though it is done sincerely;

For we are quickly defiled and captivated by pride.

Often I wish that I had held my peace instead of speaking, and that I had not been in the company of others.

Why do we so willingly speak and talk one with another, when we seldom stop speaking before we have hurt our conscience?[2]

The reason why we so willingly spend time in conversation with others is that we try to receive comfort from them, and hope to ease our mind when it is over-burdened with our own thoughts.

So we willingly talk and think of those things that we most love or desire, or of those things that we feel are the most trouble to us.

2. But, alas, often its useless and accomplishes nothing, for any outward comfort we get results in our losing some measure of inward and divine comfort.[3]

Therefore we must watch and pray so that our time will not be wasted.

If there is an opportune and appropriate time for you to speak, say something that will instruct and encourage.

Evil habits and neglect of our own spiritual progress cause us to speak too freely in thoughtless ways.

By contrast, devout conversation about spiritual things greatly promotes our spiritual growth, especially when persons of one mind and spirit are gathered together in God.[4]

1 Matthew 5:1, 14:32; John 6:15
2 Matthew 7:1, Romans 2:1
3 2 Corinthians 1:3-4
4 Acts 1:14, Romans 15:5-6

# 11
## OBTAINING PEACE, AND ZEALOUS DESIRE FOR PROGRESS IN GRACE

We might enjoy much peace if we would not busy ourselves with the words and deeds of other people—with those things that are not our concern.

How can we live long in peace when we thrust ourselves into the concerns of others, even looking around for chances to do so, and too little or infrequently concentrate on our own thoughts?

Blessed are those whose hearts are fixed [on spiritual matters], for they shall enjoy much peace.

2. Why were some of the saints so perfect and given to meditation?

Because they labored to rid themselves of all earthly desires, and so were able to fix themselves wholeheartedly upon God and be free for spiritual meditation.

We are too much led by our passions, and too concerned about temporary things.

We also seldom overcome any one vice perfectly, are not inflamed with a fervent desire to grow better every day, and so we remain cold and lukewarm.

3. If we were perfectly dead to ourselves and not entangled within our own hearts, then we would be able to taste divine things, and have some experience of heavenly meditation.

The greatest, and indeed the whole obstruction, is that we are not disentangled from our passions and lusts, we do not endeavor to enter into that path of perfection that saints have walked before us, and when we encounter any small adversity we are too quickly depressed and turn to human comforts.

4. If we would be courageous people and endeavor to stand in the [spiritual] battle, we would surely receive God's favorable assistance from heaven.

For He gives us opportunity to fight so that we will be victorious, and is ready to bring relief to those who fight courageously and trust in His grace.

If we consider our progress in religious life to consist only in keeping external things, our devotion will quickly come to an end.

Therefore, let us lay the ax to the root[1] so that we may be freed from our passions and find rest for our souls.

5. If every year we would root out one vice, we would soon become perfect people.

But often it is contrary to that, and we realize that we were better and purer at the beginning of our conversion than we are after many years of professing our faith.

Our [spiritual] fervor and progress should increase daily, but now it is regarded as something great if we retain even some part of our first zeal.

If we would force ourselves forward even a little at the beginning,[2] we would be able to do all things after that with ease and delight.

6. It is hard to lay aside those things to which we are accustomed, but it is harder to go against our own wills.

But if we do not overcome small and easy things, how will we overcome harder things?

In the very beginning, resist those things you still want to do and unlearn evil habits, otherwise they will draw you little by little into greater difficulty.

Oh, if you thought carefully about how much inward peace you would bring to yourself and joy to others, I think you would be more careful of your spiritual progress.

1 Matthew 3:10
2 Hebrews 6:1-2

# 12
## The Benefit of Adversity

It is good that we sometimes have troubles and crosses, for they often make us think about ourselves and help us realize that we are not part of this world[1] and should not place our trust in any worldly thing.

It is good that we are sometimes contradicted, and that others think ill of us or think that we are inadequate, even though we do and mean well.

These things often help us to become humble, and keep us safe from unwarranted pride in ourselves. For it is when we are outwardly condemned by others, and no credit is given to us, that we especially seek God for our inward witness.

2. We should, therefore, rest ourselves so fully in God that we do not need to seek many comforts from other people.

When good people are afflicted, tempted, or troubled with evil thoughts, then they understand better the great need they have of God, realizing that without Him they can do nothing that is good.

Then, also, they sorrow, mourn, and pray because of the miseries they suffer.

Often they weary of living longer and wish that death would come so that they might depart and be with Christ.[2]

It is then that they understand that perfect security and complete peace cannot be had in this world.

1 John 17:14-16
2 Philippians 1:23

## 13
### RESISTING TEMPTATION

So long as we live in this world we cannot be without tribulation and temptation.

Thus it is written in Job, "The life of man upon earth is a life of temptation" [see note[1]].

All of us, therefore, should guard ourselves against temptations and watch in prayer,[2] so that the devil, who never sleeps but goes about seeking whom he may devour,[3] will not find an occasion to deceive us

None of us are so perfect and holy but that we sometimes have temptations, and we can never be totally without them.

2. Nevertheless, temptations are often very beneficial to us, even though they are troublesome and grievous, for in them we are humbled, purified, and instructed.

All saints passed through many tribulations and temptations, and benefited because of that.

Those who could not resist temptations became morally unprincipled and fell away.[4]

There is no state so holy, no place so secret, that there are not temptations or adversities.

3. None of us are altogether free from temptations while we live on earth, for we are born with an inclination to evil and the root of it is within us.

No sooner does one temptation or tribulation go away then another one comes, and we will always have something to suffer because the original state of happiness was lost [in the Garden of Eden].

Many try to run away from temptations, but only fall more seriously into them.

We cannot overcome by running away, but by patience and true humility we can become stronger than all our enemies.

4. Those who only avoid the temptations outwardly but do not uproot them will have little benefit. The temptations will soon return to them and they will feel as if they are in a worse state than before.

By patience and long-suffering though God's help, you will more easily overcome the temptations little by little than with violence and your own demanding urgency.

Often get counsel from others when you are tempted, and do not deal roughly with the person who is tempted, but give that person comfort as you would wish to be comforted yourself.[5]

5. Evil temptations begin in an unsteady mind and little trust of God.

For as a ship without a rudder is tossed back and forth with the waves, so a careless and unsteady person is tempted in many ways.

Fire tries iron, and temptation tries a just person.

Often we do not know what we are able to do, but temptations show us what we are.

Yet we must be watchful, especially in the beginning of the temptation, for the enemy is more easily overcome in the beginning if he is not allowed to enter the door of our hearts, but is resisted outside the gate at his first knock.

Therefore someone said, "Withstand the beginnings, for later the remedy comes too late" [see note[6]].

For first a simple thought comes to the mind, then a strong imagination, followed by delight, an evil impulse, and then consent.[7]

So when our wicked enemy is not resisted in the beginning, little by little he gets complete entrance.

And the longer we wait before resisting, the weaker we daily become in ourselves, and the stronger the enemy is against us.

6. Some suffer great temptations in the beginning of their conversion, others at the end.

And there are some who are much troubled almost through the whole of their life.

Some are lightly tempted, according to the wisdom and justice of God's appointment. He measures the conditions and worth of people, and ordains all things for the welfare of His chosen ones.[8]

7. We should not despair, therefore, when we are tempted, but ask God more fervently to grant us help in all tribulations, for according to the words of St. Paul, with the temptation He will provide a way of escape so that we may be able to endure it.[9]

So let us humble our souls under the hand of God in all temptations and tribulations, for He will save and exalt the humble in spirit.[10]

8. Temptations and afflictions prove how much we have progressed, and by going through them our rewards are greater and God's graces are more prominently shown.

It is no great thing if we are devout and fervent when we are not being afflicted, but if during adversity we bear ourselves patiently, there is hope then of great progress in grace.

Some who are kept from great temptations are often overcome by small ones that occur daily. This happens so that having failed in small matters they will never presume that they are able to withstand the greater temptations in their own strength.

1  Job 7:1 (marginal reading: "warfare")—The NIV translates
   this verse as, "Does not man have hard service on earth?"
   Most other current Bible versions agree with this, except the
   KJV, which reads, "Is there not an appointed time to man
   upon earth?"
2  Matthew 26:41
3  1 Peter 5:8
4  Matthew 13:21-22, 2 Timothy 4:10
5  2 Corinthians 1:4
6  Kempis is paraphrasing the Roman poet Ovid (43 B.C. to
   A.D. 17). The actual quotation is, "Resist beginnings; the
   prescription comes too late when the disease has gained
   strength by long delays. (Remedia Amoris, 91Í)
7  James 1:15
8  Romans 8:28
9  1 Corinthians 10:13
10 James 4:6

# 14
## Avoiding Rash Judgment

Keep your eyes on yourself and be careful that you don't judge the deeds of others.[1] The effort of judging others is fruitless, and you'll often make mistakes and easily sin,[2] but the effort of judging and examining yourself always bears fruit.

We often judge things according to the way we imagine them, for self-love easily takes true judgement from us.

If God was always the single object of our desire, we would not be so easily troubled by the opposition of our worldly mind.

2. But frequently something lurks inside us, or else something happens outside us and draws us to it.

Many secretly seek an advantage to themselves in things they do, and do not even know they are doing it.

They seem also to have good peace of mind when things go according to their will and opinion, but if anything happens other than what they desire, they are immediately stirred up and highly irritated.

Differences of judgments and opinions often cause disagreements between friends and between citizens of a country, and even between religious and devout people.[3]

3. An old habit is not easy to break, and none of us are willing to be guided further than we can understand.

If you rely more upon your own reason and diligence than upon that power [grace] that brings you into obedience to Jesus Christ, it will be a long time before you are enlightened, for God wants us to be completely subject to Him and so inflamed with love [for Him] that we pass beyond the restrictive boundaries of human reason.

1 Matthew 7:1, Romans 15:1
2 Matthew 12:25, Luke 21:51
3 Ecclesiastes 3:16

# 15

## WORKS DONE IN CHARITY

Never do evil for worldly things or for the love of any person. Nevertheless, for the benefit of a person in need, a good work may sometimes be postponed without a guilty conscience, or even changed for a better work.

For by doing this, a good work is not lost but changed into a better one.

Without love external works are of no profit,[1] but whatever is done out of love, no matter how little and contemptible it is in the sight of the world, it becomes wholly fruitful.

For God weighs more the love with which we work than how much work we do.

2. We do much when we do well, and we do well when we serve the common good rather than our own interests.[2]

Often what seems to be love is really pleasure-seeking, because our natural inclination, self-will, hope of reward, and self-interest are seldom absent.

3. Those who have true and perfect love seek nothing for themselves,[3] but only desire that the glory of God be exalted in all things.

They also envy no one because they do not seek good for themselves and do not rejoice in themselves, but wish above all things to be made happy by their enjoyment of God.[4]

They attribute nothing that is good to any person, but wholly attribute it to God, from Whom all things proceed as from a fountain, and in whom finally all the saints rest as their highest enjoyment and accomplishment.

Oh, those that have but one spark of true love would certainly discern that all earthly things are completely worthless.

1  1 Corinthians 13:3, Luke 7:47
2  Philippians 2:17
3  Philippians 2:21, 1 Corinthians 13:5
4  Psalm 17:15, 24:6

# 16
## ENDURING THE FAULTS OF OTHERS

Those things that we cannot amend [change for the better] in ourselves or in others we should endure patiently until God decrees those things to change.

Consider that perhaps it is better that way for your trial [of endurance or belief] and your patience, without which all our good deeds are not worthy of much esteem.

Nevertheless, when you have things that impede you, pray that God will grant you help so that you will be able to endure them in an appropriate way.[1]

2. If you warn someone about a fault once or twice and that person will not listen, do not mention the sin again, but commit it all to God that His will may be fulfilled[2] and His name honored in all His servants, for He well knows how to turn evil into good.[3]

Endeavor to be patient in enduring the failures and weaknesses of others, no matter what kind they are, for you yourself have many failings that must be endured by others.[4]

If you cannot make yourself into the kind of person you want to be, how can you expect to influence someone else to be what you like?

We are eager to have others perfect, but yet we do not correct our own faults.

3. We desire that others be severely corrected, and will not be corrected ourselves.

The great freedom that others have displeases us, and yet we will not have our own desires restricted.

We are eager to have others restrained by strict laws, but in no way will we be restrained ourselves.

So it is easily seen how seldom we weigh our neighbor in the same balance with ourselves.

If everyone were perfect, why would we have to suffer anything from our neighbor for God?

4. But God has thus decreed it so that we will learn to bear one another's burdens,[5] for none of us are without fault, none of us are without burdens, none of us are sufficient

of ourselves, none of us are wise enough of ourselves—and so we should bear with one another, comfort one another, help, instruct, and admonish one another.[6]

Times of adversity best reveal how much righteousness or strength we have.

For such times do not weaken us, but rather reveal what we are.

1 Matthew 6:13, Luke 11:4
2 Matthew 6:10
3 Romans 8:28
4 1 Thessalonians 5:14, Galatians 6:1
5 Galatians 6:2
6 1 Thessalonians 5:14, 1 Corinthians 12:25

# 17

## A COMMUNITY LIFE [SEE NOTE[1]]

If you want to have peace and harmony with others, you must learn to break your will in many things.

It is no small matter to live in a religious community or congregation, to communicate with others who are there without complaining, and to persevere in that place faithfully until death.[2]

Blessed is the one who lived there well and ended happily.

If you want to persevere and grow in grace as you should, you will have to consider yourself a stranger and pilgrim on earth.[3]

To live a spiritual life you must be contented to be considered a fool in this world for Christ's sake.[4]

2. Wearing a religious habit and shaving the hair off the crown of the head [see note[5]] only change the appearance

and are of little profit, but the perfect disciplining of fleshly passions make a truly religious person.

Those who seek anything else but God and the salvation of their souls, shall find nothing but tribulations and sorrows [see note[6]].

No one can remain long in peace who does not seek to be the least and subject to all.[7]

3. We came to serve, not to rule.[8]

Understand that we are called to suffer and to labor, not to be idle or spend our time in idle talk with others.

Here, therefore, we are proved as gold in the furnace.

Here we cannot stand unless we humble ourselves with our whole heart for the love of God.

1　Kempis addresses this chapter specifically to those living in a monastery—the monks of his day. But there are principles in it that can be applied to anyone who wants to live a more spiritual life.

2　Luke 16:10

3　1 Peter 2:11

4　1 Corinthians 4:10

5　This is called *tonsure*, which is the act of shaving the head or part of the head, especially as a preliminary to becoming a priest or a member of a monastic order. Also, the part of a monk's or priest's head that has been shaved.

6　Ecclesiastes 1:17-18, Ecclesiasticus 1:18 - Ecclesiasticus (or the Wisdom of Jesus, son of Sirach, or just Sirach), is one of the books accepted into the Old Testament by the Roman Catholic and Eastern Orthodox churches. The collection in which they are contained is called the Apocrypha, a Greek term meaning "hidden things." The books in the Apocrypha were never accepted by Judaism as authoritative, have not been accepted by the vast majority of Protestant churches, and are contained in only a few Protestant Bibles, such as the *New American Standard Version of the Bible with Apocrypha*. Ecclesiasticus 1:18 (or Sirach) reads: "The fear of the Lord is the crown of wisdom, making peace and perfect health to flourish."

7   1 Peter 5:5
8   Matthew 20:26-28

# 18
## EXAMPLES OF THE HOLY SAINTS

Consider the dynamic examples of the holy saints in whom true perfection and religion shone[1] and you will see how little—almost nothing—that we do in these days.

Alas! What is our life when it is compared to theirs!

The saints and friends of Christ served the Lord in hunger and thirst, in cold and nakedness, in labor and weariness, in watchings and fastings,[2] in prayer and holy meditations, in many persecutions and reproaches.[3]

2. Oh, many and grievous were the tribulations suffered by the apostles, martyrs, confessors, virgins, and all the rest that endeavored to follow the steps of Christ!

For they hated their lives in this world, that they might keep them to life eternal.[4]

Oh, how strict and self-renouncing a life was led those holy saints in the wilderness![5] How long and grievous temptations they suffered! How often they were assaulted by the enemy! What frequent and fervent prayers they offered to God! What rigorous abstinences they practiced! How great zeal and care they had for their spiritual progress! How strong a battle they fought to  overcome their lusts! How pure and upright intentions they kept toward God!

In the day they labored and in the night they attended to continual prayer, and even when they labored they did not cease from mental [silent] prayer.

3. They spent all their time profitably, and every hour seemed too short for serving God.

When contemplating [the things of God] they felt such great sweetness that they often forgot that they needed bodily refreshments.

They renounced all riches, dignities, honors, friends, and relatives;[6] they desired to have nothing that belonged to the world; they scarcely took things necessary to sustain life; and they grieved when it was necessary to supply their bodies. As a result, they were poor in earthly things but very rich in grace and virtues.

Outwardly they were destitute, but inwardly they were refreshed with grace and divine comfort.[7]

4. They were strangers to the world but close and familiar friends to God.[8]

They saw themselves as nothing and this present world saw them as contemptible, but in the eyes of God they were precious and beloved.

They were grounded in true humility, lived in simple obedience, and walked in love and patience; therefore they profited daily in the spirit and obtained great grace in God's sight.

They were given for an example to all religious people,[9] and they should stimulate us to strive for spiritual excellence far more than all those who live lukewarm lives should tempt us to be lax.

5. Oh, how great was the fervor of all religious persons in the beginning of their holy relationship to God!

How great was their devotion to prayer! What ambition to excel others in virtue! How strict and complete their discipline flourished at that time! How great was the reverence and obedience with which they kept all things under the guidance of their spiritual superiors!

Their footsteps still remain to testify that they were indeed holy and perfect people who fought valiantly and trod the world under their feet.

Today, those who are not transgressors and who can patiently endure what they have undertaken are considered to be great.

Oh, our times are so lukewarm and negligent that we have quickly declined from that ancient fervor and have come to the state where the very laziness and lukewarmness of spirit makes our own life weary to us.

Would to God the desire to grow in virtues does not completely sleep in you who has often seen the many examples of devout and religious persons.

1 Hebrews 11:
2 2 Corinthians 11:27
3 2 Corinthians 12:10
4 John 12:25
5 Matthew 7:14
6 Matthew 19:29
7 2 Corinthians 1:3-4
8 James 4:4
9 Philippians 3:17

# 19

## Spiritual Exercises of Good Religious People

The lives of good religious people should be adorned with all moral excellence and righteousness, so that they will inwardly be the same as they seem outwardly.

Actually, there are good reasons why there should be much more inwardly than is perceived outwardly. For God looks upon us,[1] and it is our spiritual duty to reverence

Him most highly wherever we are, and to walk pure as the angels in His sight.[2]

We should daily renew our purposes and stir ourselves up to greater fervor, as though this were the first day of our conversion, and say:

*"Help me, my God, in this my good purpose and in Your holy service, and grant that this day I may begin perfectly, for everything that I have done before this is as nothing."*

2. Our spiritual progress will be in accordance with our purpose, and to show progress it is necessary that we be very diligent.

If those who firmly purpose often fail, what will those do who seldom purpose anything or purpose with little resolution?

It may turn out that there are various ways of forsaking our purpose, yet even a slight omission of spiritual exercises [see note[3]] seldom passes without some loss to our souls.

The purpose of just people depends not upon their own wisdom, but upon God's grace, which they always rely upon for whatever they make themselves responsible.

For man proposes, but God disposes,[4] and neither is the way of just people in themselves.

3. If a regular exercise is sometimes omitted because of some act of piety or profit to another, it may easily be taken up again afterward.

But if we lightly forsake the exercise because of weariness or carelessness, it is a great offense to God and will prove to be detrimental to us. Let us do the best we can, because even then we still fail too easily in many things.[5]

Yet we must always have a fixed course, especially against those weaknesses that hinder us most of all.

We must diligently search into and set in order both the outward and the inward person, because both of them are of importance to our progress in godliness.

4. If you cannot continually recall to mind your inward and outward activities, do it at least once a day, preferably in the morning or evening.

In the morning set your daily good purpose, and at night examine yourself as to what you did and how you behaved yourself in word, deed, and thought,[6] for in these things perhaps you have often offended God and other people.

Summon up your inner resources to resist the devil's evil assaults, curb your appetite, and you will be better able to keep under the unruly desires of the flesh.

Never be entirely idle, but either be reading, writing, praying, meditating, or endeavoring something for the good of others.

As for bodily exercises, those disciplines must be used with discretion and are not to be practiced the same way by everyone.

5. Uncommon spiritual exercises are not to be exposed to public view, for private things are practiced more safely at home.

Nevertheless, beware that you do not neglect those exercises that are common,[7] because you are more eager to do those that are private.

Once you have fully and faithfully accomplished all the things for which you are responsible and directed to do, use whatever spare time you may have for yourself and any devotions you desire.

All can not use one kind of spiritual exercise, but one is more beneficial for this person, another for that.

Different exercises are also more appropriate for different times—some are better suited for working days and others for holy days.

Certain exercises are beneficial in times of temptation, and others in times of peace and quiet.

Some we practice when we are melancholy, and others when we rejoice in the Lord.

6. About the time of the chief festivals [see note[8]] good exercises should be renewed and the prayers of holy people more fervently requested.

From festival to festival, we should make some good resolution, as though we were immediately going to depart out of this world and come to the everlasting feast in heaven.

Therefore, at holy times we should carefully prepare ourselves to live more devoutly and keep more strictly all things that we are to observe, as though we were shortly to be in God's presence to receive the reward of our labors.

7. But if that end is deferred, let us realize that we are not sufficiently prepared and are yet unworthy of the great glory that will be revealed in us[9] in due time—so let us endeavor to prepare ourselves better for our departure.

"Blessed is that slave," said Jesus, "whom his master will find at work when he arrives. Truly I tell you, he will put that one in charge of all his possessions."[10]

1  Psalm 33:13, Hebrews 4:12-13
2  Psalm 15:2
3  As used the text, exercises are activities that require spiritual and mental exertion, especially when intended to develop or maintain spiritual growth.
4  Proverbs 16:9
5  Ecclesiastes 7:20
6  Deuteronomy 4
7  Hebrews 10:25
8  An occasion for feasting or celebration, especially a day or time of religious significance that recurs at regular intervals.
9  Romans 7:18
10 Luke 12:43-44

## 20
### LOVE OF SOLITUDE AND SILENCE

Seek a convenient time[1] to be by yourself, and meditate often upon God's loving kindnesses.

Do not bother with writings about unusual matters, but read the things that speak to your conscience more than the things that occupy your head.

If you will withdraw yourself from worthless conversations and from roaming about idly, as well as from listening to new things and rumors, you will find enough free time that is suitable for meditation on good things.[2]

The greatest saints avoided the company of others[3] when it was appropriate and proper to do so, and choose instead to serve God in secret.

2. One writer said, "As often as I have been among men I returned home less a man than I was *before*" [see note[4]]

This we find true when we have long conversations. It is easier not to speak a word at all, than not to speak more words than we should.

It is easier to remain home, than to keep yourself well when you are away.

The person therefore who intends to achieve the more inward and spiritual things of religion, must go apart with Jesus from the influence of the multitudes.[5]

No one can securely appear in public, but those are secure who would gladly stay at home out of sight.

No one is secure when they speak, but those that hold their peace willingly.[6]

No one rules securely except those who are willing to be ruled.

No one commands securely, but those that have learned to willingly obey.

3. No one rejoices securely unless they have within them the testimony of a good conscience.

Nevertheless, the security of the saints was always filled with the fear of God.

Neither were they any less anxious and humble within themselves because outwardly they manifested grace and great virtues.

But the security of wicked people arises from pride and presumption, and in the end it deceives them.

Although you seem to be a good religious person, never promise yourself security in this life.

4. Often those whom others have greatly esteemed and considered important have fallen into the greatest danger by being too self-confident.

Therefore, it is more beneficial to many not to be totally free from temptations, but to be often tempted so that they do not become too secure and so be puffed up with pride—or too freely give themselves to worldly comforts.

Oh, how clear a conscience a person could have by never seeking after short-lived joys and never being entangled in the things of the world!

Oh, what great peace and quietness a person would have by cutting off all worthless worry, and thinking only upon divine things and those things that are beneficial to the soul, and placing all confidence in God!

5. None of us are worthy of heavenly comfort unless we diligently exercise ourselves in holy repentance.

If you desire true repentance of heart, enter into your secret place and shut out the din and commotion of the world, as it is written, "In your chambers, be ye grieved" [see note[7]]. In your secret place you will find what you will too often lose when you are away from home.

The more time you spend in your secret place the more you will like it, and the less time you spend there the more you will loath it. If in the beginning of your conversion you are content to be in it and find it satisfying, it will soon become a dear friend to you and a source of great comfort.

6. In silence and stillness a spiritual soul advances and learns the hidden truths of the holy Scriptures.

There is found a river of tears in which the soul may every night be washed and cleansed,[8] so that the more it lives away from all worldly disturbances the more it becomes familiar with its Creator.

Whoever, therefore, withdraws from acquaintances and friends, God will draw near to Himself with His holy angels.

It is better for you to live privately and take care of yourself than it is to neglect your soul even though you could work wonders in the world.

It is commendable for a spiritual person to seldom travel widely and to be hesitant about seeing others or being seen by them.

7. Why do you desire to see what it is unlawful for you to have? "The world passeth away, and the lust thereof."[9]

Our sensual desires entice us to wander about, but when the time is over what do you carry home with you but a burdened conscience and a distracted heart?

A happy going out often brings an unhappy going home, and a joyful evening often makes a sad morning.[10]

All carnal joy therefore enters gently, but in the end it bites and stings to death.

What can you see somewhere else that you cannot see at home?[11] Behold the heaven and the earth and all the elements, for of these are all things created.

8. What can you see anywhere under the sun that can continue long?

Perhaps you think you will satisfy yourself, but you can never achieve it.

Should you see all things that exist right before your eyes, what would it be but a worthless sight? [see note[12]].

Lift your eyes up[13] to God in the highest and pray that He will pardon your sins and omissions.

Leave worthless things to the foolish, and you concentrate upon those things that God has commanded you.

Shut the door of your secret place[14] and call upon your beloved Jesus.

Stay with Him in your closet, for you will not find greater peace anywhere else.

If you had not wandered around and paid attention to idle rumors, you would have better kept your happy peace of mind. But since you sometimes delight in hearing about new and unusual things, it is right that you should suffer some uneasiness of heart from it.

1   Ecclesiastes 3:1
2   Philippians 4:8-9
3   Hebrews 11:38
4   Kempis is quoting Lucius Annaeus Seneca (Epistle 8).
    Seneca, known as "the Younger, lived from about 4 B.C.
    to A.D. 65. He was a Roman Stoic philosopher, writer, and
    tutor of Nero. His works include treatises on rhetoric and
    governance and numerous plays that influenced Renaissance
    and Elizabethan drama.
5   Matthew 5:1
6   Ecclesiastes 3:7
7   Psalm 4:4 - Our current Bible versions agree that the verse
    reads, in effect, "Be angry, and do not sin. Meditate within
    your heart on your bed, and be still. Selah."
8   Psalm 6:6
9   1 John 2:17
10  Proverbs 14:13
11  Ecclesiastes 1:10
12  Original text reference was Ecclesiastes 3:2, but Ecclesiastes
    1:14 and 4:7 seem more appropriate.

13  Psalm 121:1
14  Matthew 6:6

## 21
### COMPUNCTION OF HEART

If you want to make any progress in godliness, keep yourself in the fear of God[1] and do not desire too much freedom. Keep all your senses under control by severe discipline, and do not indulge in foolish merriment.

Yield yourself to compunction [see note[2]] of heart, and you will thereby increase greatly in inward devotion [to God].

Compunction opens the way to much good, which lack of moral restrain quickly destroys.

It is a wonder that any of us who seriously consider and meditate upon our state of exile and the many perils that surround our soul can ever perfectly rejoice in this life [see note[3]].

2. Through lightness of heart and little concern for our failings we become insensitive to the real sorrows of our souls, and often we indulge in foolish laughter when we have valid reasons to weep.[4]

There is no true freedom or genuine joy except when the fear of God is accompanied by a good conscience.

Happy are those who can rid themselves of every distracting thing that impedes their progress, and can dedicate themselves to the desired result of holy compunction.

Happy is the one who can abandon all that may defile or burden the conscience.

Resist courageously, one habit overcomes another.

If you will leave others alone in the things they are doing, they will in the same way not interfere with the things you are doing.

3. Do not meddle in matters that concern others, and do not entangle yourself in the business of your superiors.

Keep your eyes on yourself first,[5] and be especially sure to admonish yourself before you admonish any of your close friends.

If you do not have the fervor of others, do not be grieved by it,[6] but take this to heart that you do not behave yourself as cautiously and prudently as a servant of God and a devout religious person should.

It is often better and safer not to have too many comforts in this life,[7] especially those that have to do with the flesh.

But if we do not have divine comforts at all or have them rarely, the fault is ours because we do not seek compunction of heart and do not completely forsake worthless and outward comforts.

4. Know that you are unworthy of divine comfort and are instead worthy of much tribulation.

When we have perfect repentance, then the whole world is grievous and bitter to us.

A good person always finds sufficient reason to mourn and weep.

For whether we consider our own or our neighbor's circumstances, we know that no one lives here without tribulation.

And when we look deeper into ourselves, we find much more that saddens us.

Our sins and wickedness in which we are so entangled that we can seldom apply ourselves to meditation of heavenly matters, minister to us feelings of just sorrow and inward repentance.

5. If you would often think of your death[8] instead of your living long, there is no question but that you would be more zealous to improve [spiritually].

If you also meditated on the pains of hell that await many in the other world, I believe you would willingly undergo any labor or sorrow in this world and not be afraid of the greatest hardship or discipline.

But because these things do not enter into the heart and we still love only those things that delight us, we remain cold and dull in our religion.

6. It is often our lack of a vibrant spirit that makes our miserable bodies complain so easily.

With all humility, therefore, pray to the Lord that He will grant you the spirit of compunction. And say with the prophet, "Feed me, O Lord, with the bread of tears, and give me plenteousness of tears to drink" [see note[9]].

1  Proverbs 19:23
2  Compunction's central meaning is: "a feeling of regret for one's sins or misdeeds." Repentance is a similar word.
3  Hebrews 11:13—Exile is used to mean the state of being here on earth as opposed to being in heaven—being "strangers and pilgrims on the earth."
4  James 4:8-9
5  James 1:23
6  Galatians 1:10
7  Psalm 76:5
8  Ecclesiastes 7:1-2
9  Psalm 80:5—This is what we might call a prayer-paraphrase of Psalm 80:5 and not an exact quote. In the NRSV the verse reads: "You have fed them with the bread of tears, and given them tears to drink in full measure."

# 22
## CONSIDERATION OF HUMAN MISERY

Miserable you are, whoever you are and wherever you go, unless you turn yourself over to God.

Why are you troubled when things do not succeed as you want or desire them to? For who has all things that they desire?[1]—neither I nor you nor any person on earth.

There is no one in this world, even if a king or bishop, without some tribulation or problem.

Who then is in the best circumstance?—the one who is able to suffer something for God.

2. Many weak and unstable people say, Behold! what a happy life that one [king or bishop] leads, how wealthy, how great, in what power and dignity!

But lift up your eyes to the riches of Heaven and you will see that all the goods of this life are nothing. They are uncertain and more burdensome than not because they are never possessed without anxiety and fear.

Our happiness does not consist in having an abundance of temporal goods,[2] for a moderate amount is enough for us.

Truly it is misery even to live upon the earth.

The more spiritual we desire to be, the more bitter this present life becomes to us because we see clearer and understand better the defects of human corruption.

To eat and drink, sleep and watch, labor and rest, and be subject to other necessities of nature is certainly a great source of misery and affliction to the spiritual person who would gladly be released and be free from all sin.[3]

3. For the inner person is greatly weighed down by these bodily necessities while we live in this world.

Therefore the prophet prayed with great zeal to be enabled to be free from them, saying, "Bring me, O Lord, out of my necessities" [see note[4]].

But woe to those who do not know their own misery, and a greater woe to those who love this miserable and corruptible life![5]

For there are some who can scarcely get their mere necessities by working or begging [see note[6]], and yet love this world so much that if they were able to live here always they would care nothing at all for the kingdom of God.

4. Oh, how senseless and unbelieving in heart are those people who are so strongly tied to this earth that they have an appetite for nothing but carnal things![7]

But contemptible as they are, they will in the end see to their distress how vile and worthless were the things that they loved.

While on the contrary, the saints of God and all the devout followers of Christ did not consider those things that pleased the flesh or that flourished in this life, but longed for the everlasting riches with all their hope and earnest intention.

They directed their whole desire upward to things everlasting and invisible, so that the desire for things visible could not draw them to things below [on this earth].

5. Oh, do not lose your confidence in making progress in godliness—there is still time, the hour has not yet passed.[8]

Why put off your purpose from day to day? Arise and begin at once and say, "Now is the time to act, now is the time to strive, now is the time to improve."

When you are uneasy and much troubled, that is the time of true blessing.

You must pass through fire and through water before you come to the place of refreshing.[9]

Unless you earnestly force yourself, you will never get victory over sin.

So long as we carry about us this frail body of ours, we can never be without sin or live without weariness and pain.

We would gladly be at rest and freed from all misery, but because through sin we have lost our innocence, we have together with that lost also true happiness.[10]

It is therefore appropriate that we have patience and wait for the mercy of God, until this iniquity pass away and mortality is swallowed up by life![11]

6. Oh, how great is human frailty, it is always prone to evil![12]

Today you confess your sins and tomorrow you commit the very same ones that you have confessed.

One moment you resolve to be more careful how you act, and a short while later you behave as though you had never had any such purpose at all.

Since we are so frail and inconsistent, we have good reason to humble ourselves and never be conceited about ourselves [see note[13]].

Moreover, we may quickly lose by our own negligence that which by the grace of God we have scarcely obtained through long and hard labor.

7. In the end, what will become of those of us who begin so early to grow lukewarm?

Woe to us if we begin to rest as if everything were peaceful and secure when so far there is no sign of true holiness in the way we live!

Like young beginners, we need to be newly instructed again in how to live a good life, if perhaps there is some hope that we can amend our future and make greater progress in spiritual things.

1  Ecclesiastes 6:2
2  Proverbs 19:1
3  Philippians 1:23
4  Psalm 25:17—Current Bible versions agree that this verse reads, in effect, "The troubles of my heart have enlarged;

Bring me out of my distresses!"

5 Romans 8:22

6 In Kempis's day, begging was a common occupation or necessity. There were also many begging monks upon the land. Desiderius Erasmus, Dutch Renaissance scholar and Roman Catholic theologian (1466? – 1536), wrote: "The world is burdened with men's institutions, and with the tyranny of begging friars."

7 Romans 8:5

8 Romans 13:11, Hebrews 10:35

9 Psalm 66:12

10 Romans 7:24, Genesis 3:17

11 2 Corinthians 5:4

12 Genesis 6:5, 8:12

13 2 Maccabees 9:11–This is one of two Maccabees books in the Apocrypha. The verse reads: "Then it was that, broken in spirit, he began to lose much of his arrogance and to come to his senses under the scourge of God, for he was tortured with pain every moment."

# 23

## MEDITATION ON DEATH

The end of your days here will come very swiftly,[1] so consider what will become of you in the next world.

Today we are here, tomorrow we have disappeared.

And when we are out of sight, we are quickly out of mind.

Oh, the stupidity and hardness of a person's heart who thinks only upon this present life and does not care about the life that is to come!

You should arrange yourself and all your thoughts and actions as if today you were going to die.[2]

If you had a good conscience you would not have a great fear of death.[3]

It is better to avoid sins than try to avoid death [see note[4]].

If you are not prepared today, how will you be prepared tomorrow?[5]

Tomorrow is uncertain, and how do you know if you will live until tomorrow?

2. What good is it to live long when there is so little improvement in our habits!

Alas!—a long life more often makes our sins greater rather than our lives better.

Oh, that in this world we had spent but one day thoroughly well!

Many can tell how long ago they were converted, and yet often the fruit of spiritual improvements in their lives is very small.

It is considered dreadful to die, but perhaps to live long may prove more dangerous.

Happy are those who always have the hour of their death before their eyes[6] and daily prepare themselves to die.

If at any time you have seen another person die, consider that you also must pass the same way.[7]

3. When it is morning, consider that you may die before evening.

And when evening comes, do not dare to promise yourself the next morning.

Be always ready, therefore, and live in a way that death will never take you unprepared.[8]

Many die suddenly and unexpectedly, for the Son Man will come at an hour when you do not expect Him.[9]

When that last hour comes, you will begin to have a different opinion of your entire past life, and you will be exceedingly sorry that you had been so careless and remiss.

4. Oh, how wise and happy is the one that strives now to be the person in life that they wish to be found at the hour of death.

A perfect contempt of the world, a fervent desire to excel in virtue, the love of discipline, the diligence of repentance, the readiness to obey, the denial of ourselves, and the patient bearing of any affliction for the love of Christ, will give us great confidence that we will die happy.

When you are healthy you can do much good, but when you are sick there is not much that you are able to do.

Few become better or reform because of sickness, just as those who travel many places are seldom made holy by it.

5. Do not trust yourself to friends and relatives, or put off the care of your soul's welfare to some future time, for people will forget you sooner than you realize.

It is better to look to your soul early and do some good in advance than to trust in help from other people.[10]

If you are not careful for yourself now, who will be careful for you in the future?

This present time is very precious—now are the days of salvation, now is the acceptable time.[11]

How sad that you waste so much time here when you could be working out your salvation and making sure your hope of eternal life.[12]

The time will come when you will desire one day or hour in which to make amends, and I cannot say that it will be granted to you.

6. Oh beloved, if you would be ever fearful and mindful of death, you would free yourself from great fear and deliver yourself from great danger.

Strive to live now so that at the hour of death you may rejoice rather than fear.

Strive now to die to the world so that you may begin to live with Christ.[13]

Learn now to despise all earthly things so that you may freely live with Christ.

Discipline your body now and bring it into subjection so that you may have assured confidence.[14]

7. Ah, foolish me, why do you plan to live long when you cannot promise yourself one more day.[15]

How many have been deceived and suddenly snatched away!

How often do you hear reports like this: one person is killed, another drowns, another's neck is broken from a fall from a high place, this one died while eating, and that one while playing!

One perished by fire, another by the sword, another of the plague, another was slain by thieves. Death is the end of everyone, and a person's life suddenly passes away like a shadow.[16]

8. Who will remember you when you are dead, and who will pray for you? [see note [17]].

Do now, beloved, what you are able to do, for you do not know when you will die or what your fate will be after your death [see note[18]].

Now while you have time store up for yourself everlasting riches.[19]

Think of nothing but the salvation of your soul, care for nothing but the things of God.

Make friends for yourself by honoring the saints of God and imitating their actions, so that when you leave this short life they may receive you into everlasting habitations.[20]

Keep yourself as a stranger and pilgrim upon the earth,[21] and as one to whom the concerns of this world do not belong.

Keep your heart free and lifted up to God, because here you do not have an enduring city.[22]

Send your daily prayers and sighs heavenward to Him, along with your tears, so that after death your virtuous spirit will journey with much happiness to the Lord. *Amen.*

1 Job 9:25-26, 14:1-2; Luke 12:20; Hebrews 9:27
2 Matthew 25:13
3 Luke 12:37
4 Wisdom 4:16—The Wisdom of Solomon is an Apocrypha book. The verse reads: "The righteous who have died will condemn the ungodly who are living, and youth that is quickly perfected will condemn the prolonged old age of the unrighteous."
5 Matthew 25:44, 25:10
6 Ecclesiastes 7:1
7 Hebrews 9:27
8 Luke 21:36
9 Matthew 24:44, Luke 12:40
10 Isaiah 30:5, 31:1; Jeremiah 17:5, 48:7; Matthew 6:20
11 2 Corinthians 6:2
12 Philippians 2:12, 1 Thessalonians 5:8-9, Hebrews 2:2-3
13 Romans 6:8
14 1 Corinthians 9:27
15 Luke 12:20
16 Job 14:2
17 This is from the doctrine in certain churches that specifies prayers for those in purgatory to lessen their time of punishment, and prayers for those awaiting judgment.
18 This is based on a doctrine that states you cannot know whether you have eternal life until after you die and are judged for your works. See also John 3:16, Romans 5:1, and Ephesians 2:10; also Psalms 37:3, James 2:20,26.
19 Matthew 6:20, Luke 12:33, Galatians 6:8
20 Luke 16:9, Hebrews 11
21 1 Peter 2:11
22 Hebrews 13:14

## 24
### JUDGMENT AND PUNISHMENT OF SINNERS

In everything have a distinct purpose that is directed toward the end of your life and how you will stand before the judgement seat of Christ[1] from whom nothing is hidden,[2] who is not pacified with gifts, but who will judge righteously and justly.[3]

O wretched and foolish sinner, who sometimes fears the look of an angry person, what answer will you give to Christ who knows all your sins.[4]

Why do you not spiritually provide for yourself against that great day of judgment,[5] when no one can excuse or answer for another, for we each will have enough to answer for ourselves.

In this life your labor is profitable, your tears acceptable,[6] your groans heard, your grief satisfying and purifying.

2. Those who are patient have a great and wholesome cleansing,[7] for though they receive harm they grieve more about the ill will of the one who harmed them than for their own injury, they pray willing for their adversary and from their heart forgive the offences committed against them, they instantly ask forgiveness of anyone whom they have offended, they are more quickly moved to compassion than to anger, and they often do holy violence to themselves and labor to bring their entire body into submission to the Spirit.

It is better to purge out our sins and cut off our vices while we are here, than to keep them to account for in the hereafter.[8]

In truth we deceive ourselves through an excessive love of the flesh.[9]

3. The fuel that feeds the fire of hell is sin.

Sinners who spare themselves now and follow the desires of their flesh will in the hereafter be severely punished, and even now store up greater fuel for the flame.

In whatever way a person has sinned, it is in that sin they will be more severely punished.

The slothful will be prodded forward with burning goads, the gluttons tormented with hunger and thirst.

There the sensuous and pleasure-lovers will be bathed in burning pitch and stinking brimstone, and the envious will howl with grief like mad dogs.

4. Every sin will have its proper punishment.

There the proud will be filled with confusion, and the covetous will be bound with miserable poverty.

One hour of pain there will be more bitter than a thousand years of the most excruciating repentance here!

There will be no rest or comfort for the damned there, but here we have some rest from our labors and enjoy the comfort of our loved ones.

Be concerned and repentant for your sins now,[10] so that at the day of judgement you will stand secure with the company of the blessed.[11]

For then will the righteous stand with great boldness against those who afflicted and oppressed them [see note[12]].

Then those who humbly submitted themselves to the judgment of others will stand as a witness against their tormentors.

Then will the poor and humble have great confidence in Christ, but the proud ones will be surrounded and seized by fear.

5. Then it will be seen that those who were truly wise in the world were those who learned to be foolish and despised for Christ.[13]

Then every affliction that we patiently went through will delight us, and the mouth of iniquity will be silenced.[14]

Then the devout will rejoice and the profane will mourn.

Than those who disciplined their flesh will rejoice more than those who satiated themselves with pleasures and delights.[15]

Then the garments of the poor will shine gloriously, and the clothing of the rich will seem vile and contemptible.

Then the dwellings of the poor will be commended more than the ornate houses of the rich.

Then steadfast patience will be rewarded more than all the power in the world.

Then simple obedience will be exalted above all worldly wisdom.[16]

6. Then a good and clear conscience will be more to rejoice about than any profound knowledge of philosophy.

Then the contempt of riches will be worth more than all the world's treasures.

Then you will be more comforted for having prayed devoutly than if you had fared bountifully.

Then you will be happy that you often kept silent rather than often speaking.[17]

Then good works will be of more value than many eloquent words.

Then a disciplined life and earnest repentance will be more pleasing than all earthly delights.

Learn to suffer little things now so that you can sustain through more grievous pains later.

Prove to yourself now what you can endure later.

If you cannot endure a little suffering now, what would you do if you had to endure the torments of hell?

If a little suffering makes you so impatient now, what would the fires of hell do?

Be assured that you cannot have two paradises—it is impossible to enjoy excessive pleasures in this world and reign with Christ in the next world.

7. Suppose up to now you had always lived in honors and delights, what worth would that be to you if you were to die at this instant?[18]

All is worthless, therefore, except to love God and serve Him only.

For those that love God with all their heart are not afraid of death or punishment, of judgment or hell, for perfect love gives sure and certain access to God through Jesus Christ.[19]

But why should it be any wonder that those who delight in sin are afraid of death and judgment?

Yet it is good if love alone cannot withhold you from sin that the fear of hell helps to restrain you.

The person who completely lays aside the fear of God[20] never continues long in good spiritual condition, but quickly falls into the snares of the devil.

1  Romans 14:10, 2 Corinthians 5:10, 2 Timothy 4:1
2  Luke 8:17
3  2 Timothy 4:8
4  Romans 2:16
5  1 Corinthians 3:8, 14-15, 24
6  2 Corinthians 6:4
7  James 1:4
8  Romans 14:12, Hebrews 4:13
9  Philippians 3:19
10 1 John 1:9
11 Revelation 7:9
12 Wisdom of Solomon 5:1—This is an Apocrypha book.
   The verse reads: "Then the righteous will stand with great confidence in the presence of those who have oppressed them and those who make light of their labors."
13 1 Corinthians 1:20, 27
14 Psalm 107:42

15 2 Corinthians 4:17
16 1 Samuel 5:22, Titus 3:1
17 Ecclesiastes 3:7, Habakkuk 2:20
18 Luke 12:20
19 1 John 4:18, Romans 8:39
20 1 Peter 2:17

# 25
## ZEAL IN IMPROVING YOUR LIFE

Be watchful and diligent in your service to God,[1] and often think of why you came to Christ[2] and why you were separated from the world.[3] Was it not so that you might live for God and become a spiritual person?[4]

Be fervent then in moving forward,[5] for in a short time you will receive the reward for your efforts,[6] and you will have nothing to fear or be sad about when you die.[7]

So work a little now, for you will have great rest later—yes, perpetual joy [see note[8]].

If you continue to be faithful and zealous in doing good, God will certainly be faithful and liberal in rewarding you.[9]

You should have a good hope[10] of obtaining victory, but you must not get careless or you may grow negligent or spiritually proud.

2. There was a man who was anxious about his salvation and often wavered between fear and hope.[11] One day he was oppressed with grief and he humbly prostrated himself before an altar and prayed silently, "Oh, if I only knew for certain that I would persevere!" He soon received an answer within himself: "What would you do if you did know? Do what you would do if you were certain, and you *will* persevere."[12]

That so comforted and strengthened him that he surrendered himself completely to the will of God, and all anxiety left him.

He also lost all curiosity to search further to know what his future would be, and instead strove to understand what the will of God was in the starting and completing of every good work.

3. "Hope in the Lord and do good," says the prophet, "and inhabit the land, and thou shalt be fed with its riches" [see note[13]].

One thing that draws many away from spiritual progress and diligently improving their lives is extreme fear of the difficulty and work of the battle.[14]

The ones, however, who improve more than others in virtue are those who endeavor most to overcome the things that are extremely painful and unfavorable to them.

For we improve more and obtain greater grace in those areas where we most overcome ourselves and discipline our wills.

4. But everyone does not have the same number of things to overcome and discipline.

Yet those who have many things to overcome and are diligent in their efforts, will improve more in virtue than those who have few things to overcome and are less fervent in their pursuit of virtue.

Two things especially further improvement—to withdraw ourselves violently from those things to which human nature is immorally inclined, and to work earnestly for the virtue that we most want.

Be careful and strenuous to avoid those things in yourself that frequently displease you in others.

5. If you see or hear about any good example of virtuously living, stir yourself up and imitate that person so that you will benefit your soul wherever you are.[15]

But if you see anything evil, be careful you do not do the same[16]—and if at any time you have done it, work quickly to amend it.

Remember, in the same way that you watch what others do,[17] others watch what you do.

Oh, how delightful and pleasant it is to see brothers and sisters who are fervent and devout, well-mannered and disciplined![18]

But it is a sad and grievous thing to see them live dissolute and disorderly lives and not apply themselves to the life to which they were called![19]

How hurtful it is to them when they neglect the good purposes of their calling[20] and busy themselves with things that are not their concern!

6. Be mindful of the confession you have made,[21] and always keep the image of your crucified Savior before the eyes of your soul.

Even though you have lived God's way for a long time, you still have good reason to be ashamed of yourself when you look at the life of Jesus Christ, for you have not yet endeavored to make yourself more like Him.

Religious people who seriously and actively imitate the most holy life and passion of our Lord,[22] will find there in abundance whatever is necessary and beneficial to them, and they will never need to look for anything better than Jesus.

Oh, if the crucified Christ truly lived in our hearts,[23] we would quickly and completely be instructed in all truth.[24]

7. Fervent religious people accept and do well all that is commanded of them.

But religious people that are negligent and cold have trial after trial and are afflicted on all sides, for they have no inward comfort, and external comforts that they seek are refused them [see note[25]].

Religious people who do not live disciplined lives are open to great evil that could ruin their souls.

Those who seek freedom[26] and ease will always live in distress, for one thing or another will always displease them.

8. Oh, that we had nothing else to do in life but always praise our Lord God with our whole mouth and heart!

Oh, that you never needed to eat, drink, or sleep, but could spend all your time praising God and doing spiritual work, then you would be much happier than you are now when you must do so many things that are necessary to serve the flesh.

Would to God[27] that such necessities did not exist, but only the spiritual meditations of the soul, which, alas, we enjoy too seldom!

9. When we come to the condition that we do not seek comfort from any creature, then we will begin to enjoy God perfectly. Then we will be content with whatever befalls us in this life.

Then we will not rejoice in great matters or be sorrowful in small, but we will completely and confidently surrender ourselves to God, who will be to us our all in all[28]—to Him nothing perishes or dies, but all things live for Him and serve Him in all matters without delay.

10. Be mindful always of the end of your life [see note[29]], and how that time lost never returns. Without care and diligence you will never grow in virtue.

If you begin to grow cold spiritually,[30] things will begin to be evil for you.

But if you keep yourself spiritually fervent, then you will have great peace and experience less hardship through your love of virtue and the assistance of God's grace.

A fervent and diligent person is prepared for all things.

It is harder to resist vices and passions than it is to do manual labor.

The person who does not get rid of small faults will gradually fall into greater ones [see note[31]].

You will always rejoice in the evening if you spend your day profitably.

Watch over yourself, stir yourself up, warn yourself, and whatever may become of others, do not neglect yourself.

The more strict you are with yourself, the more spiritual progress you will make. Amen.

1   2 Timothy 4:5
2   Matthew 11:28-30
3   John 17:14
4   1 Corinthians 2:14-15
5   Matthew 5:48, Hebrews 6:1
6   2 Timothy 4:7-8
7   Revelation 21:4, 22:3
8   Ecclesiasticus 51:27—Ecclesiasticus is an Apocrypha book.
    The verse reads: "See with your own eyes that I have labored
    but little and found for myself much serenity."
9   Matthew 6:20, 25:23
10 Romans 5:5, Colossians 1:27, Hebrews 6:19
11 James 1:6
12 Philippians 3:17-19, 2 Timothy 2:12
13 Psalm 37:3—The NKJV translates this verse as, "Trust in
    the LORD, and do good; Dwell in the land, and feed on His
    faithfulness." The NIV translates it as, "Trust in the LORD
    and do good; dwell in the land and enjoy safe pasture."
14 Ephesians 6:12
15 1 Corinthians 4:6, 11:1; Hebrews 6:12
16 3 John 1:11
17 Matthew 7:3

18 Ephesians 4:1-3, 14:16, 5:1-31, 6:1-9
19 Ephesians 4:1
20 Galatians 1:6, Ephesians 4:4, 2 Thessalonians 2:14
21 Romans 10:10; 2 Corinthians 9:13; 1 Timothy 6:12;
    Hebrews 3:1, 4:14, 10:23
22 1 Corinthians 11:1
23 Ephesians 3:17
24 John 14:17, 15:26, 16:13-14; 1 Corinthians 2:14
25 Or, ... and are forbidden [by God] to seek external comforts.
26 Galatians 5:13
27 Acts 26:29 (KJV, NKJV)
28 Romans 11:36; 1 Corinthians 8:6, 12:6, 15:28
29 Ecclesiasticus 7:36 – Ecclesiasticus (or Sirach) is an
    Apocrypha book. The verse reads: "In all you do, remember
    the end of your life, and then you will never sin."
30 Revelation 3:16
31 Ecclesiasticus 19:1–Ecclesiasticus (or Sirach) is an
    Apocrypha book. The verse reads: "The one who does this
    will not become rich; one who despises small things will fail
    little by little."

## BOOK TWO

# ADVICE ABOUT
# INTERNAL THINGS

## 1
### THE INWARD LIFE

"The kingdom of God is within you," says the Lord.[1] Turn with your whole heart to the Lord[2] and forsake this miserable world and your soul will find rest.

Learn to despise outward things and to give yourself to inward things and you will see the kingdom of God within you.

"For the kingdom of God is ... righteousness and peace and joy in the Holy Spirit,"[3] and these are not given to the unholy.

Christ will come to you and comfort you if you will prepare a worthy dwelling for Him within you.[4]

All His glory and beauty is revealed from within,[5] and He delights to be within you.

His visits with the inward person are frequent, and with Him He brings sweet conversations, pleasant comfort, great peace, and friendship that is exceedingly wonderful.

2. O faithful soul, make your heart ready for this Bridegroom so that He can come to you and dwell within you.

For Jesus said, "If anyone loves Me, he will keep My word; and My Father will love him, and We will come to him and make Our home with him."[6]

Open your heart to Christ, therefore, and deny entrance to all others.

When you have Christ you are rich and have all you need. He will be your faithful helper in all things[7] and provide all your future needs so that you will not need to rely upon others.

For people soon change and quickly fail, but Christ remains the same forever and stands by us firmly to the end.[8]

3. We should not put great trust in frail and mortal people,[9] even though they may be beneficial and dear to us, and we should not be upset if sometimes they obstruct and oppose us.

Those that take your part today will be against you tomorrow, and often they change directions like the wind.

Put all your trust in God,[10] let Him be your fear and your love, and He will answer for you and will do what is best for you.

You do not have a lasting city here,[11] you are a stranger and pilgrim wherever you are,[12] and you will never have rest unless you are inwardly one with Christ.[13]

4. Why do you look around here when this is not the place where you will have rest? Heaven is your home,[14] and you should look upon all earthly things as if they were passing away.

All things pass away [see note[15]], and you together with them.

Be careful that you do not cling to them or you may be caught and thereby perish. Fix your thoughts on the Highest and pray unceasingly through Christ[16] for help and mercy.[17]

If you can not contemplate high and heavenly things, rest yourself in the suffering of Christ and trust willingly in His sacred wounds.

For if you trust sincerely in the wounds and precious scars of the Lord Jesus, you will feel great comfort during tribulations, you will not be greatly concerned about the slight of others , and you will easily endure their disparaging words.

5. Remember, Christ also was in the world, despised by people, and forsaken by his acquaintances and friends when He was being falsely accused and had the greatest need of them.[18]

If Christ was willing to suffer and be despised, how do you dare to complain about anyone?

Christ had adversaries and backbiters, and you want everyone to be your friend and benefactor!

How will your patience gain a crown if you have no adversity to test you?[19]

If you are not willing to suffer adversity, how will you be a friend of Christ?[20]

If you want to reign with Christ, then suffer with Christ and for Christ.[21]

6. If you once perfectly entered into the inner life of Christ and tasted a little of His ardent love, then you would no longer be concerned about your own convenience or inconvenience, but would take pleasure in reproaches,[22] for His love makes us see ourselves as we truly are.

Those who are true inward Christians and love Jesus and the truth, and are free of excessive emotions, can freely turn themselves to God and rise above themselves in spirit, and joyously remain at rest.[23]

7. Those who judge all things as they truly are and not as they are said or seem to be are truly wise and taught of God rather than people.[24]

Those who can live inwardly and place small value on outward things, do not require special places or expect special times to perform spiritual exercises [see note[25]].

Spiritual people can quickly withdraw inwardly because they never totally give themselves over to outward things.

They are not hindered by work or business that may be necessary for a while, but as things occur they adjust themselves to them.

Those who are well organized and settled within themselves are not bothered by the strange and perverse behavior of others.

People are hindered and distracted in proportion to how much they involve themselves in external matters.

8. If things were well with you and you were purified from sin, all things would work out to your good[26] and your spiritual advancement.

But many things displease and often trouble you because you are not yet perfectly dead to yourself or separated from all worldly things.[27]

Nothing so defiles and entangles the heart of a person as impure love for others.

If you refuse outward comfort, you will be able to contemplate the things of heaven and receive inward joy.

1   Luke 17:21
2   Joel 2:12
3   Romans 14:17
4   Matthew 11:28-30
5   Psalm 45:13
6   John 14:23 (NKJV)
7   Hebrews 13:6

8   Hebrews 13:5, 8
9   Jeremiah 17:5
10  1 Peter 5:6-7
11  Hebrews 13:14
12  Hebrews 11:13
13  John 17:21
14  Philippians 3:20
15  Wisdom of Solomon 5:9—Wisdom of Solomon is an
    Apocrypha book. The verse reads: "All those things have
    vanished like a shadow, and like a rumor that passes by."
16  Ephesians 2:18
17  Hebrews 4:16
18  Matthew 16:21, 26:56; Luke 22:61; John 15:20
19  2 Timothy 4:7-8
20  John 15:14
21  Philippians 3:8, Revelations 3:21
22  2 Corinthians 12:10
23  Matthew 11:28-30
24  Isaiah 54:13
25  As used in the text, exercises are activities that require
    spiritual and mental exertion, especially when intended to
    develop or maintain spiritual growth.
26  Romans 8:28
27  2 Corinthians 6:17

# 2

## HUMBLE SUBMISSION

Do not consider much who is for you or against,[1] but consider only what you are doing and be careful that God is with you in everything you do.

Have a good conscience and God will defend you.[2]

For no one's perverseness can harm anyone whom God will help.

If you can suffer in silence, you will without doubt see that the Lord will help you.

He knows when and how to deliver you, and therefore you should submit yourself to Him.

It is God's purpose to help and to deliver from all confusion.

To make us more humble, it is often beneficial for others to know and rebuke our faults.

2. When we humble ourselves for our failings, then we easily pacify others and quickly satisfy those that are angry with us.

It is the humble whom God protects and delivers,[3] loves and comforts, favors with Himself,[4] gives great grace,[5] and after their humiliation raises to glory.

He reveals His secrets to the humble[6] and sweetly draws and invites them to Himself.[7]

When the humble are rebuked they remain in peace because their rest is from God and not from the world.

Do not think that you have made any [spiritual] progress unless you feel that you are inferior to all others.

1   Romans 8:31, 1 Corinthians 4:3
2   Psalm 28:7
3   Job 5:11
4   Genesis 15:1
5   James 4:6
6   Matthew 11:25
7   John 6:44

# 3
## A Good Peaceful Person

Keep yourself in peace first, and then you will be able to bring peace to others.

A peaceful person does more good than one who is knowledgeable.

A person dominated by powerful emotions turns even good into evil, and easily believes evil.

A good peaceful person turns all things to good.[1]

The person who is at peace is not suspicious of others. But the person who is discontented and troubled is tossed about with various suspicions, and not being at rest does not allow others to be at rest.

Such a person often speaks when nothing should be said, and omits doing the things that should be done.

Also, that person is concerned with the responsibilities of others,[2] but neglects personal responsibilities.

Therefore, be zealous about your responsibilities first, and then you can justly be zealous about your neighbor's welfare.

2. You know well how to excuse and color your own deeds, but you are not willing to accept the excuses of others.

It would more just for you to accuse yourself and excuse others.

If you want to be endured, learn to endure others.[3]

Look how far you still are from true love and humility, for those virtues do not know how to be angry or indignant with others but only with one's self.

It is no great matter to associate with the good and gentle, for this is naturally pleasing to all, and everyone willingly enjoys peace and loves best those who agree with them.

But to live peacefully with people who are hard, perverse, disorderly, or contrary to us, is a great grace and a most commendable and courageous thing.

3. There are some who keep themselves in peace and are at peace with others, also.

And there are some that are neither at peace themselves or allow others be in peace—they are troublesome to others, but always more troublesome to themselves.

Then there are those who keep themselves in peace and carefully consider how to bring peace to others.

In any case, complete peace in this difficult life comes from our humbly suffering adversities  rather than trying to be free from them.

Those who best know how to suffer will best keep themselves in peace. They are conquerors of themselves,[4] controllers of the world, friends of Christ,[5] and heirs of heaven.[6]

1   1 Corinthians 13:5
2   Matthew 7:3
3   1 Corinthians 13:7, Galatians 6:2
4   Romans 8:37
5   John 15:14
6   Romans 8:17, James 2:5

# 4

## A PURE MIND AND SIMPLE INTENTIONS

There are two wings that lift a person up from earthly things: simplicity and purity.

Simplicity should be in our intentions [see note[1]], purity in our feelings. Simplicity reaches toward God, purity apprehends and enjoys Him.

Nothing will delay your spiritual progress if you are inwardly free from immoderate feelings.

If it is your intention to seek nothing else but the will of God and the welfare of your neighbor, you will thoroughly enjoy internal liberty.

If your heart was sincere and upright, then every creature would be a mirror of life to you and a book of holy teaching.

There is no creature so small and lowly that it does not illustrate the glory of God.[2]

2. If you were inwardly good and pure,[3] then you would be able to see and understand all things well without obstruction.

A pure heart penetrates heaven and hell.

In the way we are inwardly, we judge outwardly.[4]

If there is joy in the world, surely those of a pure heart possess it.

If there is tribulation and anxiety anywhere, an evil conscience knows it best.

In the same way that iron put into the fire loses its rust and glows red hot, so the one who turns completely to God puts off all laziness and is transformed into a new creation.[5]

3. When we begin to grow lukewarm, we become afraid of a little [inward spiritual] work and willingly accept external comforts.

But when we begin to overcome ourselves perfectly and walk courageously in the ways of God, then we consider those things to be light that seemed grievous to us before.

1   The course of action a person proposes, or intends, to follow.
2   Romans 1:20
3   Proverbs 3:3-4, Psalm 119:100
4   Titus 1:15
5   2 Corinthians 5:17

# 5
## CONSIDERATION OF OURSELVES

We cannot trust ourselves too much[1] because grace and understanding are often lacking in us.

There is only a little light in us, and that which we have we quickly lose by our negligence.

Often, too, we are not aware of our own inward blindness.

We often do wrong, and then do something worse[2] by excusing ourselves.

Sometimes we are moved by a strong emotion and think it is zeal.

We reprove small things in others and pass over greater things in ourselves.[3]

We are quick to feel and evaluate what we suffer at the hands of others, but we give little thought to what others suffer from us.

Those who properly and truthfully consider their own works, will find little reason to judge others severely.

2. Inward Christians put their spiritual progress before all other concerns,[4] and those who diligently attend to themselves seldom have much to say about others.

You will never be truly devout inwardly unless you pass silently over the affairs of others and look especially to yourself.

If you keep your attention completely upon God and yourself, you will be moved only a little by whatever you see outwardly.[5]

Where are you when you are not with yourself? And when you have occupied yourself with all things, how have you benefited if you have neglected yourself.

If you desire peace of mind and true unity of purpose, you must increasingly put all things behind you and look only to yourself.[6]

3. If you keep yourself free from all temporal concerns, you will make great progress.

You will greatly fall back, however, if you regard anything temporal as having value.

Let nothing be great to you, nothing high, nothing pleasing, nothing acceptable, but only God Himself or that which is of God.

Consider all comfort worthless[7] when you it receive from any creature.

A soul that loves God despises all things that are inferior to God.

God alone is everlasting and of infinite greatness, filling all creation—the soul's solace and the true joy of the heart.

1   Proverbs 3:5, Jeremiah 17:5
2   Psalm 141:4
3   Matthew 7:5
4   Matthew 16:26
5   1 Corinthians 4:3, Galatians 1:10
6   Philippians 3:13
7   Ecclesiastes 1:14

# 6
## JOY OF A GOOD CONSCIENCE

The glory of a good person is the testimony of a good conscience.[1]

Have a good conscience and you will always have joy,

A good conscience is able to endure a great deal and is truly cheerful in adversities.

An evil conscience is always fearful and restless [see note[2]].

You will have a gratifying rest if your heart does not condemn you.

Rejoice only when you have done well.

Sinners never have true joy or feel inward peace, because "there is no peace," says the LORD, "for the wicked."[3]

If sinners should say, "We are in peace, no evil shall fall upon us,[4] and who shall dare to hurt us?" do not believe them, for the wrath of God will suddenly come upon them, and their deeds will be brought to nothing and their thoughts will perish [see note[5]].

2. To glory [rejoice triumphantly] in tribulations is not hard for a person who loves, for glorying in that way is to glory in the Cross of the Lord.[6]

The glory that is given and received from people is short-lived.[7]

Sorrow always accompanies the world's glory.

The glory of the good is in their consciences, and not in the words of people. The gladness of the just is of God and in God,[8] and their joy comes from the truth.[9]

The person who desires true and everlasting glory does not care for the things that are temporal.

Those who seek temporal glory or do not despise it with their hearts, show that they have little love for the glory of heaven.

The person who cares nothing about the approval or disapproval of people enjoys great peace of mind.

3. If your conscience is pure you will easily be satisfied and restored to peace.

You are not more holy when you are praised, or more worthless when you are disparaged.

You are what you are, and you cannot be said to be greater than what you are in the sight of God.

If you consider what you are within you, then you will not be concerned about what people say about you.

"People look at the outward appearance, but the LORD looks at the heart."[10] They consider the deeds a person does, but God considers the motives.[11]

To be always doing well and have little regard for yourself is the sign of a humble soul.

It is a sign of great purity and inward confidence not to look for comfort from any person.

4. Those who seek no witness outside themselves, show that they have fully committed themselves to God.

"For it is not those who commend themselves that are approved," says Paul, "but those whom the Lord commends"[12]

Spiritual people walk inwardly with God and are not sustained by any outward feelings.

1   1 Corinthians 1:31
2   Wisdom of Solomon 17:11—Wisdom of Solomon is an Apocrypha book. The verse reads: "For wickedness is a cowardly thing, condemned by its own testimony; distressed by conscience, it has always exaggerated the difficulties."
3   Isaiah 48:22
4   Luke 12:17
5   Kempis's words were once quoted by Arthur James Balfour, First Earl of Balfour (1848-1930): "Man will go down into the pit, and all his thoughts will perish." A British prime minister (1902-1905), Balfour later served as foreign secretary under David Lloyd George (1916-1919). In 1917 he promised British support for a national homeland for Jews in Palestine, provided that the rights of existing communities would be safeguarded.
6   Romans 5:31; 1 Corinthians 1:31, 2 Corinthians 10:17; Galatians 6:14
7   John 5:44
8   Psalm 63:11, Romans 5:11
9   1 Corinthians 13:6
10  1 Samuel 16:7—This is a paraphrase of the Scripture.
11  Proverbs 16:2, 1 Corinthians 4:5
12  2 Corinthians 10:18, NRSV

## 7
### Loving Jesus Above All Things

Blessed are those who understand[1] what it is to love Jesus and to despise themselves for His sake.

All your other loves must be as nothing compared to your love for Jesus, for He and the Father desire to be loved above all things.[2]

The love of created beings is deceitful and fickle, but Jesus' love is faithful and permanent.

The person who clings to others will fall with those who are frail, but the person who holds fast to Jesus will stand firmly forever.

Love Jesus and keep Him for your friend, for when all others go away He will not forsake you or allow you to perish in the end.[3]

You must someday be separated from everything whether you want to be or not.[4]

2. Keep close to Jesus in life and in death and commit yourself into His trust, for He alone can help you when all others fail.

It is the nature of your Beloved to permit no rivals, and to have your heart alone and be enthroned within it as its King.[5]

If you could free yourself completely from all others, Jesus would willingly dwell with you.[6]

Most of the trust you place in people instead of Jesus is little better than lost.

Do not trust or lean upon a weed blown by the wind, for "all flesh is grass," and all its glory will wither away like the flower of the field.[7]

3. You will quickly be deceived if you look only at the outward appearance of people.

For if you seek comfort and benefit from them, you will too often be disappointed.

If you seek Jesus in all things, you will surely find Him.

But if you seek yourself, you will also find yourself—to your own harm.

For if you do not seek Jesus, you hurt yourself more than the whole world and all your adversaries hurt you.

1  Psalm 119:1-2
2  Deuteronomy 6:5, Matthew 22:37, Luke 14:27
3  Hebrews 13:5
4  Mark 10:28-30, 2 Corinthians 6:17
5  Ephesians 3;17, Revelation 3:20
6  ibid.
7  Isaiah 40:6-7

# 8
## FRIENDLY CONVERSATIONS WITH JESUS

When Jesus is present everything is well and nothing seems difficult, but when Jesus is absent everything is hard.

When Jesus does not speak inwardly to us all other comfort is valueless, but if Jesus speaks just one word we feel great comfort.

Did not Mary Magdalene [see note[1]] rise immediately from the place where she wept when Martha said to her, "The Teacher has come and is calling for you."[2]

It is a happy moment when Jesus calls us from tears to spiritual joy!

How dry and hard we are without Jesus! How foolish and arrogant if we desire anything except Him!

Not having Jesus is a greater loss than if we should lose the whole world.[3]

2. What can the world give you without Jesus?

Life without Jesus is a sorrowful hell, and life with Him is a sweet paradise.

If Jesus is with you, no enemy can hurt you.[4]

The one who finds Jesus finds a good treasure[5]—yes, a Good above all good!

And the one who loses Jesus loses much indeed—yes, more than the whole world!

The poorest person is the one who lives without Jesus,[6] and the richest person is the one who is in favor with Jesus.

3. It is a matter of great art to know how to hold a conversation with Jesus, and a point of great wisdom to know how to keep Him.

Be humble and peaceful and Jesus will be with you.[7]

Be devout and quiet and Jesus will stay with you.

You may soon drive away Jesus [the sense of His presence] and lose His favor if you turn to outward things.

And if you should drive Him away and lose [your awareness of] Him, where will you go and whom will you seek as a friend? [see note[8]].

Without a friend you cannot live well, and if Jesus is not above everything a friend to you, you will indeed be sad and desolate.

You therefore act like a fool if you trust or rejoice in any other than Jesus.[9]

It is better to have the whole world against us than to have Jesus offended with us.

Among all, therefore, that is dear to us, let Jesus alone be especially beloved.

4. Love everything for Jesus' sake, but Jesus for Himself.

Jesus Christ alone is to be especially beloved, for He alone is good and faithful above all friends.

For Christ and in Christ friends and enemies should equally be dear to you, and all of them should be prayed for so that they all may know and love Him.[10]

Never desire to be especially praised or beloved, for that belongs only to God, Who has no one like Himself.

Never desire that the heart of anyone be centered on you, and do not center your heart on your love for anyone, but let Jesus be the center of your heart and the heart of every good person.

5. Be pure and free within and do not entangle your heart with any creature.

You should be naked and open before God, always bringing your heart pure before Him, if you want to be free to consider and see how sweet the Lord is.

But unless His grace precedes and draws you, you will never arrive at the happiness needed to forsake and cast off everything so that you alone [see note[11]] may be united to Him alone.

For when the grace of God comes to us we are enabled to do all things. And when it goes away we are poor and weak and, in a manner of speaking, turned over to tribulations.

When that happens you should not be dejected or despair, but rest steadfast in God's will, and whatever comes upon you endure it for the glory of Jesus Christ—for after winter comes summer, after night comes day, and after the violent storm comes a great calm.

---

1   The text identifies Mary Magdalene as the sister of Martha. There are four Marys named in the gospels: Mary, the mother of Jesus; Mary Magdalene; Mary, the sister of Martha and Lazarus; and Mary, the wife of Cleopas. Modern translation of the Bible clearly points this reference is to Mary, sister of Martha.

2   John 11:28 (NKJV)

3   Matthew 16:26

4  Romans 8:31
5  Matthew 13:44
6  Luke 12.21
7  John 16:33
8  Driving Jesus away from us and losing Him is contrary
   to Hebrews 13:5b, which says: "For He Himself has said,
   'I will never leave you nor forsake you.'" We are not so
   powerful that we can drive Christ from us, though we can
   through sin or neglect lose the sense of His presence within
   us. See John 3:18-20
9  Galatians 6:14
10 Matthew 5:44, Luke 6:27-28
11 Bringing nothing with you to God, only yourself.


# 9

## WANTING ALL COMFORT

It is not difficult to despise human comfort when we have divine comfort.

It is a very great thing to lack both human and divine comfort and be willing for God's honor to cheerfully endure this banishment of your heart from all others, and not to seek comfort for yourself in anything or to esteem your own merit [see note[1]].

How greatly does it matter if when grace comes you are cheerful and devout?—such a moment is wished for by everyone.

The person whom the grace of God carries rides easily enough.

And what is there to marvel about if the person who is borne up by the Almighty and led by the sovereign Guide doesn't feel their burden?

2. We are always willing to have something to comfort us, and it is difficult for us to put off and forsake ourselves [our comfort].[2]

The holy martyr Laurence, with his priest, overcame the world because he despised whatever seemed delightful in the world, and for the love of Christ he patiently permitted God's chief priest Sixtus, whom he dearly loved, to be taken away from him [see note[3]].

He therefore overcame his love for a human being by his love for the Creator, and chose what pleased God rather than human comfort.

You should also learn to part with even a near and dear friend for the love of God.

Do not take it hard when you are deserted by a friend, for we know that all of us must eventually be separated from one another.

3. We must strive long and mightily within ourselves before we can learn to master ourselves completely and move all of our heart into God.

When we trust in ourselves, we lean easily toward human comforts

But a person who truly loves Christ and diligently seeks virtue does not fall back on worldly comforts or look for things pleasing to the senses, but instead prefers difficulties and hardships for Christ's sake.[4]

4. When God gives you spiritual comfort, therefore, receive it with thankfulness, but understand that it is given to you as a gift and not because of any merit of yours.

Do not be puffed up or overjoyed or proudly presumptuous because of the gift, but be humble for it and more watchful and fearful in all your actions, for that hour will pass and temptation will follow.

Do not quickly despair when comfort is taken from you, but wait humbly and patiently for another heavenly visit, for God is able to give you even greater comfort.[5]

Such things are nothing new or strange to those who have experience with God, for the great saints and prophets often experienced sudden spiritual changes.

5. For this reason, when David was enjoying divine grace, he proclaimed, "In my prosperity I said, 'I shall never be moved.'"[6]

But when grace departed he expressed what he found within himself: "You hid your face; I was dismayed."[7]

Yet in the midst of all this he did not despair, but prayed more earnestly to the Lord and said, "Unto Thee, 0 Lord, will I cry, and I will pray unto my God" [see note[8]].

At length he received the fruit of his prayer and testified that he was heard, saying, "The Lord hath heard me, and taken pity on me; the Lord is become my helper" [see note [9]].

What was the result? David said: "You have turned for me my mourning into dancing; You have put off my sackcloth and clothed me with gladness."[10]

If great saints [like David] were dealt with in this way, we who are weak and poor should not get depressed if we are sometimes spiritually hot and sometimes spiritually cold, for the spirit comes and goes according to the good pleasure of God's will.[11] For that reason, blessed Job said, "Thou visitest him early in the morning, and suddenly Thou provest him" [see note [12]].

6. In what then can I hope and in what should I trust?—but in the great mercy of God alone and in the only hope of heavenly grace![13]

For whether I have with me good people, spiritual brothers and sisters or faithful friends; holy books or beautiful teachings; sweet chants and hymns; all of these help and please only a little when grace leaves me and I am left in my own spiritual poverty.

At such times there is no better remedy than to have patience and to deny myself according to the will of God.[14]

7. I have never found anyone so spiritual and devout that they never at times experienced a withdrawing of grace and felt their spiritual zeal decrease.

There was never a saint so highly enraptured and enlightened who was not tempted sooner or later.

For no one is worthy of the higher contemplations of God who has not been spiritually developed by some tribulation for God's sake.

Now temptation may be a sign that precedes comfort that is to come.

For heavenly comfort is promised to those who are proved by temptations: "To him who overcomes I will give to eat from the tree of life."[15]

8. So divine comfort is given to strengthen a person to endure adversities.

Temptation then follows to prevent us from growing proud of any good we have done.[16]

The devil does not sleep[17] and the flesh is not yet dead, therefore do not stop preparing yourself for the battle, for enemies who never rest are all around you.[18]

1   Merit: Theology. Spiritual credit granted for good works.
2   Matthew 26:41
3   There is no information as to who this is, but it is not the Brother Lawrence of The Practice of the Presence of God fame, for he did not live until nearly two centuries after Kempis wrote his material. Sixtus is undoubtedly one of three popes: Sixtus I (115-125), Sixtus II (257-258), or Sixtus III (432-44).
4   2 Corinthians 12:10
5   Job 42:12

6 Psalm 30:6

7 Psalm 30:7 (NIV)

8 Psalm 30:8 (NKJV)—The verse actually reads: "I cried out to You, O LORD; And to the LORD I made supplication."

9 Psalm 30:10—The text paraphrases this verse and makes it an answer to prayer instead of a continuation of prayer, as it is in all current Bible versions: "Hear, O LORD, and have mercy on me; LORD, be my helper!"

10 Psalm 30:11

11 John 3:8

12 Job 7:18—In all current Bible versions, this verse reads: "That You should visit him every morning, And test him every moment?" Verse 18 is a continuation of the question started in verse 17: "What is man, that You should exalt him, That You should set Your heart on him, ..."

13 Galatians 5:5, Colossians 1:27, 1 Thessalonians 5:8, Hebrews 6:18-19

14 Luke 9:23

15 Revelation 2:7

16 2 Corinthians 12:7

17 1 Peter 5:8

18 Ephesians 6:12-18

# 10
## GRATITUDE FOR THE GRACE OF GOD

Why do you seek to rest when you are born to labor?[1]

Commit yourself to patience rather than to comfort, and to bearing the cross rather than to pleasure.[2]

What worldly person is there who would not willingly receive spiritual joy and comfort if they could always have it?

For spiritual comforts exceed all the delights of the world and pleasures of the flesh.

For all worldly delights are either worthless or unclean, but spiritual delights that spring from virtue are pleasant and honest and infused by God into pure minds.

No one, however, can always enjoy these divine comforts whenever desired, for the time of temptation is not long away.

2. False freedom of mind[3] and great confidence in ourselves is contrary to heavenly visitations.

God treats us well by giving us the grace of comfort, but we do evil in not returning everything back to God with thanksgiving.[4]

When we do not thank the Giver and return the gifts of grace completely to the source and fountain from which they came, they cannot flow in and from us [see note[5]].

For grace always accompanies the one who is duly thankful, and what is customarily given to the humble will be taken away from the proud.[6]

3. I do not desire comfort that takes compunction from me, nor do I desire the kind of contemplation that leads to a scornful and condescending attitude.

For everything high is not holy, everything sweet is not good, every desire is not pure, and everything precious to us is not pleasing to God.

I willingly accept the grace that will make me more humble, more influenced by holy fear, and more ready to renounce myself.

Those who are taught by the gift of grace and learn by the shock of its withdrawal, will not dare to attribute any good to themselves, but instead will acknowledge that they are spiritually impoverished and vulnerable.

Give to God what is God's[7] and attribute to yourself what is yours—that is, thank God for His grace and acknowledge that nothing can be attributed to you except sin and the punishment sin deserves.

4. Always put yourself in the lowest place and the highest place will be given to you,[8] for the highest cannot stand without the foundation of the lowest.

The greatest saints before God are the least in their own judgments and the more saintly they are, the more humble they are within themselves.

Those who are full of truth and heavenly glory have no desire for worthless [earthly] glory.

Those who are firmly settled and grounded in God cannot be proud.

Those who attribute to God all the good they have received do not seek glory from others, but wish only for the glory that is from God alone, and desire above all things that God be praised in themselves and in all the saints, and are always attending to that very thing.

5. Be thankful, therefore, for the least gift so that you will be worthy to receive greater gifts,

Let the least gift be to you as the greatest, and the most contemptible gift as of special value.

No gift will seem little or of no value to you if you consider the value of the Giver. For nothing can be little that is given by the Most High God.

Yes, even if He should chastise and rebuke us severely we should thank Him for it, because whatever He permits to happen to us He always does it for our welfare.[9]

If we desire to keep the grace of God, let us be thankful when grace is given, patient when it is taken away, prayerful so it will return, and cautious and humble lest we lose it [permanently].

1   Matthew 9:37-38
2   Luke 14:27
3   Galatians 5:13
4   1 Timothy 4:4
5   John 7:38, Ecclesiasticus 1:5—Ecclesiasticus (or Sirach) is an

Apocrypha book. The verse reads: "The source of wisdom is God's word in the highest heaven, and her ways are the eternal commandments." Some versions of Sirach do not contain this verse.

6   James 4:6
7   Matthew 22:21
8   Luke 14:10
9   Hebrews 12:5-11

# 11

## HOW FEW LOVE THE CROSS OF JESUS

Jesus now has many who love His heavenly kingdom, but few who bear His Cross.[1]

He has many who desire comfort, but few who desire tribulation.

He finds many companions at His table, but few who fast often.[2]

All desire to rejoice with Him, but few are willing to suffer anything for Him—or with Him.[3]

Many follow Jesus into the breaking of bread, but few to the drinking of the cup of His suffering.[4]

Many revere His miracles, but few follow the humiliation of His Cross.

Many love Jesus, so long as adversities do not happen to them.

Many praise and bless Him, so long as they receive comfort from Him.

But if Jesus hides His presence and leaves them for even a little while, they either start complaining or become depressed.

2. But those who love Jesus for His own sake and not for some special comfort of their own, bless Him in all

heartfelt tribulation and anguish as well as in a state of highest comfort.

And even if He should never be willing to comfort them, they would still always praise Him and want to thank Him.

3. Oh, how powerful is pure love for Jesus that is not mixed with self-interest or self-love!

Those who are always looking to receive comfort should be called "mercenary" [see note[5]].

Do they not show that they are lovers of themselves rather than of Christ—always thinking of their own profit and advantage?[6]

Where can one be found who is willing to serve God for nothing?

4. Rarely is anyone found who is so spiritual as to be stripped of love for all earthly things.

For where is anyone to be found that is truly poor in spirit and free from all creatures? "From afar, yea, from the ends of the earth, is his value" [see note[7]].

If we should give all our material possessions, yet it is nothing.

And if we should practice great repentance, still it is little.

And if we should obtain all knowledge, we are still far away.

And if we should be extremely virtuous and fervently devoted, yet we still lack much, especially one thing that is most necessary for us.[8]

What is that one thing? That we leave everything, forsake ourselves, turn completely away from ourselves,[9] and keep nothing of ourselves out of self-love.

And when we have done all that is to be done so far as we know, we must think of it as having done nothing.

5. Do not consider those things valuable that might be highly esteemed, but proclaim that you are in truth an unprofitable servant, as the Truth Himself said, "So likewise you, when you have done all those things which you are commanded, say, 'We are unprofitable servants. We have done what was our duty to do.'"[10]

Then you will truly be spiritual poor and exposed and be able to say with the prophet, "I am alone and poor" [see note [11]].

Yet no one will be richer than you, no one more powerful, no one more free, for you can freely disregard yourself and all things and set yourself in the lowest place.

1  Philippians 3:18-19
2  2 Corinthians 11:27
3  2 Corinthians 1:5, 12:10; Philippians 1:29
4  Luke 9:14, 22:41-42; Mark 10:38
5  Mercenary: One who serves or works merely for monetary or material gain.
6  Philippians 2:21
7  Proverbs 31:10—Such a person is as valuable as something brought from the farthest parts of the earth, or as valuable as everything between two distant points on the earth. The origin of the quotation could not be found.
8  Luke 18:22
9  Matthew 16:24-25
10 Luke 17:10 (NKJV)
11 Exact quotation could not be found, but may be paraphrase of Elijah's words in 1 King 19:14 (see also Romans 11:3).

## 12
### THE KING'S HIGHWAY OF THE HOLY CROSS

To many this seems a hard saying,[1] "Deny yourself, take up your cross, and follow Jesus" [see note [2]].

But it will be much harder to hear that last word, "'Depart from Me, you cursed, into the everlasting fire prepared for the devil and his angels.'"[3]

But those who now willingly hear and follow the word of the cross will not in the day of judgment fear the sentence of everlasting damnation.

The sign of the cross will be in heaven when the Lord comes to judge.

Then all those who in their lifetime conformed themselves to Christ crucified and were servants of the cross will draw near to Christ the Judge[4] with great confidence.

2. Why do you fear, therefore, to take up the cross that leads you to heaven?

In the cross is salvation, life, protection from our enemies, infusion of heavenly sweetness, strength of mind, joy of spirit, height of virtue, and the perfection of holiness.

There is no salvation of the soul or hope of everlasting life but in the cross.[5]

Take up your cross, therefore, and follow Jesus, and you will enter into eternal life. He went before bearing His Cross and died upon it for you, so that you may also bear your cross and desire to die spiritually upon it.[6]

For if you died with Him, you will also live with Him.[7] And if you share His suffering, you will also share His glory.[8]

3. Behold, then, everything is in the cross and everything depends upon our dying on it, for there is no other way to life and true inward peace but the way of the holy cross and daily discipline.[9]

Go where you will and seek what you will, you will not find a higher way above or a safer way below than the way of the holy cross.

Set in order all things according to your will and judgement, and yet you will always find that it is necessary that you suffer to some degree, either willing or unwillingly, and so you will always find the cross awaiting you.

For you will either feel pain in your body or suffer spiritual tribulation in your soul.

4. Sometimes you will feel forsaken by God, sometimes you will be troubled by others, and often you will also be a burden to yourself.

During such times you cannot be delivered or eased by any remedy or comfort—but so long as it pleases God to have it that way you should patiently endure it.

For it is God's will that you learn to suffer adversities without being comforted, and that you submit yourself completely to Him and become more humble by suffering.[10]

No one can relate to the suffering of Christ as much as the person who has suffered like Him.

The cross, therefore, is always ready and waits for you everywhere.

You cannot escape from it no matter where you run, for wherever you go you take yourself with you and will always find yourself.

Above and below, within and without, whatever way you turn yourself, everywhere you will find the cross, and everywhere it will be necessary that you have patience if you want to have inward peace and enjoy an everlasting crown.

5. If you carry the cross cheerfully it will carry you and lead you to the desired end; namely, where there will be an end of suffering,[11] although here there will never be.

If you carry the cross unwillingly you will make a new burden for yourself and increase your load, and though unwilling you must still carry it.

If you cast away one cross you will without doubt find another one, and that one may be even heavier.

6. Do you think you can escape that which no mortal person has ever avoided? Which of the saints in the world were without crosses and tribulations?

Not even our Lord Jesus Christ went one hour while He lived without the anguish of His coming suffering and crucifixion. "It was necessary for the Christ to suffer and to rise from the dead the third day, ... and to enter into His glory."[12] Why do you seek any other way than this royal way of the holy cross?

7. Christ's whole life was a cross and martyrdom, and do you seek rest and joy for yourself?

You are twice deceived if you expect anything other than suffering tribulations, for this whole mortal life is full of adversities and marked on every side with crosses.

And the higher a person advances in spirit the heavier the crosses are that are often found, because the grief of a sense of separation from God increases with love for God.

8. Nevertheless, those who are afflicted in many ways are not without refreshing comfort, for they know that by bearing the cross they are gathering many treasures for themselves.[13]

For while they *willingly* put themselves under the cross, all the burden of adversity is turned into confidence of future divine comfort.

And the more the flesh is weakened by affliction, so much the more is the spirit strengthened by inward grace.

Sometimes saints are so comforted in the desire for tribulation and adversity and love of conformity to the cross of Christ, that they do not wish to be without grief and tribulation,[14] because they believe that the more and heavier things they suffer for God the more acceptable they are to Him.

This does not come from the power of a person, it comes from the grace of Christ that can and does so much in weak flesh—so what flesh naturally hates and runs from, the fire of the spirit enables it to encounter and love.

9. It is not in keeping with human inclinations to bear the cross, to love the cross, to discipline the body and bring it into subjection, to flee honors, to suffer reproaches willingly, to despise ourselves and to wish to be despised, to endure all adversities and losses, and to desire no prosperity in this world.

If you rely upon yourself you will not be able alone to accomplish anything of this kind.[15]

But if you trust in the Lord you will be given strength from heaven, and the world and the flesh will be made subject to your word.

Neither will you fear your enemy the devil if you are armed with faith[16] and marked with the cross of Christ.

10. Set yourself, therefore, like a good and faithful servant of Christ to bear courageously the cross of Christ, who was crucified for you out of love.[17]

Prepare yourself to endure many adversities and various kinds of trouble in this difficult life, for that is the way it will be with you wherever you are, and you will find it that way no matter where you hide yourself.

That is how it must be—and there are no remedies or ways to escape from tribulations and sorrows; you can only endure them.

If you desire to be the Lord's friend and share His glory with Him,[18] drink heartily of His cup.[19] As for receiving comfort, leave that to God and let Him do [for you] whatever best pleases Him.

Set yourself to suffer tribulations and consider them the greatest comforts, for even if you alone endured all the sufferings of this present age, they are not worth comparing with the glory that will be revealed in us.[20]

11. When you come to the spiritual state that tribulations seems sweet and you take pleasure in them for Christ's sake,[21] then consider yourself fortunate, for you have found a paradise on earth.

For as long as it is hard for you to suffer and you want to run from it, you will be uneasy, and the desire to run from tribulation will follow you everywhere.

12. If you will set yourself to what you should do, follow Christ in suffering and death, it will soon be better for you and you will find peace.

Even if you should be carried up to the third heaven like Paul,[22] you will not be kept from suffering tribulations. Jesus said about Paul, "I will show him how many things he must suffer for My name's sake"[23]

If it is your desire, therefore, to love Jesus and serve Him forever, you are bound to suffer.

13. O that you were worthy to suffer something for the name of Jesus![24] What great glory would await you, what joy would spring forth in all God's saints, and how greatly those around you would be edified!

For everyone praises patience, but there are few who are willing to suffer.

With good reason, therefore, you should cheerfully suffer a little for Christ's sake, especially since many suffer more grievous things for the world.

14. Know for certain that we should live a life dying to ourselves.[25] For the more we die to ourselves, the more we begin to live unto God.

None of us are qualified to understand heavenly things unless we submit ourselves to suffering adversities for Christ's sake.

For there is nothing more acceptable to God, nothing more wholesome for us in this world, than to suffer cheerfully for Christ.

If you could choose, you should desire to suffer adversities for Christ rather than be refreshed by many comforts, because you would than be more like Christ and more submissive to all the saints.[26]

For our worthiness and the development of our spiritual condition does not lie in many delights and comforts, but rather in enduring through great afflictions and tribulations [see note[27]].

15. If there had been any better and more profitable thing to our salvation than taking up our cross and following Christ, then surely He would have showed it by word and example.

But to all His disciples that followed Him and all who desire to follow Him, he plainly exhorted bearing the cross when He said, ""If anyone would come after me, he must deny himself and take up his cross daily and follow me."[28]

So when we have thoroughly read and searched everything, here is the conclusion of the matter: "We must through many tribulations enter the kingdom of God."[29]

1 John 6:60
2 Matthew 16:24—This is a paraphrase of the actual Scripture: "Then Jesus said to His disciples, 'If anyone desires to come after Me, let him deny himself, and take up his cross, and follow Me'" (NKJV).
3 Matthew 24:41

4   2 Timothy 4:1
5   1 Corinthians 1:17-18, Colossians 1:20
6   Romans 6:6-7
7   Romans 6:8
8   Acts 5:41, Romans 8:17, 2 Corinthians 1:5, Philippians 1:29
9   Luke 14:27
10 Hebrews 2:10, 5:8
11 Revelation 21:4
12 Luke 24:46a and 26b combined—See also Luke 9:26.
13 Matthew 6:19-20
14 2 Corinthians 2:16, 11:23-30
15 2 Corinthians 3:5
16 Ephesians 6:16
17 Galatians 2:20
18 Romans 8:17
19 Matthew 20:23, John 18:11,
20 Romans 8:18
21 Romans 5:3, 2 Corinthians 12:10, Galatians 6:14
22 2 Corinthians 12:2-4
23 Acts 9:16 (NKJV)
24 Acts 5:41
25 Mark 8:35, 2 Corinthians 4:10, 6:9
26 1 Peter 5:5
27 Here the original text used the words, "thoroughly enduring
   great afflictions and tribulations." Today, "thoroughly"
   is similar to "completely." But in Middle-English days,
   "thoroughly" was still used as a variant of "through." So it
   most likely that Kempis's original thought was not to simply
   endure an affliction, but to endure it until it is over—all the
   way through.
28 Luke 9:23 (NIV)
29 Acts 14:22 (NKJV)

## BOOK THREE

# INTERNAL CONSOLATION

## 1

### CHRIST SPEAKS INWARDLY TO THE FAITHFUL SOUL

"I will hear what the Lord God will speak in me" [see note[1]].

Blessed is the person who hears the Lord speak inwardly[2] and receives from His mouth Word of consolation.

Blessed are the ears that eagerly listen for the breath of the divine whisper, and do not pay attention to the many whisperings of this world.

Blessed, indeed, are the ears that do not listen to the voice that speaks outwardly, but to the truth that is taught inwardly.

Blessed are the eyes that are closed to outward things, but are firmly fixed on inward things.

Blessed are those who enter far into internal things, and by daily spiritual exercises [see note[3]] endeavor to prepare themselves increasingly to receive heavenly secrets.

Blessed are those who are glad to have time to spend with God and shake off everything worldly that hinders them.

2. Consider these things, O my soul, and shut the door of your sensual[4] desires so that you may hear what the Lord your God will speak in you.[5]

Thus says your Beloved: "I am your salvation, your peace, and your life: keep yourself with me, and you shall find peace" [see note[6]]

Let go of all temporal things and seek those things that are eternal.

What are all temporal things but seducing snares, and of what use to you are all creatures if you are forsaken by the Creator?

Cast off all temporal things and work to please your Creator and to be faithful to Him, so that you will be able to arrive at the true blessedness.

1 Psalm 85:8—This is a paraphrase of the actual verse, which says, "I will hear what God the LORD will speak."
2 1 Samuel 3:2-9
3 As used in the text, exercises are activities that require spiritual and mental exertion, especially when intended to develop or maintain spiritual growth.
4 Relating to or affecting any of the senses or a sense organ; sensory. Not referring to sexuality as it does so much today.
5 Matthew 13:16-17
6 Psalm 85:8—This verse states, in effect, "For He will speak peace To His people and to His saints." Kempis's quotation is probably several partial verses combined.

# 2

## TRUTH SPEAKS INWARDLY WITHOUT THE SOUND OF WORDS

Speak, LORD, for Your servant hears.[1]

I am Your servant; Give me understanding, That I may know Your testimonies.[2]

Incline my heart to the Words of Your mouth:[3] let Your Words descend like dew."[4]

The children of Israel once said to Moses, "You speak with us, and we will hear; but let not God speak with us, lest we die.[5]

Let it not be so, Lord, I beseech You, but rather with the prophet Samuel I humbly and earnestly plead, "Speak, LORD, for Your servant hears."[6]

Do not let Moses or any of the prophets speak to me, but You who are the inspirer and enlightener of all the prophets speak to me—for You alone without them can perfectly instruct me, but without You they can do nothing.[7]

2. They, indeed, may utter words, but they cannot give the Spirit.

They speak beautifully, but if You are silent they cannot inflame the heart.

They teach the letter, but You open the senses—they bring forth mysteries, but You unlock the meaning of the mysteries.

They declare Your commandments, but You help us to fulfil them.

They point out the way,[8] but You give us strength to walk in it.[9]

What they do is only outwardly, but You instruct and enlighten the heart.

They water outwardly, but You give abundance.

They cry aloud in words, but You impart understanding to the hearing.

3. Do not, therefore, let Moses speak to me, but You O Lord my God speak the everlasting truth, so that I will not die and prove to have been unfruitful because I was only warned outwardly and was not aroused within.

So that the Word heard and not fulfilled, known and not loved, believed and not observed, will not turn to my condemnation.

Speak, therefore, Lord, for Your servant hears, for You have the words of eternal life.[10]

Speak to me so that my soul, however imperfect, will be comforted, my life will be amended, and You will be praised, glorified, and honored forever

1  1 Samuel 3:9
2  Psalm 119:125
3  Psalm 119:36
4  Deuteronomy 32:2
5  Exodus 20:19
6  1 Samuel 3:9
7  This passage and several that follow, and a number of similar passages throughout the book, are based upon the doctrine held by some denominations that departed saints can communicate with people.
8  John 14:6—"Jesus said to him, 'I am the way, the truth, and the life. No one comes to the Father except through Me.'"
9  Philippians 4:13
10 John 6:68

# 3

## HEAR GOD'S WORDS WITH HUMILITY [SEE NOTE[1]]
## MANY DO NOT LISTEN TO THEM

My child, hear my Words, Words of the greatest sweetness, surpassing all the learning of the philosophers and the wise of this world.

"My Words are spirit and they are life,"[2] and not to be measured by the understanding of humanity.

They are not to be brought forth for worthless praise and approval, but to be listened to in silence and received with all humility and great affection.

"Blessed are those whom You will instruct, O Lord, and will teach out of Your Word, that You may give them rest from the evil days,[3] and that they will not be alone upon the earth.

2. I taught the prophets from the beginning,[4] and have not stopped speaking to everyone even to this day, but many have hardened their hearts and are deaf to My voice.[5]

Most people are more willing to listen to the world than to God, and they would rather follow the desires of their own flesh than God's good pleasure.

The world promises things that are temporary and inferior, and it is served with great eagerness—I promise things most high and eternal, and yet the hearts of people are not receptive.

Who serves and obeys Me in all things with as great a care as the world and its lords are served? "'Be ashamed, O Sidon,' for the sea has spoken."[6] And if you ask why, this is the reason. For little pay many will undertake a long journey, but for everlasting life many will scarcely lift a foot once from the ground.

The most pitiful reward is sought after, there are sometimes shameful arguments over a small amount of money, and for something worthless and the slightest promise of reward people do not hesitate to work day and night.

3. But, alas!, for an unchangeable good, an inestimable reward, the highest honor, and glory without end, they complain about getting even a little tired.

Be ashamed, therefore, you lazy and complaining servant that they are found to be more eager for eternal death than you are for eternal life.

And they rejoice more in worthlessness than you do in the truth.

Sometimes, indeed, their hopes fail them, but My promise deceives no one, and sends no one away empty who trusts in Me.[7]

What I have promised I will give, and what I have said I will make good, if any person remain faithful in My love to the end.

I am the rewarder of all good people,[8] and the strong approver of all who are devoted to Me.

4. Write My Words in your heart and meditate diligently on them,[9] for in time of temptation they will be very necessary to you.

What you do not understand when you read, you will know in the day of your visitation [the day I visit you].[10]

I customarily visit my elect in two ways—with temptation and with consolation.

And every day I read two lessons to them—one to rebuke their vices, and the other to exhort them to increase their virtues.

Those who have My Words and despise them have one who will judge them on the last day.[11]

5. A prayer pleading for the grace of devotion.

O Lord, my God! You are to me whatever is good. And who am I that I should dare speak to You?[12] I am Your poorest [see note[13]] and most inferior servant, and a most wicked person, much poorer and contemptible than I can or dare express.

Yet remember me, O Lord, because I am nothing, I have nothing, I can do nothing.

You alone are good, just, and holy. You can do all things, You accomplish all things, You fill all things, only the sinner You leave empty.

Remember Your mercies and fill my heart with Your grace,[14] for it is not Your will that Your works should be void and worthless.

6. How can I uphold myself in this difficult life unless You strengthen me with Your mercy and grace?

Do not turn Your face from me,[15] do not delay the day of Your visit, do not withdraw Your consolation, lest [for fear that] my soul becomes as a thirsty land to You.

Teach me, O Lord, to do Your will, teach me to live worthily in Your sight. For You are my wisdom,[16] You truly know me, and You knew me before the world was made[17] and before I was born into it.[18]

---

1   Kempis writes much of Book Three and Four as he felt he heard the Lord speaking to his heart. These thoughts are revelations from the Lord and are written as a conversation between the Lord and a disciple.

2   John 6:63

3   Psalm 94:12-13

4   Hebrews 1:1

5   Hebrews 3:7-8

6   Isaiah 23:4

7   Romans 1:16, Matthew 24:35

8   Matthew 5:6, 25:21, Revelation 2:23

9   Psalm 1

10  1 Peter 2:12

11  Romans 14:10, 2 Corinthians 5:10

12  Genesis 18:27;

13  In most uses this refers to being spiritually poor or inadequate.

14  Hebrews 4:16

15  Psalm 69:17

16  1 Corinthians 1:30

17  Ephesians 1:4

18  Jeremiah 1:5, Galatians 1:15

# 4

## WE SHOULD LIVE IN TRUTH AND
## HUMILITY BEFORE GOD

My child, walk before Me in truth and always seek Me with a simple heart [see note[1]].

The one who walks before Me in truth will be guarded against evil assaults, and the truth will make that person free from seducers and from the slanders of wicked people.[2]

If the truth will make you free, you will be free indeed,[3] and will not be concerned about the foolish words of others.

O Lord, it is true. I beg You that it be with me as You have said—let Your truth teach me, guard me, and preserve me safe to the end.

Let it set me free from all evil affections [see note[4]] and inappropriate love, and I will walk with You in great freedom of heart.

2. I will teach you those things that are right and pleasing in My sight.

Think seriously on your sins with great displeasure and grief, and never consider yourself to be anything because of good works.

The truth is that you are a sinner, and you are subject to and entangled in many strong emotions. What you are always moves you toward being and doing nothing—you are quickly depressed, quickly overcome, quickly confused, and quickly destroyed.

You have nothing in which you can glory,[5] but you have many things for which you should consider yourself wicked, for you are much weaker than you are able to understand.

3. Therefore, let nothing that you do seem great to you.

Let nothing seem important, nothing valuable and wonderful, nothing worth praising, nothing truly commendable and desirable, but only that which is eternal.

Let the eternal truth please you above all things, and let your own unworthiness always displease you.

Fear nothing, blame nothing, flee nothing as much as your faults and sins, which should be more displeasing to you than losing earthly goods.

Some do not walk sincerely in My sight,[6] but led by a fixed curiosity and pride they wish to learn My secrets and understand the high things of God, and in so doing neglect themselves and their own salvation [see note[7]].

Often when I resist them, their pride and curiosity make them fall into great temptations and sins.

4. Fear the judgments of God and dread the wrath of the Almighty. Do not, however, dispute the words of the Most High, but search diligently your own iniquities—the great things in which you have offended, and the many good things that you have neglected.

Some carry their devotion only in books, some in pictures, some in outward signs and figures.

Some have Me in their mouths, but little in their hearts.[8]

Others, who have their understanding enlightened and their affections cleansed, always long for eternal things, are unwilling to listen to the things of this world, serve the necessities of nature [see note[9]] with heavy hearts, and sense what the Spirit of Truth is speaking within them.[10]

For He teaches them to despise earthly things and love heavenly things, and to disregard the world and desire heaven day and night.[11]

1 Genesis 17:1, Wisdom of Solomon 1:1—The Wisdom of Solomon is an Apocrypha book. The verse reads: "Love righteousness, you rulers of the earth, think of the Lord in goodness and seek Him with sincerity of heart."
2 Ephesians 6:14

3  John 8:32
4  Fondness for evil.
5  1 Corinthians 4:7
6  2 Corinthians 2:17
7  Ecclesiasticus 3:21-23 – Ecclesiasticus (or Sirach) is an
   Apocrypha book. The verses read: "Neither seek what is too
   difficult for you, nor investigate what is beyond your power.
   Reflect upon what you have been commanded, for what is
   hidden is not your concern. Do not meddle in matters that
   are beyond you, for more than you can understand has been
   shown you."
8  Isaiah 29:13
9  As used by Kempis—all those things that are necessary to
   sustain natural life.
10 Psalm 25:5
11 Psalm 1:2

# 5

## THE WONDERFUL EFFECTS OF DIVINE LOVE

I praise You, O Heavenly Father, Father of my Lord
Jesus Christ, for You have promised to remember a poor
creature like me.

O Father of mercies and God of all comfort,[1] thank
You for the comfort with which you sometimes refresh me,
unworthy as I am of all comfort.

I will always bless and glorify You and Your only-
begotten Son and the Holy Ghost, the Comforter, for ever
and ever.

Ah, Lord God, holy lover of my soul, when you come
into my heart everything within me rejoices.

You are my glory and the exultation of my heart—my
hope and refuge in the day of trouble.[2]

2. But because my love is still weak and my virtue
imperfect, I need to be strengthened and comforted by

You—visit me often, therefore, and teach me with holy discipline.[3]

Free me from evil passions and cleanse my heart of all improper affections, so that being inwardly healed and thoroughly cleansed, I will be fit to love, courageous to suffer, and steady to persevere.

3. Love is a great thing, yes, great and thoroughly good—by itself it makes everything light that is heavy, and endures evenly everything that is uneven.

For it carries a burden that is no burden,[4] and everything that is bitter it makes sweet and tasteful.

The noble love of Jesus stimulates us to great things, and keeps us always longing for what is more perfect.

Love desires to be lifted up, and will not be kept back by anything low and inferior.

Love desires to be free and separated from all worldly attachments, so that its inward sight will not be obstructed and it will not be entangled by any temporal prosperity or conquered by any adversity.

Nothing is sweeter than love, nothing more courageous, nothing higher, nothing wider, nothing more pleasant, nothing fuller or better in heaven and earth, for love is of God and can rest only in God, who is above all created things.

4. Those who love, fly and run and rejoice—they are free and cannot be restrained.

They give all for all and have all in all, because they rest in the one highest above all things, from whom all that is good proceeds and flows.

They do not esteem the gifts, but turn themselves above all things to the giver.

Love knows no limit, but is fervent beyond measure.

Love feels no burden, thinks nothing of trouble, attempts what is above its strength, does not complain about impossibility, for it thinks all things lawful for itself, and all things possible.

It is therefore able to undertake all things and complete many of them and cause them to take effect—where the person who does not love would faint and give up.

5. Love is watchful and alert even when it is dormant.[5]

When weary it is not tired, when pressured it is not stressed, when alarmed it is not confused, but like a living flame and burning torch it forces its way upward and securely passes through everything.

Anyone who loves knows the cry of this voice. For the ardent affection of the soul is a loud cry in the ears of God when it says, *My God, my Love, you are all mine and I am all yours!*

6. Increase my love so that with the inward mouth of my heart I may taste how sweet it is to love, to melt, and to bathe myself in Your love.

Let love possess me so that I rise up above myself in exceeding fervor and admiration.

Let me sing the song of love, let me follow You, my beloved, on high, let my soul lose itself in Your praise, rejoicing in love.

Let me love You more than myself and not love myself but for Your sake, and in You let me love all those who truly love You as the law of love that shines out from You commands.

7. Love is swift, sincere, affectionate, pleasant, amiable, courageous, patient, faithful, prudent, long-suffering, and never seeks its own.[6]

For in whatever circumstances we seek ourselves [our own interests], there we fall from love.[7]

Love is circumspect [see note[8]] humble, and upright. It does not give in easily, act frivolous, or pay attention to meaningless things, but it is sober, chaste, steady, quiet, and guards all its senses.

Love submits to its superiors and obeys them, but is unkind and contemptuous toward itself. It is devoted and thankful to God, and trusts and hopes always in Him—even when God does not impart sweetness to it, for without sorrow no one lives in love.

8. Those who are not prepared to suffer all things, and to submit to the will of their beloved, are not worthy to be called lovers of God.[9]

A lover should willingly embrace all that is hard and distasteful for the sake of God, and not turn away from Him because of adversities.

1  2 Corinthians 1:3
2  Psalm 32:7, 59:16
3  Proverbs 13:24
4  Matthew 11:30
5  Romans 8:19
6  1 Corinthians 13:5
7  1 Corinthians 10:33, Philippians 2:21
8  Heedful of circumstances and potential consequences.
9  Mark 12:30

# 6

## PROOF OF A TRUE LOVE FOR CHRIST

My child, you are not yet a courageous and considerate lover.

Why not, O Lord?

Because when you get the slightest opposition you stop what you started doing and quickly look for consolation.

Courageous lovers stand firm in temptations and do not believe the crafty persuasions of the enemy. To the same extent that I am pleasing to them in prosperity, I am not unpleasing to them in adversity.[1]

2. Wise lovers do not consider so much the gift from Him who loves them as they do the love of the giver.

They prize the good will rather than the value of the gift, and set all gifts below Him whom they love.

A noble-minded lover rests not in the gift, but in Me above every gift.

All is not lost, therefore, if sometimes you have less feeling for Me or My saints than you want to have.

That good and sweet affection that you sometimes feel is the result of grace within you, and a sort of foretaste of your heavenly home, but you must not depend too much on it, for it comes and goes.

To fight against evil thoughts that arise in the mind, and to scornfully reject the suggestions of the devil,[2] is a worthy sign of virtue, and will have great reward.

3. Do not let any strange imaginations that crowd into your mind trouble you, no matter what they are about. Keep courageously to your purpose and maintain a righteous course toward God.

It is not an illusion that sometimes you are suddenly highly enraptured, and then quickly return to the usual foolishness of the heart.

For these are evils that you suffer unwillingly rather than commit, and so long as they displease you and you fight against them, it is a matter of reward and not loss.

4. Know that the ancient enemy strives by any means he can to hinder your longing for good and to keep you away from all devotional exercises—especially from meditating on the lives of God's saints, from the devout honoring of my sufferings, from the beneficial recollection of your sins, from watching over your own heart, and from the firm purpose of advancing in virtue.

He suggests many evil thoughts to you in an attempt to make you become weary and horrified, and thus draw you away from prayer and holy reading.

Humble confession displeases him,[3] and if he could he would cause you to stay away from holy communion.[4]

Do not trust or care for him, even though he often sets snares of deceit to trap you.

Blame him when he suggests evil and unclean thoughts to you. Say to him:

"Away, you unclean spirit![5] Shame, you miserable wretch! You are a filthy creature to bring such thoughts to me.

"Leave me you evil deceiver! You will have no part of me. Jesus is with me as a valiant warrior, and you will be confounded.

"I would rather die and suffer torment than consent to you.

"Hold your peace and be silent. I will hear no more from you even though you cause me many troubles. 'The LORD is my light and my salvation, whom shall I fear?'[6]

"'If whole armies should stand together against me, my heart will not fear. The Lord is my Helper and my Redeemer.'"[7]

5. Fight like a good soldier,[8] and if you sometimes fall through weakness, put on greater strength than before,[9] trusting in my more abundant grace[10]—and be careful about selfishly pleasing yourself and pride.

This causes many to error, and sometimes makes them fall into blindness that is almost incurable.

Let the fall of the proud who are foolishly overconfident in themselves serve as a warning for you and always keep you humble.

1   Philippians 4:11-13
2   Matthew 4:10
3   1 John 1:9
4   1 Corinthians 10:16, 11:26-27
5   Matthew 4:10, 16:23
6   Psalm 27:1
7   Psalm 19:14, Hebrews 13:6
8   Psalm 27:14, 1 Timothy 6:12
9   Philippians 4:13
10  2 Corinthians 12:9-10

# 7
## CONCEALING GRACE UNDER THE COVER OF HUMILITY

It is better and safer for you to conceal the grace of devotion, not to exalt yourself or speak or think much about it, but rather to despise yourself and fear that it has been given to someone unworthy of it.

Do not depend too earnestly upon this fondness of devotion, for it may be quickly changed to the contrary.

When you have grace, think how [spiritually] miserable and impoverished you are without grace.

Your progress in the spiritual life does not consist only in having the grace of comfort, but rather when you endure its withdrawal with humility, self-denial, and patience—provided you continue in prayer and do not neglect your customary duties.

But rather gladly do what there is in you to do according to the best of your [spiritual] strength and understanding, and do not completely neglect yourself [your progress] because of the mental dryness and anxiety that you feel.

2. For there are many who quickly become impatient and lazy when they do not succeed.

The way of a person's life, however, is not always theirs to decide.[1] The power to give grace belongs to God, and he comforts when He will, how much He will, and gives to whom He will[2]—to the degree that it pleases Him and no more.

Some uninformed people who received grace for a devoted life destroyed themselves because they attempted more than they were enabled to do, not considering how weak they were, but following what their heart desired rather than the judgment of their reason.

Because they ventured into greater matters than was pleasing to God, they quickly lost His grace.

Those who tried to build higher nests for themselves in heaven were made helpless and vile outcasts, humbled and impoverished, because they tried to fly with their own wings and did not continue to trust in Mine.[3]

Unless those who are still novices and inexperienced in the way of the Lord govern themselves by the counsel of discreet people, they may easily be deceived and broken to pieces.

3. If they are unwilling to at least be drawn away from their fond conceit, and would rather follow their own ideas than trust in the advice of those who are more experienced, their end will be harmful to them.

Rarely do those who are self-wise humbly endure being governed by others.

It is better to have little understanding and a small amount of good sense with humility,[4] then have great treasures of learning with conceited self-complacency.

It is better for you to have little than much of that which may make you proud.

It is an indiscreet act to give yourself wholly over to joy and forget your former helplessness and the chaste fear of the Lord, which is the fear of losing the grace that has been offered.

Nor is it brave wisdom to become highly depressed in times of adversity and tribulation and have less confidence in Me than you should.

4. The person who is willing to be over-secure in times of peace,[5] will often be found to be highly dejected and full of fears in times of war.

If you had the wisdom to be always humble and average in your own eyes, and to control and govern your spirit thoroughly, you would not fall so quickly into being offended and danger.

This is good counsel—when your spirit is set on fire within you, consider what it will be like when that light leaves you.

When that happens, remember that the light I have withdrawn from you for a time as a warning and for my own glory may return again.[6]

5. Such trials are often more beneficial than if you always have things prosper according to your own desires.

For your worth is not determined by how many visions and consolations you have, by your knowledge of the Scriptures, or by being promoted to a higher position.

It is determined by whether you are grounded in true humility, full of divine charity [love], always purely and sincerely seeking God's honor, think nothing of and sincerely despise yourself—and even rejoice to be more despised and put low by others rather than be honored by them."

1   Jeremiah 10:23, Romans 9:26
2   Exodus 33:19, Romans 9:15
3   Isaiah 14:13-14
4   Psalm 16:2, 17:10
5   1 Thessalonians 5:6
6   Hebrews 12:10

# 8
## HAVING A LOW CONCEPT OF OURSELVES BEFORE GOD

Shall I speak to my Lord since I am but dust and ashes?[1] If I esteem myself to be anything more, behold, You stand against me, and my sins bear true witness and I can not contradict it.

But if I abase myself and reduce myself to dust and draw back from all self-esteem, Your grace will be favorable to me, Your light will be close to my heart, and all self-esteem, however little, will be swallowed up in the valley of my nothingness and perish forever.

There You show Yourself to me, and [in your light] I see what I am, what I have been, and to what I have come, for I am nothing, and I did not know it.

If I am left to myself, behold, I become nothing but mere weakness, but if You for an instant look upon me, I am instantly made strong and filled with new joy.

It is a great wonder that I am so suddenly lifted up and so graciously embraced by You, for I am always dragged downward by my own weight.

2. Your love is the cause of it, freely going before me and assisting me with so many necessities, guarding me from dangers that press against me, and snatching me from innumerable evils.

Indeed, by loving myself wrongly I lost myself,[2] and by seeking You alone and loving You purely I have found both myself and You, and by that love for You have reduced myself even more to nothing.

For you, O sweetest Lord, deal with me above all that I deserve, and above all that I dare hope for or ask.

3. Blessed are You, my God, for although I am unworthy of anything good, yet Your majestic generosity never stops doing good even to the ungrateful and to those who have turned far away from You.[3]

Turn us to You, O God, that we may be thankful, humble, and devout, for You are our salvation, courage, and strength.

1 Genesis 18:27
2 John 12:25
3 Matthew 5:45

# 9

## GOD SHOULD BE THE ULTIMATE OBJECTIVE
### OF ALL THINGS

My child, if you want to be truly blessed, I should be your supreme and ultimate objective.

This objective will purify your affections, which are too often immoderately inclined to selfishness and created things.

For if in anything you seek yourself [your own interests], you immediately weaken and become fruitless.

I desire, therefore, that you direct all things principally to Me, for I am the one who has given everything.

Consider everything as flowing from the highest good [see note[1]]—therefore, since I originated everything, all must be attributed to Me.

2. The small, great, poor, and rich draw the water of life from Me,[2] as from a living fountain, and they that willingly and freely serve Me will receive grace for grace.[3]

But those who desire to glory in things other than Me,[4] or take pleasure in some good of their own, will not be established in true joy or have their heart enlarged, but will in many ways be impeded and restricted.

You should, therefore, attribute nothing good to yourself or virtue to any person, but give everything to God, without whom no one has anything.

I have given everything and it is My will that everything be returned to Me again, and I am strict in my requirement that thanks be returned to Me.

3. This is the truth by which vainglory is put to flight.

And if heavenly grace and true charity [love] enter in [the heart], there will be no envy or narrowness of heart and self-love will no longer possess it.

For divine charity [love] overcomes all things and enlarges all the powers of the soul.

If you are truly wise you will rejoice in Me alone and hope in Me alone, for no one is good except God,[5] who is to be praised above all things,[6] and in all things to be blessed.[7]

1   Ecclesiasticus 1:5—Ecclesiasticus (or Sirach) is an
    Apocrypha book. The verse reads: "The source of wisdom
    is God's Word in the highest heaven, and her ways are the

eternal commandments." Verse 5 is not found in all versions
of Ecclesiasticus.

2  John 4:14
3  1 John 1:16
4  1 Corinthians 1:29
5  Matthew 19:17, Luke 18:19
6  Psalm 113:3
7  Colossians 1:18, 1 Peter 4:11


# 10

## TO DESPISE THE WORLD AND SERVE GOD
## IS A SWEET LIFE

Now I will speak again, O Lord, and will not be silent; I
will say in the hearing of my God, my Lord and King, who is
on high: "O how great is the abundance of Your goodness,
O Lord, which You have laid up for those that fear You."[1]

But what are You to those who love You?

What are You to those who serve You with their whole
heart?

When those who love You are contemplating You, the
sweetness that You give them is truly unspeakable.

In these things above all You have showed me the
sweetness of Your love—when I was not, You made me;
when I went far astray from You, You brought me back
again so that I might serve You; and You have commanded
me to love You.[2]

2. O Fountain of love everlasting, what can I say
concerning You?

How can I forget You, who promised to remember me
even after I had wasted away and was lost?

You have shown mercy to Your servant beyond all
expectation, and have shown favor and loving-kindness
beyond all that is deserved.

What can I give to You in return for this favor?[3] For it is not granted to all to forsake everything,[4] to renounce the world,[5] and to live a life of Christian devotion.[6]

Is it any great thing that I should serve You Whom all of creation must serve?[7]

Serving You should not seem much to me, but what *does* seem much to me and wonderful is that you have promised to receive into Your service one who is so poor and unworthy, and make me one with Your beloved servants.

3. Behold, all things that I have and use to serve You are Yours.[8]

And yet You serve me more than I serve You.

Behold, You created heaven and earth for the service of humanity, and each day they [heaven and earth] are ready and willing and do whatever You command them to do.

And this is little, for moreover You have also appointed angels to minister to us.[9]

But there is something that excels all this—You Yourself have consented to service us, and have promised to give Yourself to us.

4. What can I give You for all these thousands of benefits? I wish I could serve You all the days of my life.

I wish I was able to serve You worthily for at least one day.

Truly You are worthy of all service, honor, and everlasting praise.

Truly You are my Lord and I am your poor servant, who is resolved to serve You with all my might and never grow weary of praising You.

And this I wish and desire to do, and whatever is lacking in me, I beseech You to agree to supply it.

5. It is a great honor and glory to serve You and despise all things for Your sake.

For great grace will be given to those who willingly give themselves to Your most holy service.

Those who cast aside all carnal delights for Your love will find the sweetest consolations of the Holy Spirit.

Those who enter into the narrow way and leave off all worldly care for Your name's sake will attain great freedom of mind.

6. O sweet and delightful service of God[10] by which a person is made truly free and holy!

O sacred state of Christian service that makes a person equal to the angels, pleasing to God, terrible to devils, and worthy to be commended by all the faithful.

O welcome service, always to be desired, in which we are rewarded with the greatest good and given everlasting joy!

1   Psalm 31:19
2   Genesis 1:27, Psalm 119:73, Matthew 22:37
3   Psalm 116:12
4   John 6:65, Luke 14:33, 2 Corinthians 6:17, 1 John 2:15
5   2 Corinthians 6:17, 1 John 2:15
6   Ephesians 1:4, 4:1
7   1 Corinthians 15:28, 1 Peter 3:22
8   1 Corinthians 4:7
9   Psalm 91:11, Hebrews 1:14
10 Matthew 19:29, 20:27-28, Luke 16:13, Acts 27:23, Romans 1:9

# 11

## EXAMINING AND MODERATING THE LONGINGS AND DESIRES OF OUR HEARTS

My child, you still need to learn many more things, which you have not yet learned well.

What are these, O Lord?

That you bring your desires into complete agreement with My good pleasure,[1] and that you not be a lover of yourself, but an earnest follower of My will.

You are often inflamed by various longings and desires that drive you forward with great emotion and energy, but consider whether you act more for your advantage than for My honor.

If I am the cause of your action, then you will be contented with whatever I ordain, but if there lurks any self-seeking in you,[2] it will hinder you and weigh you down.

2. Be careful, therefore, that you do not lean too much on any preconceived desire, without asking My counsel, lest perhaps you later change your mind or be displeased with what at first pleased you, and what you were earnestly zealous for as being the best.

For not every inclination that seems good should be followed immediately, nor should every contrary feeling be rejected immediately.

It is sometimes desirable to use restraint even in good desires and endeavors, lest your mind be distracted by too much eagerness, or through a lack of self-discipline you generate a scandal for others, or when you are opposed and resisted by others you suddenly become confused and so fall.

3. Sometimes, however, you must use violence against yourself and courageously resist your sensual appetite, not paying attention to what your flesh would or would not do,[3] but forcing it even against its will to be subject to the Holy Spirit.[4]

And it should be disciplined and forced to remain in subjection until it is prepared for everything, has learned to be content with little, is pleased with plain things, and does not murmur about any inconvenience."

1 Matthew 6:10
2 Philippians 2:21
3 1 Corinthians 9:27
4 Philippians 2:12, Hebrews 12:9,

# 12
## GROWING IN PATIENCE AND
## STRIVING AGAINST CONCUPISCENCE [SEE NOTE[1]]

O Lord my God, I can plainly see that patience is very necessary for me,[2] for many adverse things happen to us in this life.

For no matter what plans I make for my own peace, my life cannot be without struggle and sorrow.

That is so, My child, but My will is not that you seek peace that is free of temptations or adversity, but that you consider that you have found peace when you are stirred by various trials[3] and tried by many adversities.

2. If you say that you are not able to suffer much now, how then will you endure the [possible] punishment hereafter?[4]

The lesser of two evils should always be chosen.

So that you will avoid any future punishment [loss of reward], endeavor to endure patiently any present evils for God's sake.

Do you think that the people of this world do not suffer or suffer only a little? Ask even those who enjoy the greatest pleasure and you learn differently.

But you will say that they enjoy many pleasures and do what they wish and, therefore, do not think much of their troubles.

Even if it is so that they do whatever they wish, how long do you think it will last?

3. Behold, the rich of this world will be consumed like smoke,[5] and there will be no memory of their past joys.[6]

Yes, even while they are still alive they have no inward rest without bitterness, weariness, and fear.

For they often receive the penalty of sorrow from the same thing that they thought would be pleasurable.

It is right that pleasures that they immoderately sought after and followed should not be enjoyed without shame and bitterness.

4. Oh, how brief, how false, how immoderate and obscene, are all those pleasures!

Yet some people are so satiated and blind that they do not understand it, but like dumb animals they incur the death of their souls for the sake of a little enjoyment in this corruptible life.

Do not, therefore, My child, "go after your lusts, but refrain yourself from your appetites" [see note[7]]. "Delight yourself also in the LORD, And He shall give you the desires of your heart."[8]

5. If you desire true delight and to be abundantly comforted by Me, behold, your blessing comes from holding all worldly things in contempt and cutting off all base pleasures—then abundant consolation will be given to you.

The more you withdraw yourself from any solace from creatures, the more powerful consolations you will find in Me.

But in the beginning you will not gain these consolations without some sadness and laborious conflict.

Old inbred habits will resist you, but they will be overcome completely by developing better habits.

Your flesh will murmur against you, but it will be controlled by fervency of spirit.

That old serpent will provoke and trouble you, but prayer will put him to flight, and useful activities will prevent his having access to you.[9]

1  A strong sexual desire, especially lust.
2  Hebrews 10:36
3  James 1:2
4  1 Corinthians 3:14-15, Colossians 2:18, Hebrews 2:2-4, 2 John 1:8, Revelation 11:18
5  Psalm 68:2
6  Matthew 19:24
7  Ecclesiasticus 18:30—Ecclesiasticus (or Sirach) is an Apocrypha book. The verse reads: "Do not follow your base desires, but restrain your appetites."
8  Psalm 37:4
9  1 Timothy 5:13, 1 Peter 5:8

# 13

## OBEYING IN HUMBLE SUBJECTION, AFTER THE EXAMPLE OF JESUS

My child, those who strive to withdraw themselves from obedience, withdraw themselves from grace, and those who seek for themselves special privileges,[1] lose those that are common to all.[2]

Those who do not cheerfully and freely submit themselves to their [spiritual] superiors, show that their flesh is not yet perfectly obedient to them, but opposes and murmurs against them.

Therefore, if you desire to keep your flesh under control, learn to quickly submit yourself to your superior.

For the outward enemy is more speedily overcome if the inward person is not suppressed.

If you are not in harmony with the Spirit, there is no enemy who is worse or more troublesome to the soul than you yourself.

It is absolutely necessary that you develop true contempt for yourself if you wish to prevail against flesh and blood.

2. Because you still love yourself excessively, you are afraid to submit yourself completely to the will of others.

And yet, what great matter is it if you who are but dust and nothing subject yourself to others for God's sake, when I, the Almighty and Most Highest who created all things of nothing, humbly subjected myself to humanity for your sake?[3]

I became the most humble and abject of all men so that you might overcome your pride with My humility.[4]

O dust, learn to be obedient. Learn to humble yourself, you earth and clay, and to bow yourself down under the feet of everyone.

Learn to break your own will, and to yield yourself to all subjection.

3. Be violent against yourself and allow no pride to live in you, but be so humble and small that everyone will be able to walk over you and press you down like the dust in the streets. You prideful person, what do you have to complain about?

What can you say, wicked sinner, to those who rebuke you, when you have so often offended God and so many times deserved hell? But My eye has spared you because your soul was precious in my sight, and so you might know My love and be eternally thankful for My favors.

Also that you might continually give yourself to true subjection and humility, and patiently endure any contempt from others.

1 Mark 10:37
2 Matthew 16:24
3 Luke 2:7
4 John 13:14

# 14

## CONSIDER GOD'S SECRET JUDGMENTS, SO YOU WILL NOT BE LIFTED UP FOR ANYTHING GOOD IN YOU

You, O Lord, thunder forth Your judgments over me, you shake all my bones with fear and trembling, and my soul is exceedingly afraid.

I stand astonished, and I consider that "the heavens are not pure in Your sight."[1]

If You found wickedness in angels[2] and did not spare even them, what shall become of me?

Even stars fell from heaven[3]—what then can I who am but dust presume [will happen to me]?

Many of those whose works seemed commendable have fallen into abject misery, and those who [once] ate the bread of angels[4] I have seen delighting themselves with the food of swine.

2. O Lord, there is no holiness if You withdraw Your hand.

No wisdom avails if You cease to govern us.

No courage helps if You cease to preserve us.

No purity is secure if You do not protect it.

No guard of our own is of any value if You do not watch over us.

For if we are left to ourselves we sink and perish, but when we are visited by You we are raised up and live.

Indeed we are unstable, but You support us—we grow cold, but You inflame us.

3. Oh, I should think of myself as humble and lowly, and if I seem to have any good I should consider it as nothing.

With profound humility, O Lord, I should submit myself to Your unfathomable judgments, in which I find myself to be nothing else but nothing—and still nothing.

O immeasurable weight! O sea that can never be crossed, in which I find nothing of myself except that I am wholly nothing.

Where then is the hiding place of glory? Where is the confidence born of virtue?

All boastful pride is swallowed up in the depths of Your judgments of me.

4. What is all flesh in Your sight?[5]

Shall the clay glory against Him who formed it?[6]

How can those whose hearts are truly subject to God be puffed up by meaningless words? [see note[7]].

Not all the world can make those proud whom the truth has made subject to itself, and those who have set their entire hope in God cannot be moved by the praises of others.

For, behold, even those who speak are themselves nothing, for they will pass away with the sound of their own words, but the truth of the Lord remains forever.[8]

1  Job 15:15
2  Job 4:18, Jude 1:6
3  Revelations 12:4
4  Psalm 28:25
5  Romans 8:8, Galatians 3:11, Colossians 1:21-23
6  Isaiah 29:16, Romans 9:20-21
7  Isaiah 29:16, Ecclesiasticus 23:4-5—Ecclesiasticus (or Sirach) is an Apocrypha book. The verses read: "O Lord, Father and God of my life, do not give me haughty eyes, and remove evil desire from me."
8  Isaiah 40:7

## 15

### HOW WE SHOULD BE AFFECTED BY THE THINGS WE DESIRE, AND WHAT WE SHOULD SAY

My child, say this in everything: "Lord, if this is pleasing to You, let it be so."

"Lord, if it is to Your honor, in Your name let it be done.

"Lord, if You see it is good and beneficial to me, then grant that I may use this to Your honor.

"But if You know it will be harmful to me and not beneficial to the health of my soul, take away any desire for it from me."

For not every desire is of the Holy Spirit, even though it may seem to be right and good.

It is difficult to judge correctly whether a good spirit or an evil one has prompted you to desire this or that, or whether you are being motivated by your own spirit.

Many who seemed at first to be led by a good spirit have been deceived in the end.

2. Therefore, whatever comes to mind as desirable must always be desired and prayed for with humility of heart and fear of God, and, most of all, you must commit the whole matter to Me with true resignation and say:

"O Lord, You know what is best for us, therefore let this or that be done as You will.

"Give what You will, how much You will, and when You will.

"Deal with me as You think good, as best pleases You, and is most for Your honor.

"Put me where You will and deal with me in all things as You will.

"I am in Your hand, turn me around and back again, whichever way You please.

"Behold, I am Your servant and I am prepared for all things, for I do not desire to live for myself but for You—and oh that I could do it worthily and perfectly!

3. A prayer that the will of God may be fulfilled:

O most merciful Jesus, grant me Your grace, that it may be with me and work with me [see note[1]], and continue with me even to the end.

Grant that I may always desire and will that which is most acceptable and pleasing to You.

Let Your will be mine, and let my will follow Yours and agree perfectly with it.

Let my willingness or unwillingness be all one with You, and let me not be able to will or not will anything else but what You will or not will.

4. Grant that I may die to all things that are in the world, and for Your sake love to be despised and not known in this world.

Grant that above all things I may rest in You, and in You have my heart at peace.

You are the true peace of the heart and its only rest—outside of You all things are hard and restless. In this very peace—that is, in You the highest eternal good—I will sleep and rest.[2] Amen.

---

1   Wisdom of Solomon 9:10—This is an Apocrypha book.
    The verse reads: "Send her forth from the holy heavens, and
    from the throne of your glory send her, that she may labor at
    my side, and that I may learn what is pleasing to you."
2   Psalm 4:8

## 16
### TRUE COMFORT IS TO BE SOUGHT IN GOD ALONE

Whatever I can desire or imagine for my comfort, I do not look for it here, but hereafter.

For even if I alone could have all the comforts of the world and enjoy all its delights,[1] it is certain that they could not long endure.

Therefore, O my soul, you cannot be fully comforted[2] or have perfect refreshment except in God, the comforter of the poor and patron of the humble.

Wait a little while, O my soul, wait for the divine promise and you will have an abundance of all good things in heaven.

If you have excessive desire for the things that are present and temporal, you will lose the things that are celestial and eternal.

Use temporal things, but desire eternal things.

You cannot be satisfied with any temporal goods because you were not created to enjoy them.

2. Even if you possessed all created good you could not be happy and blessed by it, for your [true]blessedness and happiness is in God who created all things [see note[3]]—not the blessedness and happiness that is seen and commended by the foolish lovers of the world, but that for which the good and faithful servants of Christ wait, and of which the spiritual and pure in heart, whose conversation [citizenship] is in heaven,[4] sometimes have a foretaste.

Empty and brief is all human comfort.

Blessed and true is the comfort that is received inwardly from the truth.

Devout people carry their comforter Jesus with them everywhere, and say to Him: "Be present with me, O Lord Jesus, in every place and time.

"Let this be my consolation, to be cheerfully willing to do without all human comfort.

"And if Your consolation is lacking, let Your will and just trial of me be to me like my greatest comfort, for You will not always chide and You will not keep Your anger forever."[5]

1 Matthew 16:26
2 Psalm 77:1-2
3 Wisdom of Solomon 2:23—This is an Apocrypha book. The verse reads: "for God created us for incorruption, and made us in the image of his own eternity."
4 Philippians 3:20
5 Psalm 103:9

# 17
## All Our Anxieties Are to Be Placed on God

My child, allow Me to do with you what I please. I know what is best for you.

You think as a human being—you judge in many things as human feelings persuade you.

O Lord, what You say is true. Your concern for me is greater[1] than all the care that I can have for myself.

For those who do not cast all their cares upon You stand very unstable.

O Lord, if only my will may remain right and firm toward You, do with me whatever will please You.

For whatever You will do with me cannot be anything but good.

2. If it is Your will that I be in darkness, be blessed—and if it is Your will that I be in light, be blessed again. If You grant me comfort, be blessed—and if you wish me afflicted, be equally blessed.

My child, if you desire to walk with Me this should be your condition.

You must be as ready to suffer as to rejoice.

And when you are destitute and poor, you must be as cheerful as you are when you are full and rich.[2]

3. O Lord, for Your sake I will cheerfully suffer whatever befalls me with Your permission.

From Your hand I am willing to receive without concern good and evil, sweet and bitter, joy and sorrow,[3] and for all that happens to me I will be thankful.

Keep me safe from all sin and I will fear neither death[4] nor hell.

No tribulation will hurt me so long as You do not cast me from You forever or blot my name out of the Book of Life.[5]

1   Matthew 6:30, 1 Peter 5:7
2   Philippians 4:11-13, 1 Timothy 6:6-8
3   Job 2:10
4   Psalm 23:4
5   Philippians 4:3, Revelation 3:5, 13:8, 17:8, 20:12-15, 21:7, 22:19

# 18
## TEMPORAL SUFFERINGS MUST BE BORNE PATIENTLY, AFTER THE EXAMPLE OF JESUS

My child, I descended from heaven[1] for your salvation and took your sufferings upon Myself,[2] not out of necessity but out of love, so you might learn patience and endure your temporal sufferings without complaining.

For from the hour of My birth[3] until My death on the Cross, I was not without suffering or grief.

I suffered from great lack of temporal things, often heard complaints against Me, and meekly endured disgraces and reviles. In return for benefits, I received ingratitude; for miracles, blasphemies; for [heavenly] doctrine,[4] reproofs.

2. O Lord, because You were patient in Your lifetime, especially in fulfilling the commandment of Your Father,[5] it is right that I, a most miserable sinner, should conduct myself patiently according to Your will, and for my soul's welfare endure the burden of this corruptible life for as long as You choose for me.

For although this present life is burdensome, it is, nevertheless, made profitable by Your grace, and made clearer and more endurable for the weak by the examples and footsteps of Your saints.

It also has more consolation than it formerly had under the old Law when the gate of heaven remained shut, when the way to heaven seemed more obscure, and when so few concerned themselves with seeking the kingdom of heaven.[6]

Moreover, the just and the elect could not enter into the heavenly kingdom before Your suffering and holy death had paid our debt.

3. Oh, what great thanks I must give to You for having consented to show me and all faithful people the good and right way to Your eternal kingdom.[7]

For Your life is our way,[8] and by holy patience we walk toward You our crown.

If You had not gone before us and taught us, few would have cared to follow.

Alas, many would remain far behind if they did not have Your most noble example to consider.

Behold, if we are still cold even after we have heard of so many of Your miracles and teachings, what would become of us if we did not have such great light[9] by which to follow You?

1   John 3:13
2   Isaiah 53:4-5
3   Luke 2:7
4   John 3:12
5   John 12:49
6   Matthew 7:14
7   John 14:6
8   Romans 5:10
9   John 12:46

# 19

## ENDURING SUFFERING AND PROOF OF TRUE PATIENCE

What have you been saying, my child? Consider My suffering and that of other holy saints and stop complaining.

"You have not yet resisted unto blood, striving against sin."[1]

You have suffered little in comparison to those who suffered greatly by being so strongly tempted, so grievously afflicted, so many ways tested and tormented.[2]

You should, therefore, think of the greater sufferings of others so you can endure your own small troubles easier.

And if they do not seem small to you, then be careful that your impatience is not the reason they seem greater.

But whether they are small or great, endeavor to endure them all patiently.

2. The more you willingly accept suffering, the wiser you act and the greater is the reward you will receive—and if you have diligently prepared yourself in mind and habit to accept suffering, the more easily you will endure it.

Do not say: "I cannot endure suffering these things at the hands of such a person, nor should I suffer these kind of things, for that person has done me great wrong and accused me of things that I never thought of—but from someone else I will willingly suffer things that I see I should suffer."

Such a thought is foolish, for it does not consider the virtue of patience or Who will give a crown for it [God], but instead evaluates the persons and the offenses committed.

3. A person who will only suffer as much as seems good and from whom they are willing to accept it is not truly patient.

A truly patient person does not mind by whom the [spiritual] exercise comes a superior, an equal, an inferior, a good and holy person, or someone perverse and unworthy.

But no matter how much or how often adversity comes to such a person, it is accepted indifferently from all creatures, received thankfully as being from the hands of God, and considered a great benefit.

For with God it is impossible that anything suffered for His sake, however small, can pass without a reward.[3]

4. [Always] be prepared to fight, therefore, if you want to obtain the victory.[4]

Without a fight you cannot win the crown of patience.[5]

If you are unwilling to suffer, you refuse the crown. But if you desire to be crowned, fight courageously, endure patiently.

Without labor there is no rest, and without fighting there is no victory.

O Lord, let that which naturally seems impossible to me become possible by Your grace.

You know that I can endure only a little suffering, and that I am quickly discouraged when even a slight adversity arises.

For Your name's sake, therefore, let every exercise [see note[6]] of tribulation be desirable to me, for suffering and being troubled for Your name's sake is very wholesome for my soul.

1   Hebrews 12:24
2   Hebrews 10:30
3   Genesis 15:1, Job 42:12, Psalm 19:11, Hebrews 10:35
4   1 John 5:4
5   2 Timothy 4:7-8
6   As used in the original text, exercise is an activity that requires spiritual and mental exertion, especially when intended to develop or maintain spiritual growth.

# 20
## ACKNOWLEDGING INFIRMITIES
## AMID THE DIFFICULTIES OF THIS LIFE

I will witness against myself for my unrighteousness,[1] I will confess my weakness to You, O Lord.

Often just a small matter will make me sad and troubled.

I resolve to act with courage, but when a small temptation comes I am immediately in great distress.

Sometimes it is a trifling thing that causes great temptation.

And when I think I am reasonably safe and least expect it, I sometimes find myself almost entirely overcome by the slightest stirring.

2. Look, therefore, O Lord, at my low condition and my frailty that You know in every way.

Have mercy on me and deliver me out of the mire so I will not be embedded there and be utterly discouraged forever.

Because I am so subject to failing and weak in resisting my passions, I am often driving backwards and shamed before You.

I do not fully consent to them, and their continual assaults are troublesome and grievous to me, and it tires me extremely to live in such daily conflict.

By this my weakness is shown to me—hateful imaginations always rush into my mind much more easily than they leave it.

3. Most mighty God of Israel, zealous lover of faithful souls! Oh, that You would consider the labor and sorrow of Your servant and assist me in whatever I undertake.

Strengthen me with heavenly courage lest the old man,[2] the miserable flesh that is not yet fully subject to the spirit, prevail and get the upper hand—it is a battle I must fight so long as I draw a breath in this difficult life.

Alas, what kind of life is it where tribulation and sorrows are never lacking, and where everything is full of snares and enemies?

For when one tribulation or temptation retreats, another advances, and while the first conflict still rages, many others unexpectedly come one after the other.

4. And how can a life be loved that has such great bitterness and is subject to so many calamities and miseries?

Again, how can it be called life when it generates so many plagues and deaths?

And yet it is the object of people's love and many seek their delight in it.

The world is often blamed for being deceitful and foolish, and yet no one easily parts with it because the desires of the flesh are too powerful.

But some things draw us to love the world, others to despise it.

The lust of the flesh, the lust of the eyes, and the pride of life[3] cause us to love the world, but the pains and miseries that justly follow those things cause us to hate and loath the world.

5. But, alas, the fondness for wicked pleasure overcomes the minds of those who are addicted to the world, and they consider it delightful to be under thorns [see note[4]], because they have not seen or tasted the sweetness of God and the inward pleasure of virtue.

But those who perfectly despise the world and study to live for God under holy discipline, are not ignorant of the divine sweetness promised to those who truly forsake the world, and they clearly see how grievously mistaken the world is, and how it is deceived in so many ways.

1   Psalm 32:5
2   Romans 6:6, Ephesians 4:22
3   1 John 2:16
4   Job 30:7—*be under thorns*: live under irritations, pains, and discomforts.

## 21

### WE ARE TO REST IN GOD ABOVE ALL THINGS THAT ARE GOOD, AND ABOVE ALL HIS GIFTS

Above all things and in all things, O my soul, you will rest in the Lord always, for He is the everlasting rest of all saints.

Grant me, O most sweet and loving Lord, to rest in You above all creatures,[1] all health and beauty, all glory and honor, all power and position, all knowledge and cleverness, all riches and art, all joy and gladness, all fame and praise, all sweetness and comfort, all hope and promise, all merit and desire:

Above all gifts and presents that You can give and impart to us, and all joy and merriment that our minds can receive and feel:

Finally, above angels and archangels, all the heavenly host, all visible and invisible things, and all that You are not, O my God.

2. Because You, O Lord my God, are supremely good above all. You alone are most high, most powerful, most full and sufficient, most sweet, and most full of consolation.

You alone are most beautiful and loving, and most noble and glorious above all things. In You all good things together are perfect, and ever have been and will be.

Therefore, whatever You give me besides Yourself, reveal to me about Yourself, or whatever You promise, is too small and unsatisfying while You are not seen and fully possessed.

For my heart cannot truly rest or be totally content unless it rises above all gifts and creatures and rests in You alone.

3. O most beloved spouse of my soul, Jesus Christ, You most pure lover, You Lord of all creation—Oh, that I had the wings of true liberty so I might fly away and rest in You![2]

Oh, when will it be fully granted to me to have a quiet mind to contemplate how sweet You are, my Lord God?

When will I fully gather myself in You, so that above all sense and measure, in a way not known to everyone, I will, because of my love for You, not be aware of myself at all but You alone.

But now I often mourn and endure my unhappiness with grief.

Because many evils occur in this valley of miseries and they often trouble, grieve, and cover me like a cloud, hindering and distracting me, alluring and entangling me, so that I have neither free access to You nor enjoy the sweet pleasures that are ever ready for blessed spirits.

Oh, let my mourning and many miseries here on earth stir You [on my behalf].

4. O Jesus, brightness of eternal glory, comfort of the pilgrim soul, in your presence my mouth is without sound and my very silence speaks to You.

How long will my Lord delay His coming?

Let Him come to His unworthy servant and make me glad. Let Him put forth His hand and deliver this poor person from all anguish.

Come, oh, come, for without You I will not have a joyful day or hour, for You are my joy and without You my table is empty.

I am a miserable person, in a way imprisoned and burden with chains, until You refresh me with the light of Your presence and give me liberty—and look with favor upon me.

5. Let others seek what they please instead of You, but as for me, nothing does or will delight me but You only, my God, my hope, my everlasting salvation.

I will not hold my peace or stop praying until Your grace returns and You speak inwardly to me.

Behold, I am here. Behold, I have come to you because you called upon Me. Your tears and the desire of your soul, your humility and your contrite heart, have influenced and brought Me to you.

Lord, I called You and desired to enjoy You, and I am ready to refuse all things for You.

For You first stirred me up so I might seek You.

Be blessed, therefore, O Lord, for having shown this goodness to Your servant according to the multitude of Your mercies.

6. What more can Your servant say to You? Keeping always in mind my iniquities and wickedness, I can only humble myself before You.

For among everything that is wonderful in heaven and earth there is none like You.[3]

Your works are exceedingly good, Your judgments true, and Your providence rules the universe.

Therefore praise and glory be to You, O wisdom of the Father—let my mouth and soul and all creatures together praise and bless You.

1   Romans 8:19-22
2   Psalm 55:6
3   Psalm 35:10, 71:19, 86:8, 89:8

## 22

### REMEMBERING GOD'S MANY AND VARIED BENEFITS

Open my heart, O Lord, to Your Word, and teach me to walk in Your commandments.[1]

Enable me to understand Your will, and to remember both your general and specific benefits with great reverence and diligent consideration, so that from this day forward I can give You worthy thanks for them.

Yet I know and admit that I am not able in any measure to give You ample thanks for the favors that You bestow on me.

I am less than the least of Your benefits, and when I consider Your generosity, its greatness makes my spirit lose its strength.

2. All that we have in our body and soul, and all that we possess outwardly and inwardly, naturally or supernaturally, are Your benefits, and they proclaim how generous, merciful, and good You are, from Whom we have received all good things.

Even though one receives more and another less, all are still Yours, and without You not even the smallest blessing can be received.

We who receive more cannot glory about our worthiness or extol ourselves above others or insult those who receive less, for those are greater who attribute least to themselves and are the most humble and devote in giving thanks.

And those who consider themselves the most wicked of all people, and judge themselves to be the most unworthy, are the most fit to receive the greater blessings.

3. But those of us who receive fewer blessings should not be saddened or grieve over it, or envy those who are enriched with greater things, but rather turn our minds to You and praise You highly for Your goodness by which You

have given gifts so generously, freely, and willingly, without respect of persons [see note[2]].

All things come from You, and therefore You are to be praised in everything.

You know what is best to give to each of us, and why this person has less and that one more. It is not for us to judge, but for You who knows exactly what is appropriate for every person.

4. Therefore, O Lord God, I consider it a great mercy not to have much of the outward things that people consider worthy of glory and applause. For those who consider the poverty and unworthiness of themselves should not be grieved or saddened or discouraged, but rather be comforted and glad, because You, O God, have the chosen the poor, the humble, and the despised in this world for Yourself,[3] and as Your friends and servants.

The apostles, whom You made princes over all the earth, are themselves witnesses of this.[4]

Yet they lived in the world without complaining,[5] and were so humble and simple and so without malice and deceit that they even rejoiced to suffer reproach for Your name[6]—and what the world despised they affectionately embraced.

5. When we love You, therefore, and acknowledge Your benefits, nothing should rejoice us as much as Your will toward us and the good pleasure of Your eternal decree.

Along with this, we should be so contented and comforted that we would as willingly be the least as others would desire to be the greatest.

And be as peaceful and contented in last place as in first, and be as willing to be a despised castaway of no name or character, as to be given preference and honor before others, and be greater in the world than they.

For Your will and the love of Your glory should be preferred before all things, and should comfort us more and please us better than all the benefits we have received or will receive.

1 Psalm 119
2 Romans 2:11—*respect of persons*: deferential treatment or regard because of their position in life.
3 1 Corinthians 1:26-29
4 Psalm 45:16
5 1 Thessalonians 2:10
6 Acts 5:41

# 23
## FOUR THINGS THAT BRING GREAT INWARD PEACE

My child, I will now teach you the way of peace and true liberty.

O Lord, I beseech You, do as You say, for this is joyous for me to hear.

Endeavor, my child, to do the will of another rather than your own.[1]
Choose always to have less rather than more.[2]
Seek always the lowest place and consider others better than yourself.[3]
Wish and pray always that the will of God be completely fulfilled in you.
Behold, such a person enters into the realm of peace and rest.

2. O Lord, this short speech of Yours contains great perfection.[4]

It is few in words, but full in meaning and abundant in fruit.

For if I faithfully observed it I would not be so easily troubled.

For whenever I feel uneasy and troubled, I find that I have wandered from this teaching.

But You who can do all things and always loves benefiting my soul, increase Your grace in me so that I can fulfil Your works and work out my own salvation.

3. A prayer against evil thoughts:

O Lord my God, be not far from me. My God, hurry to help me,[5] for various evil thoughts and great fears have risen up against me and are afflicting my soul.

How shall I pass through them unharmed? How shall I destroy them?

I will go before you, and will humble the great ones of the earth. I will open the prison doors and reveal hidden secrets to you.[6]

Do, O Lord, as You say, and let all my evil thoughts fly away from Your face.

My only comfort and hope is to run to You in every tribulation, to trust in You, to call upon You with all my heart, and to wait patiently for Your consolation.

4. A prayer for mental enlightenment:

O merciful Jesus, enlighten me with a clear and bright inward light, and drive away all darkness still dwelling in my heart.

Subdue my many wandering thoughts, and destroy those temptations that violently assault me.

Fight strongly for me and vanquish the evil beasts—the alluring desires of the flesh—so I may obtain peace by your power, and so Your abundant praises may resound in Your holy court—that is, in a pure conscience.

Command the winds and storms and say to the sea, "Be still,"[7] and to the north wind, "Blow not," and there shall be a great calm.

5. Send out Your light and Your truth[8] so they shine upon the earth, for until You enlighten me I am as the earth [once was], without form and void.[9]

Pour down Your grace from above, fill my heart with heavenly dew, supply fresh streams of devotion to water the face of the earth so it may bring forth good and excellent fruit.

My mind is pressed down by a load of sins, lift it up and draw all my desire to heavenly things, so that having tasted the sweetness of divine happiness it will be tedious to me to even think about earthly things.

6. Yank me away and deliver me from all temporary comfort of creatures, for no created thing can give complete comfort and rest to my desires.

Join us together with an inseparable band of love, for You alone satisfy the one who loves You, and without You all things are worthless and foolish.

1   Matthew 26:39; John 5:30, 6:38
2   1 Corinthians 10:24
3   Luke 14:10, Philippians 2:3
4   Matthew 5:48
5   Psalm 71:12
6   Daniel 2:29
7   Mark 4:39
8   Psalm 43:3
9   Genesis 1:1

# 24
## AVOIDING CURIOUS INQUIRY INTO OTHER PEOPLE'S LIVES

My child, do not be curious or bother with unimportant things [see note[1]].

What does this or that matter to you? You follow Me.[2]

For what is it to you if that person is such or such, or whether this person does or talks about this or that?

You will not need to answer for others, but you will give account for yourself,[3] so why do you involve yourself in their affairs?

Behold, I know everyone and see all things that are done under the sun, and I understand how it is with everyone—what they think, what they wish, and what objective they are trying to achieve.

Therefore, commit all things to Me, keep yourself gently at peace, and let those who are restless be as restless as they want to be.

Whatever they have done or said will come upon themselves, for they cannot deceive Me.

2. Do not be anxious to live in the shadow of someone great, for the close friendship of many, or for the personal affection of individuals.

For these things distract the heart and greatly darken it.

I would gladly speak My Word and reveal My secrets to you if you would watch diligently for My coming and open the door of Your heart to Me.[4]

Be careful, therefore, and watchful in prayer, and humble yourself in all things.

---

1    1 Timothy 5:13, Ecclesiasticus 3:23—Ecclesiasticus is an
     Apocrypha book. The verse reads: "For their conceit has led
     many astray, and wrong opinion has impaired their judgment."

2 John 21:21-22
3 Galatians 6:4-5
4 Revelation 3:20

## 25

### THE BASIS OF A CONSTANT PEACEFUL HEART AND TRUE SPIRITUAL PROGRESS

My child, I have said, "Peace I leave with you, My peace I give to you; not as the world gives do I give to you."[1]

Peace is what everyone desires, but not all care for the things needed for true peace.

My peace is with the humble and gentle of heart—your peace is in having much patience.

If you will listen to Me and follow My voice [do what I say], you will enjoy much peace.

What then should I do, O Lord?

In all matters be careful what you do and say. Direct your whole attention to this so that you will please Me alone, and neither desire nor seek anything besides Me.

Do not judge the words or actions of others rashly, and do not involve yourself in things that are not your concern—by doing this you will scarcely or seldom be disturbed.

2. To never feel any grief at all, however, or never suffer mental or physical troubles, does not belong to this life but to the realm of eternal rest.

Do not think, therefore, that you have found true peace if you feel no burden, or that all is well if you have no enemy, or "to be perfect" is to have everything go the way you wish.

And do not think highly of yourself or consider yourself especially beloved if you are in a condition of great devotion and sweetness, for a true lover of virtue is not known by these things, and the [spiritual] progress and perfection of a person does not consist of these things.

3. In what do they then consist, O Lord?

In giving yourself and your whole heart to the divine will, and not seeking your own interests in either small or great things, in either time or eternity.

By so doing, you will remain steadfast and give thanks in both prosperity and adversity, and will judge all things properly.

Be so courageous and patiently hopeful that when inward comfort is withdrawn, you can prepare your heart to suffer even greater things. And do not justify yourself as if you should not suffer these afflictions or even greater ones, but acknowledge Me in whatever I decree for you and continue to praise My holy name.

Then you will walk in the true and right way of peace and will have certain hope of joyfully seeing My face again.

For if you come to the place of complete contempt for yourself, then you will enjoy as much peace as you are capable of having in this earthly life.

1   John 14:27

## 26
### THE EXCELLENCE OF A FREE MIND, WHICH IS GAINED QUICKER BY HUMBLE PRAYER THAN BY STUDYING

O Lord, it is the work of a perfect person never to stop thinking carefully of heavenly things, and so go through many cares as if they had no cares—not by being without feelings, but by the power of a free mind that clings to nothing with unreasonable affection.

2. I beseech You, my most gracious God, keep me from the cares of this life, lest I become too entangled in them; from the many necessities of the body, lest I be captured by pleasure; and from whatever is an obstacle to my soul, lest I become broken by troubles and overthrown.

I am not speaking of those things that so are earnestly coveted by worldly vanity, but of those miseries that as punishments and the common curse of mortality[1] weigh down and hinder the soul of Your servant, and prevent it from entering into the freedom of the spirit as often as it wishes.

3. O my God, You who are indescribable sweetness, make bitter to me all temporal comfort that draws me away from the love of eternal things, and wickedly draws me to itself by showing me some delightful benefit that I can have now.

Let me not be overcome, O Lord, let me not be overcome by flesh and blood;[2] let not the world and it's temporary glory deceive me; let not the devil and his subtle craftiness remove me from my place [in You].

Give me strength to resist, patience to endure, and faithfulness to persevere.

Instead of all the comforts of the world give me the sweet balm of Your Spirit, and instead of love for worldly things fill me with love for Your name.

4. Behold—food, drink, clothes and other necessities for maintaining the body are a burden [see note³] to a fervent spirit.

Give me the grace to use such refreshments moderately, and not be entangled with an excessive desire for them.

It is not lawful to do away with all things, for nature has to be sustained. But the holy law forbids the desire for what is not required and for things that are merely for delight, for then the flesh would rebel against the spirit. In this I beseech You, let Your hand govern and teach me so that I will not exceed what is lawful.

1  Genesis 3:17, Romans 7:11
2  Romans 12:21
3  The burden is the necessary time and effort required to obtain them.

# 27

## It Is Self-Love That Is the Most Hindrance to the Highest Good

My child, you must give all for all and keep nothing of yourself.

Understand that love of yourself hurts you more than anything in the world.

The degree to which things cling more or less to you is determined by how much love you have for them.

If your love is pure,¹ simple, and disciplined, you will be free from the bondage of things.

Do not covet what is not lawful for you to have. Do not covet what may hinder you and deprive you of inward liberty.

It is strange that you do not commit yourself, and all things that you can have or desire, completely to Me from the bottom of your heart.

2. Why do you waste away with worthless grief?[2] Why tire yourself with needless cares?

Accept the good pleasure of My will[3] and you will suffer no harm or loss at all.

If you look for this or that, or want to be here or there, so you can better enjoy your own pleasure and benefit, you will never be at rest or free from troubled thoughts, for there will be something lacking in everything, and in every place there will be someone to afflict you.

Our welfare is not in getting and piling up external things, but rather in despising them and completely rooting them out of the heart.

3. This is true not only of income and wealth, but also of seeking after honor and desiring empty praise, all of which will pass away with this world.

The place is of little value if a fervent spirit is lacking, and the peace that you look for outwardly will not last long[4] if the condition of your heart does not have a true foundation; that is, unless you stand steadfast in Me—you may change, but not for the better.

For when the opportunity [for self-fulfillment] comes to you and is taken, you will find what you ran from and more, too.

4. A prayer for a clean heart and heavenly wisdom:

Strengthen me, O God, by the grace of Your Holy Spirit.

Grant that I be strengthened with might in my inner being,[5] take out of my heart all useless care and anguish,[6] and do not let me be drawn away by various desires for anything, whether wicked or valuable, but enable me to look upon everything as passing away, and on myself as passing away with them.

For nothing is permanent under the sun, where all things are meaningless and annoying to the spirit.[7] Oh, how wise is the person who understands that!

5. O Lord, give me heavenly wisdom [see note[8]] so I may learn above all things to seek and find You alone, appreciate and love You above all things, and understand all other things as they are—in keeping with the way your wisdom has made them.

Grant that I may wisely avoid those who flatter me, and endure patiently those who oppose me.

For it is a great part of wisdom not to be moved by every gust of words,[9] or listen to an evil, flattering, person, for then we will continue securely in the direction we started.

1  Matthew 6:22
2  Exodus 18:18, Micah 4:9
3  Luke 12:32; Ephesians 1:5, 9;Philippians 2:13; 2 Thessalonians 1:11
4  Isaiah 41:13
5  Ephesians 3:16
6  Matthew 6:34
7  Ecclesiastes 1:14, 2:1
8  Wisdom of Solomon 9:4—Wisdom of Solomon is an Apocrypha book. The verse reads: "give me the wisdom that sits by your throne, and do not reject me from among your servants."
9  Ephesians 4:14

28

## STRENGTH AGAINST THE TONGUES OF SLANDERERS

My child, do not take it to heart if some think badly of you and say offensive things about you.[1]

You should judge yourself as even worse, and believe that no person is weaker than you are.

If you walk spiritually, you will not be bothered by fleeting words.

It is wise to keep silent in an evil time, turn yourself inwardly to Me, and not be troubled by the judgment of others.

2. Do not let your peace depend on the words of people, for whether they speak well or ill of you does not make you a different person. Where are true peace and glory? Are they not in Me.[2]

Those who are not anxious to please people or fear to displease them will enjoy much peace.

A restless heart and a distracted mind come from immoderate love and meaningless fear.

1   1 Corinthians 4:13
2   John 16:33

# 29

## WE SHOULD CALL UPON GOD AND BLESS HIM WHEN TRIBULATION COMES TO US

O Lord, blessed be Your name forever,[1] for it is Your will that this temptation and tribulation come to me.

I cannot escape it, but must run to You so that You can help me and turn it to my good.

Lord, I am now being afflicted, and my heart is troubled by my present suffering and not at peace.

And now, dear Father, what shall I say?—I am caught in the middle of trouble, "save me from this hour."[2]

Yet I came to this hour so You might be glorified when I am greatly humbled and delivered by You.

Therefore, let it please You, Lord, to deliver me, for what can a poor wretch like I am do, or where can I go, without You?

Give me patience, O Lord, even now in this emergency. Help me, my God, and then I will not be afraid of how much I may be afflicted.

2. And now in these troubles what shall I say?

"Lord, Your will be done."[3] I very much deserve to be afflicted and distressed.

Surely I should endure it—and, oh, that I may endure it with patience until the storm passes and it becomes calm!

But Your all-powerful hand is able to take even this temptation from me, and lessen its violence so that I do not completely sink under it, as You have so often done for me in the past, O my God, my mercy!

And the more difficult this temptation is for me, the easier it is for You to change it by the right hand [power] of the Most High.

1   Job 1:21, Psalm 113:2
2   John 12:27
3   Matthew 6:10

# 30
## SEEKING DIVINE HELP AND
## BEING CONFIDENT OF REGAINING GRACE

My child, I am the Lord who gives strength in the day of trouble.[1]

Come to Me when things are not well with you.[2]

The thing that keeps you from receiving heavenly comfort the most is that you are too slow in turning to prayer.

For before you earnestly pray to Me, you look in the meantime for many comforts and delight yourself in outward things.

And so all of those things are of little benefit to you until you realize that I am the one who delivers those who trust in Me, and that outside of Me there is no strong help, beneficial counsel, or lasting remedy.

But now that you have recovered your breath after the storm, be strengthened by the light of My mercies, for I am near, says the Lord, to repair everything completely and abundantly above measure.

2. Is anything too difficult for me? Or am I like a person who promises and does not do it?[3]

Where is your faith?[4] Stand strong and steadfast and be courageous and patient, comfort will come to you in sufficient time.

Wait, wait, for Me—I will come and heal you.

It is but temptation that distresses you and useless fear that troubles you.

What does anxiety about future possibilities bring you but sorrow upon sorrow? "Each day has enough trouble of its own."[5]

It is useless and unprofitable to be either disturbed or pleased about future things, which perhaps will never happen.

3. But it is human nature to be deluded by imaginary happenings, and being easily drawn away by the suggestions of the enemy is a sign of a mind that is still [spiritually] weak.

For the enemy does not care whether he deludes and deceives you with true or false suggestions, or whether he overthrows you with love for the present or worry about the future.

"Let not your heart be troubled, neither let it be afraid."[6]

Trust in Me and be confident of My mercy.[7]

When you think you are furthest from Me, often I am nearest to you.

When you think that almost everything is lost, often your greatest reward is close at hand.

Everything is not lost when anything is contrary to what you wish.

You must not judge by the way you presently feel, or be so grieved by your trouble, wherever it comes from, that you give in to it as if all hopes of recovery were gone.

4. Do not think you are entirely forsaken if I send you some temporary trouble or withdraw the comfort you desire, for this is the way to the kingdom of heaven.

And without doubt it is better for you and the rest of My servants to be tried in adversities than to have everything in the way that you desire them.

I know the hidden thoughts of your heart, and that it is better for your welfare that you sometimes be left in a dry condition without the taste of spiritual sweetness, lest perhaps you become proud of your prosperous [spiritual] condition and become pleased with yourself about something that you are not.

What I have given I can take away, and restore it again when it pleases Me.

5. What I give remains Mine, and when I withdraw it I do not take anything that is yours, for every good and perfect gift is Mine.[8]

Do not be sad or let your heart fail if I send you affliction or trouble, for I can quickly relieve you and turn all your heaviness into joy.

When I deal with you that way, I am still righteous and greatly to be praised.[9]

6. If you are wise and think of this correctly, you will never be mournful or disheartened because of any adversity that happens to you, but instead you will rejoice and give thanks.

Yes, you will consider it a special joy that I afflict you with sorrow and do not spare you.

"As the Father has loved Me, so have I loved you."[10] I said this to My beloved disciples, whom I certainly did not send out to temporal joys, but to great conflicts; not to honors, but to contempt; not to idleness, but to labor; not to rest, but to patiently bring forth much fruit. Remember these words, O My child!

1 Nahum 1:7
2 Matthew 11:28
3 Isaiah 55:11
4 Luke 8:25
5 Matthew 6:34, NIV
6 John 14:27
7 Psalm 91:1
8 James 1:17
9 1 Chronicles 16:25; Psalm 48:1, 96:4, 145:3
10 John 15:9

## 31
### FINDING THE CREATOR BY FORSAKING EVERYTHING

O Lord, I need even greater grace if I am to reach that place where neither human nor creature will be a hindrance to me.

For as long as anything hinders me, I cannot fly freely to You.

The one who wrote, "Who will give me wings like a dove, and I will flee away and be at rest?" [see note[1]], wanted to fly freely to You.

What is more at rest than a heart focused solely upon You, and what is more free than the person who desires nothing on earth?

We should rise above all creatures, therefore, and perfectly forsake ourselves and remain in an intense joy of mind as we see that among all creatures there is nothing like You, the creator of all things.

Unless we are disentangled from all creatures, we cannot freely attend to divine things.

That is why there are so few who truly meditate on spiritual matters, they cannot completely withdraw themselves from created things that are temporal.

2. To get to this spiritual level requires great grace—grace that elevates the soul and lifts it up above itself.

And unless we are lifted up in spirit, freed from all creatures, and wholly united to God, whatever we know and have are of no great importance.

Whoever considers anything great but the only infinite, eternal, God, will remain small a long time and lie groveling below that level.

And whatever is not God is nothing and should be considered as nothing.

There is a great difference between the wisdom of an enlightened and devout person, and the knowledge of a learned and studious person.

For the knowledge that flows from the divine source above is wiser than that which is diligently gotten by human efforts.

3. There are many who desire to live a meditative life, but are not willing to practice the things that are needed to do so.

It is a great hindrance that we rest in [spiritual] signs and things perceived by the senses and have little concern about perfectly humbling ourselves.

I do not know what it is—what spirit leads us or what we pretend—that we who want to be spiritual are so concerned and full of anxiety about transitory and meaningless things, and so seldom concentrate fully on our inward condition.

4. Alas, after thinking about it only slightly, we break our concentration and do not strictly examine our works and evaluate them.

We are not careful about where our affections lie, or sorrow over the impurity in all our actions.

"For all flesh had corrupted their way on the earth,"[2] and therefore the great flood followed.[3]

Since our inward affections are highly corrupted, our actions that proceed from them are naturally corrupted also, which is proof of our lack of inward strength.

From a pure heart proceeds the fruit of a good life.

5. We ask how much a person has done, but never seriously consider the amount of virtue with which they act.

We ask whether the person is courageous, rich, attractive, skilful, a good writer, singer, or laborer; but never ask how poor in spirit, patient and meek, devout and spiritual.

Nature looks at the outward things of a person, grace looks at the inward things.

The one is often wrong, but the other trusts in God and is rarely wrong.

1 Psalm 55:6—The verse reads: "Oh, that I had wings like a
　　dove! I would fly away and be at rest."
2 Genesis 6:12
3 Genesis 7:11-12

# 32
## Self-Denial and Renouncing Every Evil Appetite

My child, you cannot have perfect liberty unless you completely deny yourself.[1]

Those who only seek their own interests and are lovers of themselves are in chains—they are covetous, curious, wanderers who always seek things that appeal to them and not the things of Jesus Christ, and often devise and plan things that will not succeed. For all that is not of God will fail.

Keep this short and perfect word: "Give up everything and you will find everything."[2] Give up every immoderate desire, and you will find rest.

Consider this well, and when you have put it into practice you will understand all things.

O Lord, this is not the work of one day or the sport of children—indeed, in that short sentence is all the perfection of spiritual people.

2. My child, do not turn back or be discouraged when you are told of the way to perfection, but instead be stirred

to move up to higher things, or at the least strongly desire to have them.

I wish you had come far enough to no longer be a lover of yourself, but simply waited for My bidding—and that of the one whom I have appointed spiritual leader over you—then you would please Me exceedingly and all your life would pass in joy and peace.

You still have many things to give up, and unless you give them completely to Me you will not gain the objective you desire.

"I counsel you to buy from Me gold refined in the fire, that you may be rich,"[3]—that is, rich in heavenly wisdom that treads underfoot all inferior and earthly things.

Set little value on earthly wisdom, and do not overly desire to please others or yourself.

3. I said that [heavenly] things that seem inferior must be bought with things that people consider precious and of great value.

For true heavenly wisdom that has no high thoughts of itself or seeks to be exalted on earth does seem ordinary and of little value—and is almost forgotten among people. Many do, indeed, praise such wisdom with their words, but in their lives they stay far from it—yet it is a precious pearl,[4] which is hidden from many.

1  Matthew 16:24-25
2  Matthew 19:27-29
3  Revelation 3:18
4  Matthew 13:46

## 33

## A Changing Heart and
## Directing Our Objective Toward God

My child, do not trust what you feel, for it will quickly change into something else.

As long as you live you are subject to change, even against your will, and so you are merry one time, then sad, then peaceful, then troubled, then worldly, then diligent, then listless, then grave, and soon frivolous.

But those who are wise and well instructed in spiritual matters stay steady during these changeable times, pay no attention to what they feel within themselves or which way the wind of instability is blowing, but concentrate their mind solely upon what is the right and best end.

That way they are able to continue as they are, steady and unshaken, in the middle of numerous and various events, while continuing to direct their single objective toward Me.

2. And the purer the objective is, the steadier people pass through the several kinds of storms that assail them.

But in many the focus of a pure objective grows blurry, for they quickly look at whatever pleasurable object that comes their way.

For it is rare to find someone who is totally free from all defects of self-seeking.

Such as when the Jews came to Bethany to Martha and Mary, not only because of Jesus but also to see Lazarus.[1]

The focus of your objective, therefore, is to be purified so that it is concentrated and right, and is to be directed toward Me, despite all the various circumstances that may come between [you and your objective].

1  John 12:9

## 34
## GOD IS SWEET ABOVE ALL THINGS AND IN ALL THINGS TO THOSE WHO LOVE HIM

Behold, my God, and my all! What more can I want, and what greater happiness can I desire?

O sweet and delicious Word!—but only to those who love the Word, and not the world or the things in the world.

"My God, and my all!" These words are enough to those who understand, and to those who love [God] it is a joy to say them often.

For when You are present everything is delightful, but when You are absent everything is tedious.

You give rest to the heart, great peace, and festive joy.

You cause us to think well of everything and praise You in everything, and nothing can bring lasting pleasure without You—for anything to be pleasant and agreeable Your grace must be present, and it must be seasoned with the sweetness of Your wisdom.

2. What is not pleasing to the person who delights in You?

And what can be pleasing to the person who does not delight in You?

But the wise people of the world and those who relish the things of the flesh come short of Your wisdom,[1] for in one there is great pride and in the other death.

But those who follow You by disdaining worldly things and mortifying their flesh are truly wise, for they have changed from pride to truth, from flesh to spirit.

These relish God, and for whatever good is found in creatures they give praise to their Maker.

However, great—yes, very great—is the difference between the sweetness of the Creator and the creature, of eternity and time, of light uncreated and light enlightened.

3. O You who are everlasting light and surpass all created lights, send the rays of Your brightness from above and pierce all of the most inward recesses of my heart.

Purify, rejoice, enlighten, and enliven my spirit with all the power needed so I may cling to You with abundant joy and triumph.

Oh, when will that blessed and desired hour come, so that You can fill me with Your presence and be to me my all in all?

Until this is granted to me, I will not have complete joy.

Alas! The old nature still lives in me[2] and is not wholly crucified, not perfectly dead.

It still fights mightily against the Spirit, causes inward battles, and will not allow the kingdom of my soul to be in peace.

4. You, O God, who rules the power of the sea and still its rising waves,[3] arise and help me!

Scatter the people who delight in war,[4] crush them by Your might.

I beseech You to display Your greatness and let Your right hand [power] be glorified, for there is no other hope or refuge for me except in You, O Lord my God.[5]

---

1  1 Corinthians 1:26, Romans 8:5, 1 John 2:16
2  Romans 7
3  Psalm 89:9
4  Psalm 68:30
5  Psalm 31:14

# 35
## THERE IS NO SECURITY FROM TEMPTATION IN THIS LIFE

My child, you are never secure in this life, and while you live you will always need spiritual armor.[1]

You live among enemies and are continually assaulted on the right hand and on the left.[2]

Therefore, if you do not use the shield of patience to defend yourself on every side, you will not be long without a wound.

Moreover, if you do not fix your heart on Me with a sincere willingness to suffer all things for Me, you cannot endure the heat of this combat or attain the crown[3] of the saints in heaven.

You should, therefore, go courageously through it all, and stand strongly against whatever opposes you.

To the one who overcomes, manna is given,[4] but for the one too lazy [to fight], there is only much misery.

2. If you seek rest [from spiritual battles] in this world, how will you attain to everlasting rest?

Do not train yourself for much rest, but for much patience.

Do not seek true peace on earth, but in heaven—not in people or any other creature, but in God alone.

For the love of God you should cheerfully undergo all things—work, grief, temptation, annoyance, anxiety, necessity, infirmity, injury, detraction, reproof, humiliation, shame, correction, and contempt.

These are helps to virtue, the trials of a babe in Christ, the construction of the heavenly crown.

I will give an eternal reward for a short labor, and infinite glory for passing shame.

3. Do you think you will always have spiritual consolation when you desire it?

My saints did not, but they had many afflictions, various temptations, and great discomforts.

Yet in all these they bore themselves patiently and trusted in God rather than in themselves, knowing that the sufferings of this present time are not worthy to be compared with our future glory.[5]

Would you have at once what others scarcely obtained after many tears and great labors?[6]

Wait for the Lord, act bravely, and be strong.[7] Do not despair or turn back, but steadily offer your body and soul for the glory of God.

I will reward you abundantly, and I will be with you in every tribulation.

1  Ephesians 6:11
2  2 Corinthians 6:7
3  2 Timothy 4:8
4  Revelation 2:17
5  Romans 8:18
6  1 Peter 4:18
7  Psalm 27:14

# 36
## THE WORTHLESS JUDGMENTS OF PEOPLE

My child, fix your heart firmly on the Lord, and do not fear the judgement of people when your conscience witnesses to your piety and innocence.

It is a good and happy thing to suffer that way, and it will not be a burden to a heart that is humble and trusts in God rather than in itself.[1]

Most people talk a great deal, and therefore little trust should be placed in them.

Moreover, it is impossible to satisfy everyone.

Although Paul tried to please everyone in the Lord, and became all things to all people,[2] yet he considered it a very small thing that he should be judged by others.[3]

Although he labored with everything in him at doing whatever he could for the salvation and edification of others, he could not prevent people from sometimes judging and despising him.

Therefore, he committed everything to God who knows everything, and used patience and humility to defend himself again unjust tongues, those who thought foolishness and lies, and those who boasted whenever they wished.

Sometimes he did answer, however, so that the weak would not be hurt by his silence.[4]

3. Who are you, then, that you fear mortal people? Today they are here, tomorrow they are gone [see note[5]].

Fear God, and you will not be frightened by people.

What harm can the words or abuses of people do to you? They harm themselves rather than you, and they cannot avoid God's judgment whoever they might be.[6]

Keep your eyes focused on God, and do not contend against complaining words.

And if it seems to you that at the present you are overcome and suffer undeserved shame, do not be grieved or lessen your crown by being impatient.[7]

Instead, look up to Me in heaven, for I am able to deliver you from all wrong and shame and give to every person according to their works.

1   1 Peter 2:20
2   1 Corinthians 9:22, 2 Corinthians 4:2
3   1 Corinthians 4:3
4   Acts 26, 2 Corinthians 11, 12
5   1 Maccabees 2:62-62—1st and 2nd Maccabees are
    Apocrypha books. The verses read: "Do not fear the words
    of sinners, for their splendor will turn into dung and worms.

Today they will be exalted, but tomorrow they will not be found, because they will have returned to the dust, and their plans will have perished."

6 Romans 2:3, 1 Corinthians 11:32

7 Hebrews 12:1-2

# 37

## Pure and Entire Resignation of Ourselves to Obtain Freedom of Heart

My child, forsake [abandon] yourself and you will find Me.[1]

Choose nothing out of concern for yourself, or set apart anything for yourself, and you will always gain.

For greater grace will be given to you the moment you perfectly resign [give up] yourself—unless you turn back and take yourself up again.

Lord, how often should I resign myself, and in what way should I forsake myself?

Always and every hour, in small things as well as great. I exclude nothing, for I desire that you be stripped of all things.

Otherwise, how can you be Mine and I be yours unless you are stripped of all self-will inwardly and outwardly.

The sooner you do this the better it will be for you, and the more fully and sincerely you do it the more you will please Me and the more [merit] you will gain.

2. There are some who resign themselves, but exclude certain things, for they do not trust God completely and so try to learn how to provide for themselves.

Also, some offer everything at first, but later when they are assaulted with temptation they go back to where they were, and thereby make no progress on the path of virtue.[2]

These will not obtain the true liberty of a pure heart, or the grace of My closest friendship, unless first they completely resign themselves and daily sacrifice themselves to Me.[3] For without this, there is not and cannot be a fruitful union with Me.

3. I have often said this to you, and now I say it again: forsake yourself,[4] resign yourself, and you will enjoy great inward peace.

Give [your] all for [My] all, require nothing back, abide purely and with firm confidence in Me,[5] and you will possess Me—then you will be free in heart and darkness will not weigh you down.

Let this be your whole endeavor, your prayer, your desire—being stripped of all selfishness, you can with great simplicity follow Jesus only,[6] and having died to self you can live eternally with Me.

Then all foolish imaginations, evil disturbances, and needless cares will fly away.

Then, also, all unreasonable fear will leave you, and all immoderate love will die.

1   Matthew 16:24
2   Matthew 13:20-21
3   Luke 9:23
4   Matthew 16:24
5   John 15:4-7
6   2 Corinthians 11:3

## 38
### GOVERNING EXTERNAL THINGS PROPERLY, AND HAVING RECOURSE TO GOD WHEN IN DANGER

My child, you should earnestly endeavor to be inwardly free in every place and activity and in all external actions, and you should thoroughly master yourself so that all things are under you and you are not under them.

You must rule and control your actions, not let them rule and control you—as if you were a slave or a hireling [see note[1]].

You should, instead, be a free person and a true Hebrew who has passed into the kingdom and freedom of the children of God.[2]

For though they see the things that are present, they contemplate the things that are eternal.

They look at the temporal things [of earth] with their left eye, and with their right eye they behold the [eternal] things of heaven.

Temporal things cannot so draw them that they cling to them—instead, they use temporal things to serve them in the ways ordained and appointed by God, the Great Workmaster, who has left nothing unordered in His creation.

2. If you stand steadfast in all circumstances and do not evaluate the things that you see and hear by their outward appearance or with a worldly eye, but immediately enter with Moses into the Tabernacle[3] to ask counsel of the Lord, you will sometimes hear the divine answer and will return instructed about many things, both those present and those to come.

For Moses always had recourse to the Tabernacle for answers to doubts and questions, and fled to prayer for assistance and support when facing danger and the wickedness of others.

So in like manner you should fly to the secret place in your heart and earnestly ask for God's grace.[4]

For we read that Joshua and the children of Israel were deceived by the Gibeonites because they did not ask the Lord for counsel, but trusted too much in their crafty words and were deceived by their counterfeit piety.[5]

1  *Hireling*—one who works solely for compensation, especially a person willing to perform for a fee tasks considered menial or offensive.
2  Colossians 1:13
3  Exodus 33:9
4  Matthew 6:6, Hebrews 4:16
5  Joshua 9

# 39

## A Person Should Not Be Anxious in Business Affairs

My child, always commit your affair to Me—I will take care of it in a beneficial way in due time.

Wait for My arrangements, and you will find it will be to your good.

O Lord, I most cheerfully commit all things to You, for my efforts are of little value.

I wish that I was not so much concerned about future events, but could myself give myself without hesitation to Your good pleasure.

2. My child, people often feverishly pursue something they want, and when they obtain it they begin to change their mind, for people's affections do not remain long on one object, but instead drive them from one thing to another.

It is no small advantage, therefore, for you to forsake yourself even in the smallest things.

3. True [spiritual] progress consists in denying yourself, and those who have so denied themselves live in great freedom and security.

However, that old enemy who always opposes those who are pious never stops from tempting, but day and night lies dangerously in wait to cast the unwary ones that he can into the snare of deceit.[1]

Therefore says the Lord, "Watch and pray, lest you enter into temptation."[2]

1    1 Peter 5:8
2    Matthew 26:41

# 40

## WE HAVE NO GOOD IN OURSELVES, AND NOTHING IN WHICH WE CAN GLORY

Lord, "what is man that You are mindful of him, And the son of man that You visit him?"[1]

What have we deserved that You should grant us Your grace?

O Lord, what reason have I to complain if You abandon me? Or if You do not do what I ask, what can I rightly say against Your decision?

What I should truly think and say is this: Lord, I am nothing, I can do nothing, I have nothing of myself that is good, and I am defective in all things and continually tend to achieve nothing.

And unless You help me and inwardly instruct me, I will become totally lukewarm and ineffective.

2. But You, O Lord, are always the same and endure forever.[2] You are always good, just, and holy—and You do all things well, justly, sacredly, and arrange all things with wisdom.

But I am more ready to go backward than forward and never stay in one condition, for I change with the seasons [see note[3]].

Yet my condition becomes better when it so pleases You, and You agree [in answer to prayer] to stretch forth Your helping hand, for You can help me by Yourself without human aid, and so strengthen me that my heart will remain unchanged and turn to You alone and be at rest.

3. Therefore, if I could totally cast aside all human comfort—for reasons of gaining a state of devotion, or out of necessities that force me to seek You because no mortal person can comfort me—then I could well hope in Your grace and rejoice in the gift of new consolation.

4. Thanks be to You from whom everything comes when it goes well with me.

But in Your sight I am self-centered and nothing, an unsteady and weak person.

For what reason then can I glory, or for what do I wish to be respected—is it for being nothing? That is most prideful.

Truly, empty glory is an evil plague and totally worthless, for it draws us away from true glory and robs us of heavenly grace.

For while we please ourselves we displease You, and while we pant after the praise of people we are deprived of true virtues.

5. But true glory and holy exultation is for us to glory in You[4] and not in ourselves, to rejoice in Your name and not in our own virtue and strength, and not to find pleasure in any creature except for Your sake.

Your name be praised, not mine—Your work be magnified, not mine. Let Your holy name be blessed, but let no part of human praise be given to me.[5]

You are my glory, You are the joy of my heart.

In You I will glory and rejoice all the day, but as for myself I will not glory in anything except my infirmities.[6]

6. Let others seek honor from one another, I will seek the honor that comes from the only God.[7]

For all human glory, all temporal honor, all worldly elevation, is worthless and foolish when compared to Your eternal glory.

O my God, my truth, my mercy—O Blessed Trinity, to You alone be praise, honor, power, and glory forever and ever.[8]

1  Psalm 8:4
2  Psalm 102:12
3  Original text read, "for seven times are passed over me," which is a paraphrase of Daniel 4:16, 23, and 32.
4  Habakkuk 3:18
5  Psalm 113:3, 115:1
6  2 Corinthians 12:5, 9
7  John 5:44
8  Revelation 4:11, 5:13, 7:11-12

## 41
### CONTEMPT OF ALL TEMPORAL HONOR

My child, do not concern yourself if you see others honored and advanced and you despised and degraded.

Lift your heart up to Me in heaven and the contempt of those on earth will not grieve you.

Lord, we are blinded and quickly misled by pride.

If I look within myself I cannot say that anyone has done any wrong to me, and so I cannot justly complain to You.

2. But because I have often and seriously sinned against You, it is just that all creatures war against me.

I justly deserve shame and contempt—but You praise, honor, and glory.

And unless I prepare myself to be cheerfully willing to be despised and forsaken of all creatures, and be thought of as completely nothing, I cannot obtain inward peace and stability, be spiritually enlightened, or be fully united to You.

## 42
### OUR PEACE IS NOT TO BE DERIVED FROM PEOPLE

My child, if you derive your peace from people because of your opinion of them or your close friendship, you will always be in an insecure and entangled condition.

But if you have recourse to the eternal and abiding Truth, you will not be grieved when friends die or leave you.

Your regard for your friends should be grounded in Me, and whoever you think well of and hold dear in this life should be loved for My sake.

No friendship can endure or continue without Me, and no love is true and pure that is not bound together by Me.

You should be so free from needing such affections from beloved friends, that so far as you are concerned you could easily wish to be without the companionship of others.

The further you withdraw from human consolation, the nearer you come to God.

In proportion, also, as you descend into yourself and grow inferior in your own estimation, the higher you ascend into God.

But if you attribute any good to yourself, you hinder God's grace from entering your heart, for the grace of the Holy Spirit always seeks a humble heart.[1]

If you knew how to do away with yourself completely and empty yourself of all created love, then I could flow into you with an overabundance of grace.

When you look to the creatures, the sight of the Creator is withdrawn from you.

Learn in all things to overcome yourself for the love of your Creator, and then you will acquire divine knowledge.

No matter how small something is, if it is immoderately loved and admired it keeps you back from the chief good and harms your soul.

1    1 Peter 5:5

# 43
## Against Useless and Worldly Knowledge

My child, do not let the words of people move you, no matter how beautiful or clever the words may be, "For the kingdom of God is not in word but in power."[1]

Listen well to My words [the Scriptures], for they inflame the heart, enlighten the mind, arouse the conscience, and provide an abundant variety of consolation.

Never read the Word so that you can appear more knowledgeable or wiser.

Study it to learn of your sins and how to discipline yourself, for this will benefit you more than knowing the answers to many difficult questions.

2. When you have read and know many things, you should always return to this one beginning and principle:

I am He who teaches people knowledge, and I give little children a clearer understanding [of spiritual things] than can be taught by any human.

The one to whom I speak, therefore, will soon be wise and will benefit much in the spirit.

Woe to those who seek [to learn] the skillful and clever ways of people, and care little about the way to serve Me!

The time will come when the Teacher of teachers will appear, Christ the Lord of angels, to hear the lessons that all have learned—that is, to examine everyone's conscience.

And then He will search Jerusalem with lamps,[2] and the things hidden in the dark will be brought into the light,[3] and everyone's justifications [for their sins] will be silenced.[4]

3. I am He who instantly enables the humble mind to understand more about eternal truth than could be learned by studying ten years in schools.

I teach without the noise of words, confusion of opinions, ambition for honor, and clash of arguments.

I am He who teaches people to despise earthly things, loath present things, seek eternal things, enjoy eternal things, flee honors, suffer injuries, place all hope in Me, desire nothing from Me, and, above all things, love Me ardently.

4. For by loving Me fully, a certain person learned divine things and spoke of things that were admirable.

He benefited more by forsaking all things than by studying difficult and elusive matters.

To some I speak of common things, to others of special things—to some I appear sweetly by signs and symbols, and to some I reveal mysteries with much illumination.

The voice of [biblical] books is indeed one, but it does not instruct all alike, for I am the teacher of inward truth, the searcher of the heart, the discerner of thoughts, the inspirer of good actions, giving to each person as I judge best.

1  1 Corinthians 4:20
2  Zephaniah 1:12,
3  Luke 8:17
4  Luke 16:15, 1 Corinthians 4:5

## 44
### NOT BRINGING TROUBLE TO OURSELVES FROM OUTWARD THINGS

My child, there are many things in which it is your moral obligation to be ignorant and to think of yourself as dead upon the earth, and as a person to whom the whole world is crucified.[1]

It is your moral obligation also to pass by many things with a deaf ear, and to think instead of those things that bring you [inward] peace.[2]

It is more beneficial to turn your eyes away from unpleasant things, and to leave every person to their own opinion, rather than be caught in quarrelsome conversations.

If everything is well between you and God, and you keep in mind His judgment [of earthly things], you will more easily endure being overcome [by others].

2. O Lord, what a condition we have come to! Behold, we mourn over a temporal loss, we work and rush about, and we ignore and hardly think about the spiritual damage being done to our soul.

We attend to those things that are of little or no benefit, and we ignore the things that are especially necessary to us, all because we get too involved in external things—and unless we turn away from them quickly, we willingly get engulfed in them.

1   Galatians 6:14
2   Philippians 4:8

# 45
## EVERYONE IS NOT TO BE BELIEVED, FOR WE TEND TO MAKE MISTAKES WHEN WE SPEAK

Grant me help, O Lord, in my tribulation, for the help of people is useless.[1]

I have often been deceived, and did not find faithfulness where I was certain it was.

And often I have found it where I least expected it.

It is useless, therefore, to trust in people, for the salvation of the righteous is in You, O God.

Blessed be You, O Lord my God, in all things that befall us.

We are weak and unstable, quickly deceived and soon changed.

2. Who of us is able to so wisely guard and care for ourselves that we are never deceived or confused?

But the person who trusts in You, O Lord, and seeks You with an undivided heart, does not fail so easily.[2]

And if we fall into any tribulation, no matter how much we are entangled we will either be quickly delivered through You or be comforted by You, for You will never forsake those who trust in You.[3]

A friend that remains faithful in all of a friend's troubles is rarely found.

You alone, O Lord, are faithful all the time, and there is no one else like You.

3. Oh, how wise that holy Christian was who said, "My mind is firmly settled and grounded in Christ" [see note[4]].

If that were so with me, then fear of others would not easily distress me, and the sting of their words would not disturb me.

Who can foresee everything? Who is able to prepare ahead for future troubles? If troubles we foresee often hurt us, how can troubles we do not anticipate do anything other than gravely wound us?

Knowing how wretched I am, why did I not better provide for myself? And why have I so easily had confidence in others?

We are human, however, nothing but frail human beings, even though many think highly of us and some even call us holy.

In whom shall I have faith, Lord? In whom but You? You are the truth that neither deceives nor can be deceived.

In contrast, "every person is a liar,"[5] weak, unstable, and subject to errors, especially in words—therefore, we must not easily believe even that which externally seems at first to be right.

4. O how wise was Your warning to beware of people— that because our enemies are sometimes even those of our own household,[6] we are not to believe it if someone says,

"Look, He is in the desert!" or "Look, He is in the inner rooms!"[7]

Injury has been my instructor, and I pray it has made me more cautious and less gullible.

"Be careful," they say, "be careful and keep to yourself what I tell you." Then while I keep silent, thinking it is a secret, they cannot keep to themselves the very thing they wanted me to keep, and soon they betray both me and themselves and are gone.

From such tales and such indiscreet people protect me, O Lord, that I neither fall into their hands nor ever commit such things myself.

Grant that I may be truthful and steadfast in my words, and keep a crafty tongue far from me.[8]

What I am not willing to endure in others, I should certainly avoid myself.

5. Oh how good and peaceful it is to be silent about other people, not to believe indiscriminately all that is said, and not to gossip about what we have heard.[9]

Also, it is good to open yourself to few people, and to always seek after You[10]—the discerner of the thoughts and attitudes of the heart.[11]

We should not be tossed about by every wind of words,[12] but should desire that all things inwardly and outwardly be accomplished according to the pleasure of Your will.[13]

We can securely keep heavenly grace by not being with too many people, not seeking those things in the world that people seem to admire, but pursuing with all diligence the things that change our spiritual life [for the better] and increase our zeal for godliness.

6. Many have been known for their virtue and have been hurt by being too hastily commended for it.

But grace has been highly beneficial when it has been maintained in silence, for this frail life is said to be full of temptation and warfare.

1   Psalm 60:11
2   Proverbs 10:29
3   Hebrews 13:5
4   Attributed to Agatha, who was martyred by Quintain (or Quintian), governor of Sicily—she died on February 5, 1251 (The New Foxe's Book of Martyrs, Bridge-Logos Publishers).
5   Romans 3:4
6   Micah 4:5, Matthew 10:36
7   Matthew 24:26
8   Job 15:5; Psalm 120:2; James 3:5-8; 1 Peter 3:10
9   Proverbs 25:9
10  Isaiah 26:3
11  Hebrews 4:12
12  James 1:6
13  Ephesians 1:5, 9; Philippians 2:13

# 46
## TRUSTING IN GOD WHEN EVIL WORDS ARE SPOKEN AGAINST US

My child, stand steadily and put your trust in Me,[1] for what are words but words?

They fly through the air, but do not hurt even a stone [see note[2]].

If you are guilty, consider how eager you are to improve yourself—if your conscience does not reprove you, resolve to suffer this willingly for God's sake.

It is a small matter to suffer a few words sometimes, since you do not yet have the courage to endure hard blows.

Why do such small matters go your heart if not because you are still carnal [worldly] and pay more attention to people than you should?

Because you are afraid of being despised, you will not accept reproof for your faults and you try to hide in excuses.

2. Look closer into yourself and you will see that the world is still alive in you, and you have a prideful desire to please people.

For when you deliberately avoid being humbled and reproved for your faults, it is evident that you are not truly humble or dead to the world, and that the world is not crucified to you.[3]

But pay close attention to My Words, and you will not be concerned about ten thousand words spoken by people.

Behold, if everything that could be maliciously invented was said against you, how much would it hurt you if you let it pass and gave it no more consideration than you would a blade of grass? Could those words remove as much as one hair from your head?[4]

3. But those who have no courage in them or God before their eyes are easily moved by a disparaging word.

While at the same time, those who trust in Me and are not influenced by confidence in their own judgement will be free from all fear of people.

For I am the judge and discerner of all secrets—I know how the matter came about, and I know the one who caused the injury and the one who suffered it.

This proceeded from Me—it has happened by My permission so that the thoughts of many hearts might be revealed.[5]

I will judge the guilty and the innocent—but by a secret [standard of] judgement I tried them both beforehand.

4. The testimony of people often deceives, but My judgment is true and will stand and not be overthrown.

It is commonly hidden and not known in everything, except by a few—nevertheless, it is never wrong and neither can it be, even though to the eyes of the foolish it often does not seem right.

People should, therefore, come to Me for every judgment, and not lean on their judgment.[6]

For just people will not be troubled[7] no matter what befalls them from God, and if anything is brought wrongfully against them, they will not much care.

Neither will they rejoice proudly if they are exonerated by others.

For they realize that I am the one who searches the hearts and minds,[8] and that I do not judge according to the way things look outwardly or by human appearances.[9]

For what is often thought to be commendable in the judgment of people is often found to be deserving of blame in My sight.


O Lord God, the righteous judge, strong and patient, You who know the frailty and wickedness of people, be my strength and all my trust, for my own conscience is not sufficient.

Although I know nothing against myself, yet I cannot justify myself by this,[10] for without Your grace no one living is justified [righteous] in Your sight.[11]

1   Psalm 37:3
2   Or: hurt as much as a stone does.
3   Galatians 6:14
4   Matthew 10:30, Luke 12:7
5   Luke 2:35
6   Proverbs 3:5
7   Proverbs 12:13
8   Psalm 7:9, Revelation 2:23

9    1 Samuel 16:7
10  1 Corinthians 4:4
11  Psalm 143:2

# 47

## ENDURE ALL GRIEVOUS THINGS
## FOR THE SAKE OF ETERNAL LIFE

My child, do not be discouraged by whatever difficult work you undertake for Me, or be dismayed because of tribulations that befall you, but in everything let My promises strengthen and comfort you.

I am well able to reward you above all you can measure or imagine.[1]

You will not labor here long or always be burdened with griefs.[2]

Be patience a little while and you will see a speedy end of your sorrows.

There will come an hour when all labor and trouble will cease.[3]

The things that pass away with time are valueless and fleeting.

2. Do earnestly whatever you do and labor faithfully in My vineyard[4]—I will be your reward.

Work what I put in your hands to do,[5] study the Scriptures and meditate on them,[6] sing psalms [songs of praise],[7] pray continually,[8] endure crosses courageously[9]—your eternal life is worthy of all these things,[10] and even more.

Peace will come in a day that is known [only] to the Lord,[11] and there will no longer be earthly day or night, but heavenly eternal light, infinite brightness, continual peace, and secure rest.

Then you will not say, "Who will deliver me from this body of death?"[12] or cry, "Woe is me, that my sojourning is prolonged! [see note[13]]. For death will be cast down headlong, and there will be salvation [see note[14]] that cannot fail and no more anxiety—only blessed joy and sweet and glorious companionship.

3. Oh, if you could see the everlasting crowns of the saints in heaven [see note[15]], and how gloriously they now rejoice—when in times past they were scorned by the world and considered unworthy of life itself—you would certainly humble yourself to the world[16] and seek to be subject to everyone rather than have authority over even one person.

Also, you would not desire the pleasant days of this life, but instead would rejoice to suffer affliction for God's sake, and consider it your greatest gain to be regarded as nothing among people.

4. Oh, if you had an appetite for these things and allowed them to sink deep into your heart, how could you complain even once?

Should not all painful trials be endured for the sake of eternal life [in Christ]?[17]

It is no small matter to lose or gain [the blessings] of the kingdom of God.[18]

Lift up your eyes, therefore, to heaven and see Me and all the saints with Me. In the world they had great conflicts, but now they are joyful, comforted, secure, and restful, and will remain with Me forever in the kingdom of My Father.

1  Ephesians 3:20
2  Revelation 21:3-4
3  1 Thessalonians 4:16

4   Matthew 20:1-16
5   Ephesians 6:7; 1 Thessalonians 4:11; 2 Thessalonians 3:10-
    12
6   Psalm 1:2
7   James 5:13, NIV
8   Luke 21:36, 1 Thessalonians 5:17
9   Romans 8:17, Philippians 1:29
10  Ephesians 4:1
11  Zechariah 14:7, 1 Thessalonians 5:2, 2 Peter 3:10
12  Romans 7:24
13  Psalm 120:5—Actual quotation is, "Woe is me, that I
    sojourn in Mesech, that I dwell in the tents of Kedar!" (KJV)
14  Possibly: healing
15  2 Timothy 4:8; James 1:12; 1 Peter 5:4; Revelation 2:10,
    3:11; Wisdom of Solomon 5:16—Wisdom of Solomon is
    an Apocrypha book. The verse reads: "Therefore they will
    receive a glorious crown and a beautiful diadem from the
    hand of the Lord, because with his right hand he will cover
    them, and with his arm he will shield them."
16  Philippians 2:3
17  Philippians 1:29, 2 Timothy 3:12, Revelation 2:10
18  1 Corinthians 3:15, 2 Thessalonians 1:5, 2 Timothy 2:12

# 48

## The Day of Eternity and the Distresses of This Life

O, most blessed mansion of the city above![1] O, most bright day of eternity, which no night darkens, but the highest Truth ever illuminates! O, day ever joyful, ever secure, and never changing into an opposite state!

O, that this day might soon appear and all these temporal things come to an end!

To the saints [already in heaven] it shines radiantly with everlasting brightness, but to those that are pilgrims on the earth,[2] it appears far off as if reflected dimly in a mirror.[3]

2. The citizens of heaven know how joyful that day is, but the exiled children of Eve mourn how bitter and tedious this life is.

The days of this life are short and [morally] evil, full of sorrow and trouble.

Here a person is defiled by many sins, ensnared by many passions, bound by many fears, harassed by many cares, distracted by many curiosities, entangled by many prides, surrounded by many errors, wearied by many labors, burdened by temptations, weakened by pleasures, and tormented by desires.

3. Oh, when will these evils end? When will I be delivered from the miserable bondage of my sins?[4] When will I think of You alone, O Lord?[5] When will I fully rejoice in You?

When will I enjoy true freedom without any obstacles whatever, without any mental or physical trouble?

When will I have solid peace, peace secure and undisturbed, peace inwardly and peace outwardly, peace assured in every way?

O merciful Jesus, when will I stand to look upon You? When will I contemplate the glory of Your kingdom? When will You be all in all to me?

Oh, when will I be with You in Your kingdom, which You have prepared[6] for Your beloved from all eternity?[7]

I am a poor and exiled person who has been left in the land of my enemies, where everyday there are wars and adversities.

4. Comfort my exile and lighten my sorrow, for all of my soul thirsts for You.[8]

For everything the world offers for my consolation is a burden to me.

I long to enjoy You most inwardly, but I cannot achieve it.

My desire is to be completely given up to heavenly things, but temporal things and undisciplined passions weigh me down.

With my mind I wish to be above all things, but my flesh forces me to be subject to them against my will.[9]

So I am an unhappy person—I fight with myself and have become a burden to myself, for my spirit wants to rise upward, but my flesh wants to sink downward.

5. Oh, how I suffer inwardly when I think about heavenly things, for when I pray a multitude of carnal imaginations immediately invades my thoughts! O my God, do not be far from me or turn away in anger from Your servant!

Send forth Your lightning and scatter these thoughts—shoot out Your arrows and let all the fantasies of the enemy be put to flight.

Gather my senses and draw them home to You, make me forget all worldly things, and enable me to quickly and scornfully drive away all vicious imaginations.

Help me, O everlasting Truth, so that no foolishness will affect me.

Come to me, Heavenly Sweetness, and cause all impurity to flee from before Your face.

In mercy deal gently with me, and pardon me as often as I think of anything besides You.

For I must truly confess that I am always subject to many distractions.

A multitude of times I am not where I am bodily standing or sitting, but instead I am wherever my thoughts take me.

I am where my thoughts are, and commonly my thoughts are where my emotions are.

This too easily happens to me with those things that are naturally delightful or habitually pleasing.

6. Therefore, You who are Truth itself have plainly said, "For where your treasure is, there your heart will be also."[10]

If I love heaven, I willingly think on heavenly things.

If I love the world, I rejoice at the success of the world and grieve at its adversities.

If I love the flesh, I will often fantasies on those things that are pleasing to the flesh.

If I love the spirit, I will delight in thinking about spiritual things.

For whatever I love, I willingly speak and hear about, and carry the essence of it home with me.

Blessed are those who for Your sake, O Lord, willingly give up all creatures, do violence to their [carnal] nature, through fervor of spirit crucify the lusts of the flesh, so that with an untroubled conscience they can offer pure prayers to You and, having excluded all inward and outward earthly things, be [spiritually] fit to join the heavenly choirs [even while on earth].[11]

---

1   John 14:2
2   1 Peter 2:11
3   1 Corinthians 13:12
4   Romans 7:24
5   Psalm 71:16
6   John 14:2-3
7   Ephesians 1:4
8   Psalm 42
9   Romans 7:18-23, 8:23
10 Luke 12:34
11 Revelation 5:8-14, 19:1-8

## 49

### THE DESIRE FOR ETERNAL LIFE, AND THE GREAT REWARDS PROMISED TO THOSE WHO FIGHT WITHOUT WAVERING

My child, when you feel the desire for the everlasting joy that will be given to you from above, and want to depart out of the tabernacle of the body so you can contemplate my glory without any change, open your heart wide and receive this holy inspiration [inspired desire] with all eagerness.

Give great thanks to the heavenly goodness that deals with you so favorable—visiting you mercifully, stirring you up fervently, and holding you up powerfully—lest the weight of yourself causes you to sink down to worldly things.

You do not obtain this by your own thought or effort, but by the pure condescension of heavenly grace and divine favor. This was done so you can make further progress in virtue, obtain greater humility, prepare yourself for future conflicts, strive to cling to Me with all the love of your heart, and serve Me with fervent desire.

2. My child, often the fire burns, but the flame does not ascend without smoke.

In the same way the desires of some burn toward heavenly things, and yet they are not free from the temptations of carnal affection.

Therefore, the earnest requests they make to God are not altogether purely for His honor.

Often this is the same with your desires, which you pretend are so serious and earnest.

For desires that are mixed with your own special interest and advantage are not pure and perfect.

3. Do not ask for that which is delightful and beneficial to you, but that which is acceptable to Me and promotes My honor, for if you judged rightly you would prefer and

follow My will instead of your own desire—or desired things of any kind.

I know your desire and have heard your frequent groaning.[1]

Now you long to enjoy the glorious liberty of the children of God.[2] Now you are delighted by the everlasting dwelling and the heavenly country filled with joy, but that hour has not yet come. There is yet another time—a time of war, labor, and testing.

You want to be filled with the sovereign good, but you cannot realize it now.

"I am that sovereign good, wait for Me," says the Lord, "until the kingdom of God comes."

4. You are yet to be tried upon the earth, and to be [spiritually] exercised in many things.

Consolation will sometimes be given to you, but the abundant fullness of it will not be granted.

Be courageous, therefore, and be as strong[3] in doing as in suffering things that are contrary to nature.

You should put on the new self[4] and be changed into another person.

It is often your duty [to God] to do what you would rather not do, and to leave undone what you wish to do.

What is pleasing to others will prosper, what you long for will not prosper.

What others say will be heard, what you say will be considered as nothing—others will ask and receive, you will ask and not receive.

5. Others will be greatly praised by people, but nothing will be said about you.

To others this or that work will be committed, but you will considered of no use.

When this happens, your nature will be troubled, but it is better if you endure it in silence.

In these and many similar instances, the faithful servants of the Lord are customarily tried, to see if they can deny and break themselves in all things.

There is scarcely anything in which you have more need to die to yourself than in seeing and suffering those things that are contrary to your will, especially when what is commanded seems to you inconvenient or less beneficial [than your way].

At those times, it seems hard to submit to the will of another and give up your own opinion completely, [which you must do] since you are under [secular or spiritual] authority and dare not resist your superior.

6. But if you consider, my child, the fruit of these labors, the end that is near at hand, and the reward that is exceedingly great, you will not be reluctant to endure them, but instead will receive great comfort from your patience.

For instead of the little of your will that you now readily give up, you will always have your will in heaven.

Yes, there you will find all that you wish, all that you will be able to desire.

There you will have everything good within your reach without fear of losing it.

There shall your will always be one with Me, it will not covet any outward or personal things.

There no one will oppose you, no one will complain about you, no one will hinder you, nothing will stand in your way, but all desirable things will be present there, and will refresh all your affections [for things denied for Christ's sake] and fill them up to the brim.

There I will give you glory for the reproach you suffered here, the garment of praise for [the spirit of] heaviness,[5] and an eternal kingly throne for your lowly position.[6]

There will the fruit of obedience appear, the labor of repentance rejoice, and humble subjection will be gloriously crowned.

7. At present, then, bow yourself humbly under all, and do not be concerned about who said this or commanded that.

But be careful that whether your superior, inferior, or equal require anything of you, or even hint at their desire, that you take it with good grace and sincerely endeavor to do it.

Let one seek this, another that. Let this person glory in this thing, the other in that, and both be praised a million times. But you are to rejoice in neither this or in that, but in contempt of yourself and in My good pleasure and honor.

This is what you are to wish—that God will always be glorified in you, whether it be by life or in death.[7]

1   Exodus 3:7
2   John 1:12, Romans 8:21, 1 John 3:1
3   Joshua 1:7
4   2 Corinthians 5:17, Ephesians 4:24 (NIV)
5   Isaiah 61:3
6   Revelation 3:21
7   John 21:19

# 50

## HOW DESPONDENT PEOPLE SHOULD OFFER THEMSELVES INTO THE HANDS OF GOD

O Lord God, Holy Father, be blessed now and forever, because what You will is done, and what You do is always good.

Let me, Your servant, rejoice in You, not in myself or in anything else, for You alone are true joy—You are my hope and my crown, my joy and my honor, O Lord.

What do I, Your servant, have that I have not received from You,[1] even without any merit of my own?

Everything is Yours, both what You have given and what You have made.

I am poor and have labored from my youth,[2] and sometimes my soul is sad even unto tears, and sometimes, also, it is troubled by sufferings that are about to happen.

2. I long for the joy of peace, and I earnestly beg for the peace of Your children who You feed by the light of Your consolation.

If You give peace, if You pour holy joy into my heart, the soul of Your servant will be full of melodies and will become devout in Your praise.

But if You withdraw Yourself, as You do too many times, I will not be able to walk in the way of Your commandments, but instead I will bow my knees and smite my breast, because it will not be the same with me as it was in the past when Your lamp shone upon my head, and I was protected under the shadow of Your wings from the temptations that assault me.[3]

3. O righteous Father, ever to be praised, the hour has come that Your servant is to be proved.[4]

O beloved Father, it is right and just that in this hour Your servant should suffer something for Your sake.

O Father, ever to be honored, the hour has come that You foreknow from all eternity would come—that for a short time Your servant would be outwardly oppressed, but inwardly always live with You.

It is well that for a little while I should be considered inferior and humbled, fail in the sight of people, and be ravaged by sufferings and weakness, so that I may rise again with You in the dawn of the new light and be glorified in heaven.[5]

Holy Father, You have ordained it and so will have it, and what is fulfilled is what You commanded.

4. For this is a favor to me, Your friend, that I suffer and be afflicted in the world for love of You, no matter how often and by whom You permit it to happen to me.

Nothing happens on the earth without Your guidance and providence—and without reason.

It is good for me, Lord, that You have humbled me so I will learn Your righteous judgments[6] and cast away [from me] all presumptuousness and pride of heart.

It is beneficial for me that shame has covered my face so I will seek consolation from You rather than from people.

By this means I have also learned to fear Your unsearchable judgments with which You afflict the just and the unjust, although not without fairness and justice.[7]

5. I thank You that You have not spared my sins, but have chastised me with bitter stripes, inflicting sorrows and sending anxieties upon me within and without.[8]

There is no one else under heaven who can comfort me, except You, O Lord my God, the Heavenly Physician of souls, who wounds and heals, who sends down to hell and raises up again [see note[9]].

Your discipline will watch over me, and Your rod itself will instruct me.[10]

6. Behold, O beloved Father, I am in Your hands—I submit myself to Your rod of correction.[11]

Strike my back and my neck, too, so my perverse ways will conform to Your will.

Make me a dutiful and humble disciple of Yours, as You are well used to doing, so I will be ready at every demand of Your divine will.

I commit myself and all that is mine to You to be corrected, for it is better to be chastised here than hereafter.

You know everything, both together and separately,[12] and there is nothing in a person's conscience that can be hidden from You.[13]

Before things are done You know they will come to pass, and You have no need of anyone teaching or admonishing You about the things that are done on the earth.[14]

You know what is needed for my spiritual progress, and how much tribulation serves to scour the rust off my sins.

Do with me according to Your good pleasure, and do not despise me for my sinful life, which is known to no one as completely and clearly as it is to You.

7. Grant me, O Lord, the grace to know what is worth knowing, love what is worth loving, praise what is most pleasing to You, value what is precious to You, and despise what is contemptible in Your sight.

Do not allow me to judge according to what I see, or give sentence according to what ignorant people hear [see note[15]], but enable me to discern with true judgment between things visible and spiritual, and above everything to always search for the good pleasure of Your will.

8. The minds of people are often deceived in their judgments, and the lovers of the world are deceived in loving only things they can see.

How is a person ever better by being considered great by people?

The deceitful flatter the deceitful, the proud exalt the proud, the blind commend the blind, the weak magnify the weak—and in so doing, each person deceives the other and increases their shame while foolishly praising them.

The humble St. Francis [see note[16]] said, "For what everyone is in Your sight, that they are and no more."

1   1 Corinthians 4:7
2   Psalm 88:15
3   Psalm 17:8, 36:7, 57:1, 63:7
4   Genesis 22:12, John 17:1
5   Revelation 21:24
6   Psalm 119.71
7   2 Timothy 4:1, 1 Peter 4:5
8   Hebrews 12:5-11
9   Psalm 18:16; Acts 2:27, 31; Revelation 20:13; Tobit 13:2—
    Tobit is an Apocrypha book. The verse reads: "For he
    afflicts, and he shows mercy; he leads down to Hades in
    the lowest regions of the earth, and he brings up from the
    great abyss, and there is nothing that can escape his hand."
    Kempis's statement about God sending to hell and raising up
    again is obviously taken from Tobit.
10 Proverbs 23:14, Isaiah 11:4
11 Proverbs 29:15 (NKJV)
12 Matthew 10:29-30
13 Matthew 10:26
14 Job 38, 39, 40, 41
15 Another version of Kempis reads: "Do not allow me to judge
    according to the light of my bodily eyes, nor to give sentence
    according to the hearing of ignorant men's ears."
16 Francis of Assisi—1182?-1226. Italian Roman Catholic
    monk who founded the Franciscan order (1209) and
    inspired followers with his devotion, simple living, and love
    of nature.

# 51

## WHEN WE LACK STRENGTH FOR HIGHER [DEEPER] WORKS, WE SHOULD CONCENTRATE ON HUMBLE WORKS

My child, you are not always able to continue in a fervent
desire for virtue, or to persist in a high degree of meditation,[1]
but sometimes because of the effect of the original sin [and

its resulting curse[2]] you descend to inferior things and bear the burdens of this corrupted [cursed] life, though against your will and wearily.

So long as you have a mortal body, you will feel weariness and heaviness of heart.

Therefore, while you are in the flesh you should often sorrow over the burden of the flesh that keeps you from always continuing in spiritual exercises and divine meditation

2. At those times, it is useful for you to do humble outward works and refresh yourself with good deeds, while confidently expecting My coming and heavenly visitation, and patiently enduring your [temporary] exile and dryness of mind until I again visit you and set you free from all anxieties.

For I will cause you to forget your former pains and enjoy complete inward peace.

I will lay open before you the pleasant fields of Holy Scripture, so that with an enlarged heart you will begin to walk in the way of My commandments.[3]

Then you will say, "the sufferings of this present time are not worthy to be compared with the glory which shall be revealed in us."[4]

1  Psalm 1:2
2  Genesis 3:17
3  Leviticus 26:3, Galatians 5:16, Ephesians 2:10,
   Colossians 1:10, 1 John 1:7
4  Romans 8:18

# 52

## We Should Not Consider Ourselves Worthy of Consolation, But Rather as Deserving Chastisement

O Lord, I am not worthy of Your consolation or of any spiritual visitation, and so You deal justly with me when you leave me [spiritually] poor and desolate.

For though I could shed a sea of tears, I would still not be worthy of Your consolation.

So I deserve nothing but to be scourged and punished,[1] for I have often grievously offended you and greatly sinned in many things.

All things considered, therefore, I am not worthy of even the smallest consolation.

But it is not Your will that Your works should perish, O gracious and merciful God, and so to show the richness of Your goodness upon the vessels of mercy,[2] You grant Your servants comfort far above the ways of the world.

For your consolations are not like the words of people.

2. What have I done, O Lord, that You should bestow any heavenly comfort upon me?[3]

I do not remember having done any good, but I have always been prone to sin and slow to repent and amend.

I cannot deny that this is true—if I said otherwise You would stand [in judgment] against me [see note[4]], and there would be no one to defend me.[5]

What do I deserve for my sins but hell and everlasting fire?

I confess truly that I am worthy of all scorn and contempt, and it is not fitting that I be remembered among Your devout servants.

And though I do not want to hear this, nevertheless, for Your truth's sake I will testify against myself about my sins, so that I may quickly receive mercy from Your hand.

3. Since I am guilty and full of confusion, what can I say? I can say nothing but this: O Lord, I have sinned[6]—have mercy on me and pardon me.

Have patience with me for a little while so that I can mourn my sins before I go into the land of darkness, a land covered with the shadow of death.[7]

What do you require of guilty and miserable sinners, except that they be repentant and humble themselves for their sins?[8]

Out of true repentance and humbling of the heart, hope of forgiveness arises, the troubled conscience is reconciled to God,[9] God's favor is recovered, the person is preserved from the wrath to come,[10] and God and the penitent soul greet one another with a holy kiss.[11]

4. Humble contrition for sins is an acceptable sacrifice for You, O Lord[12]—it is a sacrifice far sweeter in Your presence than the perfume of frankincense.

This is also the pleasant ointment that you desire to have poured upon Your sacred feet,[13] for a contrite and humble heart You have never despised.[14]

Here is refuge from the angry face of the enemy—here is amended and washed away whatever defilement and pollution were contracted elsewhere.

1   Hebrews 12:6
2   Romans 9:15, 23
3   Romans 9:16, 18
4   Acts 7:55-56—When Stephen saw Jesus standing at the right hand of God, it meant He was standing in judgment of those who refused Him and were now persecuting His servant.
5   Job 9:2-3, 33; 1 Timothy 2:5, Hebrews 8:6, 9:15, 12:24

6　Psalm 51
7　Job 10:21-22, Psalm 23:4
8　Micah 6:8, 1 John 1:9
9　Hebrews 10:19-23
10 1 Thessalonians 1:10
11 2 Corinthians 13:12
12 Psalm 51:17
13 Luke 7:38
14 Psalm 51:17, Isaiah 57:15

# 53

## The Grace of God Is Not with Those Who Cherish Earthly Things

My child, My grace is precious—it does not allow itself to be mingled with external things or with earthly consolations.

You should, therefore, cast away all obstacles to grace, if you want to receive it abundantly.[1]

Choose, therefore, a secret place for yourself, love to be there alone, desire conversation with no one, but instead pour out devout prayers to God so that you can keep your mind repentant and your conscience pure.

Consider the whole world as nothing, and prefer waiting upon God before all outward things.[2]

For you will not be able to wait upon Me, and at the same time delight in outward things.

You should remove yourself from your acquaintances and friends,[3] and keep your mind free from any thoughts of external comforts.

Thus the blessed apostle Peter begged the faithful in Christ to keep themselves as strangers and pilgrims in the world [see note[4]].

2. What great confidence those have who are not attached to this world by affection for anything in it.

But the feeble heart does not understand what it means to have a heart so detached from everything, and the worldly person does not know the freedom of the spiritual person.

Nevertheless, if we want to be truly spiritual, we should renounce both those far from us and those near us, and be on guard against no one more than ourselves.

If you completely conquer yourself, you will easily bring all else under control.

The perfect victory is to triumph over ourselves.

For those who keep themselves in such subjection that their sensual [see note[5]] desires obey reason and their reason obeys Me in all things, are truly conquerors of themselves and masters of this world.

3. If you desire to climb up to this height, you must begin courageously and lay the ax to the root,[6] so that you can pull up and destroy both that hidden immoderate love of yourself, and all [love of] personal and earthly goods.

From this sin of too much love for ourselves comes almost every other sin that must be uprooted. And when this evil is vanquished and brought under control, great peace and tranquillity will soon follow.

But because few endeavor to die entirely to themselves or completely turn away from themselves, they therefore remain entangled in themselves and cannot be lifted in spirit above themselves.

But those who desire to walk freely with Me must mortify all unwholesome and immoderate affections, and must not seriously cling with selfish love to any creature.

1  Psalm 84:11; Romans 5:17; 1 Corinthians 1:4; Ephesians 2:8-9, 4:7
2  Psalm 27:14, 37:9, 34, 62:5, 69:3, 6, 130:5

3  Matthew 19:29
4  1 Peter 2:11—Actually, Peter referred to the saints as
   "sojourners and pilgrims," and begged them to "abstain
   from fleshly lusts which war against the soul."
5  Relating to or affecting any of the senses or a sense organ;
   sensory. Not referring to sexuality as it does so much today.
6  Matthew 3:10

# 54
## THE DIFFERENT MOVEMENTS OF NATURE AND GRACE

My child, please note carefully the movements of nature and grace, for they move in a very contrary and subtle manner, and can scarcely be discerned except by the person who is spiritual and inwardly enlightened.[1]

Everyone indeed desires what is good, and assumes there is some good in their words and deeds—therefore, because of the assumption of good, many are deceived.

Nature is crafty and entices many, entangling and deceiving them, and always for its own purpose and goal.

But grace walks in simplicity, abstains away from all appearance of evil,[2] purposes no deceits, and does everything purely for God's sake, in whom it ultimately rests.

2. Nature will not willingly die, be kept down, be overcome, be subject to any, or be subdued without reluctance.

But grace strives for self-mortification, resists sensuality, seeks to be subject, is willing to be kept under, does not wish to use its own liberty, loves to be held under discipline, and does not desire to rule over anyone—but always desires to live and stay in those conditions and be always under God, for whose sake it is ready to bow down [submit] to everyone.[3]

Nature strives for its own advantage and considers the benefit it can reap from another person.

Grace does not consider what is beneficial and convenient to itself, but rather what may be for the good of many.

Nature willingly receives honor and respect.

But grace faithfully attributes all honor and glory to God.

3. Nature is afraid of shame and contempt.

But grace rejoices to suffer reproach for the name of Jesus.[4]

Nature loves leisure and physical rest.

But grace cannot be idle and cheerfully embraces work.

Nature seeks to have things that are rare and beautiful, and abhors things that are common and coarse.

But grace delights in what is plain and humble, not despising rough things, or refusing to wear old and patched garments.

Nature cherishes temporal things, rejoices in earthly gains, sorrows over loses, and is irritated by the slightest harmful word.

But grace looks to eternal things, does not cling to temporal things, is not troubled with losses, or irritated by hard words, because she has placed her treasure and joy in heaven where nothing perishes.[5]

4. Nature is covetous, more willing to receive than give, and loves to have personal things that it can call its own.

But grace is kind-hearted and open, shuns personal interest, is contented with a little, and judges it more blessed to give than to receive.[6]

Nature is partial to creatures, to its own flesh, to self-importance, and to running here and there.

But grace draws near to God and to every virtue, renounces creatures, avoids the world,[7] hates the desires of the flesh, restrains wandering about, and blushes at being seen in public.

Nature is willing to have some external comfort in which it can be sensually delighted.

But grace seeks consolation in God alone, and to have delight in the highest good above all visible things.

5. Nature does everything for its own gain and benefit, and cannot bear to do anything without pay, but for every kindness hopes to receive its equal or better, or at least praise or favor—and is determined to have its works and gifts valued highly.

But grace seeks nothing temporal, does not ask any other reward than God alone, and does not ask any more of temporal necessities that what will be of service in obtaining eternal things.

6. Nature rejoices in having many friends and relatives, glories in its noble position and birth, smiles on the powerful, fawns on the rich, and applauds those who are like itself.

But grace loves even its enemies, is not puffed-up at having many friends, and does not think much of noble birth, unless it is combined with even nobler virtue.

It favors the poor rather than the rich, has more compassion for the innocent than the powerful, and rejoices with the truthful person, not with the deceitful.

Grace is always exhorting the good people to strive for the best [spiritual] gifts,[8] and by practicing all virtue to become like the Son of God.

Nature quickly complains of need and trouble—grace endures need with firmness and steadfastness.

7. Nature directs all things to itself, and strives and argues for itself.

Grace directs all things back to God from whom they originally came, ascribes no good to itself, is not arrogantly presumptuous, does not contend or prefer its own opinion before others, but in every matter of sense and perception submits itself to eternal wisdom and the divine judgment.

Nature is eager to know secrets and to hear news, likes to appear abroad, and likes to give evidence of many things by its own senses—it also desires to be noticed, and to do things for which it may be praised and admired.

But grace does not care to hear news, or understand strange matters, because all this takes its rise from the old corruption of humanity, since there is nothing new upon the earth,[9] nothing that will last.[10]

Grace teaches, therefore, restraint of the senses, shunning of vain self-satisfaction and showiness, humbly hiding things that are worthy of admiration and praise, and in everything and every knowledge to seek beneficial fruit and the praise and honor of God

It will not have itself or what belongs to it praised, but desires that God, who gives all things in simple love, be blessed in His gifts.

8. This grace is a supernatural light and indisputable special gift of God, and the proper mark of the elect and pledge of everlasting salvation. It raises us up from earthly things to love the things of heaven, and it makes a carnal person a spiritual person.[11]

The more, therefore, that nature is disciplined and conquered, the more grace is given, and by daily new visitations the inward person becomes more reformed according to the image of God.[12]

1   Luke 12:56, 1 Corinthians 2:14
2   1 Thessalonians 5:22
3   1 Corinthians 16:16, Hebrews 13:15, 1 Peter 2:13, 5:5
4   Acts 5:41
5   Matthew 6:20
6   Acts 20:35

7   2 Corinthians 6:17
8   1 Corinthians 13:1
9   Ecclesiastes 1:9-10
10  2 Peter 3:10-11
11  1 Corinthians 3:1
12  1 Corinthians 15:49, 2 Corinthians 3:18

# 55

## THE CORRUPTION OF NATURE AND THE EFFECTIVENESS OF DIVINE GRACE

O Lord, my God, who created me in Your own image and likeness,[1] grant me this grace that You have shown to be so great and necessary for salvation, that I may overcome my most evil nature that draws me to sin and perdition.

For I feel in my flesh the law of sin contradicting the law of my mind[2] and leading me captive[3] to obey sensuality in many things. I cannot resist the passions that result, unless Your most holy grace is fervently infused into my heart and helps me.

2. There is need of Your grace, O Lord, and of a great amount of it, so that a nature that has been prone to evil from youth[4] may be overcome.

For through Adam, the first man, nature is fallen and weakened by sin, and the proneness to sin resulting from that stain has descended upon all humanity, so that "nature" itself, which You created good and upright, is considered a symbol for the sin and weakness of corrupted nature, because when left to itself it tends toward evil and inferior things.

The little strength remaining in it is like a spark hidden in ashes.

This is natural reason itself, encompassed about with great darkness, yet still retaining power to discern the difference between true and false, good and evil,—though it is unable to fulfil all that it approves and no longer the full light of the truth or soundness of the emotions.

3. Thus it is, my God, that I delight in Your law according to the inward person,[5] knowing that Your command is good, just, and holy, and reproving all evil and sin and teaching that it is to be avoided.

But in the flesh I serve the law of sin,[6] obeying sensuality rather than reason.

Thus it is that the will to do good is present with me, but how to accomplish it I do not know.[7]

Thus I often propose many good things, but because grace is lacking to help my weakness, I recoil and give up at the smallest resistance.

Thus it comes to pass that I know the way of perfection and see clearly how I should act, but being pressed down with the weight of my own corruption I do not rise to what is more perfect.

4. O Lord, Your grace is entirely needful for me to begin anything good, continue with it, and accomplish it.

For without it I can do nothing,[8] but in You I can do all things when Your grace strengthens me.[9]

Oh, grace truly celestial, without which our most worthy actions are nothing and no gifts of nature are to be admired.

Before You, O Lord, no arts or riches, beauty or strength, genius or eloquence, are of any value without Your grace.

For gifts of nature are common to good and bad, but the distinctive gift of Your elect is grace and love, and those who bear this honorable gift are accounted worthy of everlasting life.[10]

So valuable is this grace that the gift of prophecy, working of miracles, or any meditation—no matter how exalted—is of no value without it.

No, not even faith or hope or any other virtues are acceptable to You without love and grace.[11]

5. O most blessed grace that makes the poor in spirit rich in virtues, and makes the one who is rich in many goods humble of heart.

Come down upon me—come and refresh me soon with your comfort,[12] lest my soul faint with weariness and dryness of mind.

I beg You, O Lord, that I may find grace in Your sight,[13] for Your grace is sufficient for me,[14] even though I obtain none of the things for which nature longs.

If I am tempted and afflicted with many tribulations, I will fear no evil[15] while Your grace is with me.

This alone is my strength—this alone gives me counsel and help.

This is stronger than all enemies and wiser than all the wise.

6. This grace is the mistress of truth, the teacher of discipline, the light of the heart, the consoler in anguish, the banisher of sorrow, the expeller of fear, the nourisher of devotion, the mother of tears.

Without grace I am but a withered branch, a useless piece of wood, fit only to be cast away.[16]

Let Your grace, therefore, O Lord, always go before me and follow me, and make me always inclined to good works, through Your Son Jesus Christ. Amen.

1   Genesis 1:26
2   Romans 7:23
3   Ephesians 4:8
4   Genesis 8:21
5   Romans 7:22
6   Romans 7:25
7   Romans 7:18

8   John 15:5
9   2 Corinthians 12:9, Philippians 4:13
10 Romans 5:5, Ephesians 2:8
11 1 Corinthians 13:13
12 2 Corinthians 1:3-4
13 Exodus 33:13
14 2 Corinthians 12:9
15 Psalm 23:4
16 John 15:1-6

# 56

## WE SHOULD DENY OURSELVES AND
## IMITATE CHRIST BY BEARING THE CROSS

My child, the more you can go out of yourself, the more you will be able to enter into Me.

In the same way that being empty of all desire for external things produces inward peace, forsaking yourself inwardly unites you with God.

I want you to learn perfect abandonment of yourself to My will, without contradiction or complaint.

Follow Me: "I am the Way, the Truth, and the Life."[1] Without the Way there is no going, without the Truth there is no knowing, without the Life there is no living. I am the Way that  you must follow, the Truth that you must believe, the Life that you must hope for.

I am the inviolable Way, the infallible Truth, the endless Life.

I am the straightest [narrow] Way, the sovereign Truth— the true, blessed, and uncreated Life.

If you abide in My way you will know the Truth, and the Truth will make you free,[2] and you will attain life everlasting.

2. If you desire to enter into life, keep My commandments.[3]

If you desire to know the truth, believe in Me.[4]

If you desire to be perfect, sell all [see note[5]]

If you desire to be My disciple, deny yourself.[6]

If you desire to possess a blessed life, despise this present life.[7]

If you desire to be exalted in heaven, humble yourself in this world.[8]

If you desire to reign with Me, bear the cross with Me.[9]

For only the disciples of the cross find the Way of blessedness and of true light.

3. O Lord Jesus, because Your way is narrow[10] and despised by the world, grant me the grace to imitate You[11] in spite of the world's contempt.

For the servants are not greater than their lord,[12] or the disciples above their master.[13]

Let Your servant be trained in Your life and manner [of living], for my salvation[14] and true holiness consist in them.[15]

Whatever I read or hear about in addition to those does not refresh or fully delight me.

4. My child, now that you have read and know all these things, you will be happy if you do them.

Those who have My commandments and keep them, are those who love Me. And those who love Me will be loved by My Father, and I will love them and manifest Myself to them,[16] and will grant them to sit with Me in My Father's kingdom.[17]

O Lord Jesus, as You have said and promised, so let it occur—and grant that I may not be completely undeserving of this favor.

I have received the cross, I have received it from Your hand, and I will bear it, and bear it even onto death—in the way and degree that You have laid it on me.

Truly the life of a godly spiritual person is a cross, but it is also a guide to paradise.

We have begun, it is not lawful to look back, or right to leave that which we have undertaken.[18]

5. Let us take courage, Christians, and go forward together, Jesus will be with us.

For Jesus' sake we have taken this cross upon ourselves, and so for Jesus' sake let us persevere with it.

He who is our guide and forerunner[19] will also be our helper.[20]

Behold, our King marches before us and will fight for us.[21]

Let us follow courageously, let no one fear any terrors, let us be prepared to die valiantly in battle, and not flee from the cross and disgrace the glory [that will be revealed in us].[22]

1 John 14:6
2 John 8:31-32
3 John 14:15, 15:10
4 John 1:12, 3:18, 36; Acts 16:31; Romans 10:9,
5 Matthew 19:21—This was a specific command by Jesus to a specific person; it is not a general command to all Christians.
6 Luke 9:23, John 8:31, 13:35, 15:8
7 John 12:25
8 James 4:10, 1 Peter 5:5-6
9 Luke 14:27, 2 Timothy 2:12, Revelation 5:10
10 Matthew 7:13-14, Luke 13:24
11 1 Corinthians 11:1, 3 John 1:11
12 Matthew 10:24
13 Luke 6:40
14 Philippians 2:12-13
15 Hebrews 12:10

16 John 14:21
17 Revelation 3:21
18 Luke 10:62
19 Hebrews 7: 19-20, 9:11-14
20 John 14:16, 26, 15:26, 16:7; Hebrews 13:6
21 Exodus 13:21, Judges 7:22, 2 Kings 6:15-18
22 Romans 8:18

# 57

## WE SHOULD NOT BE OVERLY DEPRESSED WHEN WE SOMETIMES FAIL

My child, patience and humility in adversities are more pleasing to Me than [your having] much comfort and devotion when things are going well.

Why are you grieved by every little thing said against you?

Even if it had been more you should not have been disturbed.

But now let it pass—it is not the first that has happened, nor is it anything new, and it will not be the last if you live for a long time.

You are courageous enough so long as nothing adverse comes your way.

You can give good counsel, and can encourage others with your words, but when trouble suddenly comes to your door, you fail in counsel and in strength.

Consider, therefore, your great weakness, which you have too often experienced in trivial matters

Nevertheless, when these and like things happen to you they are intended for your good.

2. Put it out of your heart the best you can, and even if it has emotionally affected you, do not let it discourage or confuse you for long.

If you cannot endure it cheerfully, at least endure it patiently.

Even though you endure it unwillingly and are indignant at it, restrain yourself and let no immoderate words pass your lips that will offend Christ's little ones.

The storm that is now raised will quickly be calmed[1] and your inward grief will be sweetened by returning grace.

"I yet live," says the Lord, "and I am ready to help you[2] and give you greater comfort than before, if you put your trust in Me and call devoutly upon Me."[3]

3. Be more patient and strengthen [prepare] yourself for greater endurance.

All is not lost even though you are often afflicted or grievously tempted.

You are a human being, not God—you are flesh, not an angel.

How can you expect to always continue in the same state of virtue when an angel in heaven fell,[4] as did the first people in paradise.[5]

I am He who strengthens with comfort those who mourn, and raise up to divine glory those who know their own weakness.

4. O Lord, blessed be Your words that are sweeter to my mouth than honey and the honeycomb.[6]

What would I do in these great tribulations and needs, if You did not comfort me with Your holy words?

But what does it matter how much or what I suffer, so long as in the end I reach the haven of rest?[7]

Grant me a good end—grant me a happy passage out of this world.

Remember me, O my God, and guide me in the right way to Your kingdom. Amen.

1  Mark 4:39-40
2  Isaiah 41:10
3  1 Chronicles 5:20; Psalm 4:3, 16:1; Isaiah 55:6; Romans 10:12-13
4  Isaiah 14:12
5  Genesis 3
6  Psalm 19:9-10, 119:103; Proverbs 16:24
7  Hebrews 7:17-20

# 58
## High Matters and God's Secret Judgments Are Not to Be Closely Looked Into

My child, beware of scrutinizing high matters and God's hidden judgments—why this person is forsaken and that person greatly favored, and why this person is so afflicted and that person so greatly exalted.

These things are beyond human understanding, and it is not within the power of reason or debating to learn God's judgments.[1]

Therefore, when the enemy suggests such things to you, or when some curious people raise the question, answer them as the prophet did: "Righteous are You, O LORD, And upright are Your judgments."[2]

And again, "The judgments of the LORD are true and righteous altogether."

My judgments are to be feared, not discussed, for they cannot be understood by the understanding of human beings.

2. In like manner, I advise you not to inquire or debate about the merits of the saints—who among them is more holy than the other or which will be the greatest in the kingdom of heaven.[3]

These things often breed strife and useless contentions,[4] and nourish pride and vainglory, from which spring envy and quarrels as one proudly prefers this saint and the other another.

A desire to know and learn such things has no purpose, nor would it please the saints, for I am not a God of dissension but of peace—peace that results in true humility rather than in self-exaltation.

3. Some are drawn with zealous preference toward these or those saints, but this is human affection rather than divine.

I am He who made all the saints. I gave them grace.[5] I obtained them for glory.

I know what everyone of them deserves. I preceded them with the blessings of My goodness.

I knew My beloved ones before the beginning [foundation] of the world.[6]

I chose them out of the world—they did not choose Me.[7]

I called them by grace,[8] I drew them by mercy,[9] and I led them safely through various temptations.[10]

I poured into them glorious consolations, I gave them perseverance, and I crowned their patience.[11]

4. I know the first and the last,[12] and I embrace them all with inestimable love.

I am to be praised in all My saints, blessed above all things, and honored in everyone whom I have in this manner gloriously exalted and predestined without any previous merits of their own.[13]

Anyone who despises one of the least of My saints does not honor the greatest,[14] for I made both the least and the great [see note[15]].

And anyone who disparages one of My saints, disparages Me also,[16] and all the rest in the kingdom of heaven.

These are all one through the bond of love—they have the same thoughts, the same will, and they all love one another.

5. But what is a higher consideration is that they love Me more than they do themselves or any merits of their own.

For being lifted above self-love, they are able to love Me completely, in whom they rest with entire fulfillment.

Nothing can pull them back and nothing can depress them, for they are full of the eternal Truth and burn with the fire of unquenchable love.[17]

Therefore, let carnal and sensual people who can only love their personal joys, refrain from debating about the state of the saints. They add and take away according to their own imaginations and not as it pleases the eternal Truth.

6. Many are ignorant, especially those who are only a little enlightened, and can seldom love anyone with a perfect spiritual love.

They are still drawn by natural affection and human friendship to this person or to that one, and they base their imaginings of heavenly things on the experiences they have had in their earthly affections.

But there is an incomparable distance between the things that the imperfect imagine and those that enlightened people are enabled to understand through revelation from above.[18]

7. Be careful, therefore, my child, not to treat things beyond your knowledge with fanciful curiosity [see note[19]],

but instead so apply your endeavors that you will have a place in the kingdom of God, even if the lowest.

Even if my children were to know who exceeds another in holiness, and who is the greatest in the kingdom of heaven, what good would this knowledge do them, unless in proportion to this knowledge they humble themselves more in My sight and rise up in greater praise of My name?

Those who think of the greatness of their sins, the smallness of their graces, and how far off they are from the perfection of the saints, please God much more than those who debate about who is greater or who is less.

8. The saints [in heaven] are well and perfectly contented, so people should restrain themselves and refrain from these useless discourses.

They do not glory in their own merits, for they ascribe no goodness to themselves but attribute all to Me, for out of My infinite love I gave them all things.

They are filled with such great love for God and with such overflowing joy, that there is no glory or happiness that is or can be lacking in them.

The higher the saints are in glory the more humble they are in themselves, and the nearer and dearer they are to Me.

Therefore you find it written that they cast their crowns before God, and fell down on their faces before the Lamb and adored Him Who lives forever.[20]

9. Many who inquire about who is the greatest in the kingdom of God do not know whether they themselves will be numbered there even among the least.[21]

It is a great thing to be even the least in heaven where all are great, for all those will be called, and will be, the children of God.[22]

"The least shall be as a thousand," and "the sinner of a hundred years shall die."[23]

For when the disciples asked Jesus who would be greatest in the kingdom of heaven they were told: "Assuredly I say to you, unless you are converted and become as little children, you will by no means enter the kingdom of heaven. Therefore whoever humbles himself as this little child is the greatest in the kingdom of heaven."[24]

10. Woe to those who disdain to humble themselves willingly with the little children, for the low gate of the kingdom of heaven will not allow them to enter.

Woe also to the rich who have their consolations here, for while the poor enter into God's kingdom, they will stand outside lamenting.[25]

Rejoice you who are humble,[26] and be filled with joy you who are poor [in spirit],[27] for yours is the kingdom if you walk in the Truth.[28]

---

1   Isaiah 55:8-9
2   Psalm 119:137
3   Matthew 18:1-4, Mark 9:34, Luke 9:36, 46, 22:24
4   2 Timothy 2:23
5   Ephesians 2:4-9
6   Romans 8:29, Ephesians 1:3-5, 2 Thessalonians 2:13, 1 Peter 1:2
7   John 15:16, Ephesians 1:4
8   Galatians 1:6, 15; Ephesians 4:1; 2 Thessalonians 2:14; 2 Timothy 1:9; 1 Peter 1:15, 2:9, 5:10
9   John 6:44
10  Romans 8:14, Galatians 5:18
11  2 Timothy 4:8
12  Matthew 20:16, Revelation 1:8
13  Romans 8:30; Ephesians 1:5, 11
14  James 2:1-5
15  Wisdom of Solomon 6:7—This is an Apocrypha book. The verse states: "For the Lord of all will not stand in awe of anyone, or show deference to greatness; because he himself made both small and great, and he takes thought for all alike."

16 Acts 9:4

17 Revelation 7:9-10

18 1 Corinthians 2:14, 2 Corinthians 12:4, Galatians 1:12

19 Ecclesiasticus 3:21 – this is an Apocrypha book. The verse states: "Who knows whether the human spirit goes upward and the spirit of animals goes downward to the earth?"

20 Revelation 4:9-11, 5:13-14

21 1 Corinthians 3:11-15, Hebrews 8:11

22 1 John 3:1

23 Isaiah 60:22 reads: "A little one shall become a thousand ..." Isaiah 65:20 reads: "For the child shall die one hundred years old, But the sinner being one hundred years old shall be accursed."

24 Matthew 18:3-4

25 Matthew 21:31; Luke 16:19-31, 18:24-25

26 1 Peter 5:5-6

27 Matthew 5:3

28 Ephesians 4:1, Colossians 2:6, 1 Thessalonians 2:12, 1 John 1:6-7, 3 John 1:3-4

# 59

## OUR HOPE AND TRUST ARE TO BE FIXED IN GOD ALONE

Lord, what is the confidence that I have in this life, or what is the greatest comfort that all the things under heaven give to me?

Is it not You, O Lord, my God, whose mercies are without number?

When have things ever gone well with me without You, or when could things go badly with me when You were present?

I had rather be poor for Your sake than rich without You.

I would rather be a pilgrim on the earth with You,[1] than to possess heaven without You. Where You are there is heaven, and where You are not there are death and hell.

You are all my desire and therefore I must sigh and call and earnestly pray to You.[2]

I have none in whom I can fully trust, none who can help me at the proper time with my necessities, but only You, my God.

You are my trust and my confidence, my Comforter[3]— and in all things most faithful to me.

2. Everyone seeks their own benefit[4]—You only place my salvation and my benefit first, and work all things to my good.[5]

Although You expose me to various temptations and troubles, yet You decree all those for my good, because You habitually prove Your loved ones in a thousand ways.[6]

During this process You should not be praised or loved less than if You had filled me with heavenly consolations.

3. In You, therefore, O Lord God, I place my entire hope and refuge, and on You I cast my tribulations and anguish, for I find everything I see outside of you to be weak and unstable.

For having many friends cannot benefit, strong helpers cannot assist, wise counselors cannot give a beneficial answer, books written by knowledgeable people cannot comfort, valuable items cannot deliver, and no matter how isolated and lovely a place is it cannot shelter—unless You Yourself assist, help, strengthen, comfort, instruct, and guard us.

4. For all things that seem to be for obtaining peace and happiness are nothing without You, and truthfully bring no happiness at all.

You are the end[7] [object] of all that is good, the height of life, the depth of all that can be expressed, and to hope in You above all things is the strongest comfort of Your servants.

I look, therefore, to You my God, the Father of mercies, and in You I put my trust.

Bless and sanctify my soul with your heavenly blessings,[8] so that it may become Your holy habitation and the [mercy] seat of Your eternal glory[9]—and let nothing be found in this temple of Your dignity that will offend the eyes of Your majesty.

According to the greatness of Your goodness and the multitude of Your mercies,[10] look upon me and hear the prayers of Your poor servant,[11] who is exiled far from You in the land of the shadow of death.[12]

I am the least of Your servants,[13] yet protect and keep my soul that is surrounded by the many dangers of this corruptible life, and by Your grace accompanying me[14] direct it along the way of peace to its home of everlasting light.[15]

1 Hebrews 11:13; 1 Peter 1:1, 2:11
2 Jeremiah 33:3, Hebrews 5:7, 1 Peter 3:12
3 John 14:16, 26, 15:26, 16:7 (KJV)
4 Philippians 2:21
5 Romans 8:28
6 Hebrews 12:6
7 Revelation 1:8
8 Matthew 5:3-11
9 Leviticus 16:2, Psalm 26:8
10 Hebrews 4:16
11 1 John 3:22, 5:14-15
12 Psalm 23
13 1 Corinthians 15:9, Ephesians 3:8
14 Exodus 33:15-16
15 Revelation 22:5

## BOOK FOUR

# EXHORTATION TO RECEIVE
# HOLY COMMUNION

*The Voice of Christ*

"Come to Me, all you who labor and are heavy laden, and I will give you rest."[1]

"I am the living bread which came down from heaven. If anyone eats of this bread, he will live forever; and the bread that I shall give is My flesh, which I shall give for the life of the world."[2]

"Take, eat; this is My body which is broken for you; do this in remembrance of Me."[3]

"He who eats My flesh and drinks My blood abides in Me, and I in him."[4]

"It is the Spirit who gives life; the flesh profits nothing. The words that I speak to you are spirit, and they are life."[5]

1 Matthew 11:28
2 John 6:51
3 1 Corinthians 11:24
4 John 6:56
5 John 6:63

# 1

## RECEIVE THE EMBLEMS OF CHRIST WITH REVERENCE

### *The Voice of the Disciple*

These are Your words, O Christ, the everlasting truth, though they were not spoken all at one time or recorded together in one place [in the Bible]. And because they are Your words and true, I must accept them all with faith and gratitude.

They are Yours, and You spoke them, and so they are mine, also, because You spoke them for my salvation. I cheerfully receive them from Your lips, so they may be implanted deeply into my heart.

Words of such tenderness, full of sweetness and love, encourage me, but my offences discourage me, and an impure conscience drives me back from receiving such great mysteries.

The sweetness of Your words encourages me, but the multitude of my sins weighs me down.

2. You command me to come confidently to You if I would be part of You, and to receive the bread of immortality if I desire to obtain everlasting life and glory.

You say, "Come to Me, all you who labor and are heavy laden, and I will give you rest."[1]

O how sweet and loving in the ears of a sinner are the word by which You, my Lord God, invite the poor and needy to the communion of Your most holy body.

But who am I, Lord, that I should presume to approach You.

"Behold, heaven and the heaven of heavens cannot contain You,"[2] and You say, "Come—all of you—to Me."

3. What does this gracious honor and loving invitation mean?

How shall I dare to come, I who know of no good in myself on which to presume?

How shall I bring You into my house, I who have so often offended in Your most gracious sight?

Angels and archangels stand in awe of You, holy and righteous people fear You, and You say, "Come to Me—all of you."

If You had not said it, O Lord, who would believe it to be true?

And if You had not commanded it, who would attempt to draw near?

Behold, that just man Noah worked a hundred years to build an ark that he and a few others might be saved, and how then can I prepare myself in one hour to commune reverently with the Maker of the world?

4. Your great servant and special friend, Moses,[3] made an ark of incorruptible wood, which he covered with purest gold[4] to place in it the tablets of Your law[5]—shall then I, a creature of corruption, dare so easily to receive You, the Maker of the law and the Giver of life?

Solomon, the wisest of the kings of Israel, spent seven years building a magnificent temple in praise of Your name.[6]

He celebrated its dedication with a feast of eight [or fourteen] days,[7] sacrificed countless peace-offerings[8] in

Your honor, and solemnly set the Ark of the Covenant with trumpeting and jubilation in the place prepared for it.[9]

And I, the most miserable and poorest of all, how shall I receive You into my house—I who can scarcely spend one-half hour in true devotion?

If only I could spend even that much time in a worthy and proper manner!

5. O my God, how earnestly they studied and endeavored to please You.

Alas, how little it is that I do! How short a time I spend when I am preparing myself to receive the communion.

I am seldom wholly collected [mentally quiet]—very seldom, indeed, free from all distraction.

Yet surely in the life-giving presence of Your Godhead no unbecoming thought should intrude itself and no creature possess my heart, for I am not about to entertain an angel as my guest, but the Lord of angels.

6. Very great, too, is the difference between the Ark of the Covenant with its contents and Your most pure body with its inexpressible virtues, between those legal sacrifices that were only shadows of things to come[10] and the true sacrifice of Your body that was the fulfillment of all ancient sacrifices.

Why, then, am I not more ardent and zealous in seeking Your adorable presence?

Why do I not prepare myself with greater concern to receive the holy emblems? Inasmuch as those holy patriarchs and prophets of old, as well as kings and princes with all the people, showed such affectionate devotion to Your divine service?

7. The most devout King David danced before the Ark of God with all his might,[11] and recalled the benefits bestowed in the past upon his forefathers. He made instruments of

various kinds, wrote psalms and commanded them to be sung with joy, and he himself played upon the harp when inspired by the grace of the Holy Spirit. He taught the people of Israel to praise God with their whole hearts, and to bless and praise Him everyday with harmonious and melodious voices.

If such devotion flourished in those days, and celebrations of divine praise were continually before the Ark of the Testament, great praise and devotion should now be shown by me and all Christian people during the ministration of the sacrament [see note[12]] of communion.

8. Many people travel far to honor the relics of the departed saints [see note[13]], are filled with admiration when they hear about their wonderful deeds, look with awe upon the spacious buildings of their shrines, and kiss their sacred bones that are wrapped in silk and gold.

But, behold, You are Yourself present before me on the altar [see note[14]], my God, Saint of saints, Creator of all things, and Lord of Angels.

Often in looking at such things, people are moved by curiosity, by the novelty of the unseen, and little or no fruit of amendment of their lives is taken home, especially when they go from place to place with a light heart and without true repentance.

But here in this holy Sacrament [see note[15]] of the altar You are wholly present, my God, the man Christ Jesus, from Whom is obtained the abundant fruit of eternal salvation to those who worthily and devoutly receive You.

Indeed, we are not attracted to You by levity, curiosity, or sensuality,[16] but by firm faith, devout hope, and sincere love.

9. O God, the invisible[17] Creator of the world, how wonderfully You deal with us! How sweetly and graciously

You attend to all things for Your elect,[18] for whom You offered Yourself to be received by faith.[19]

This truly surpasses all understanding. This especially draws the hearts of the devout and inflames their love.

For even Your truly faithful servants, who give their whole life to spiritual improvement, often gain much of the grace of devotion and love of virtue through this precious sacrament.

10. Oh, the admirable and hidden grace of this sacrament, which only the faithful in Christ understand, but which the unbelievers and those that are slaves of sin cannot experience.

In this sacrament spiritual grace is conferred, strength that was lost is restored to the soul, and the beauty that sin had disfigured returns.

At times this grace is so great, that out of the fullness of devotion that is given, not only the mind, but also the weak body feels a great increase of strength.

11. Nevertheless, our coldness and neglect is much to be deplored and pitied, that we are not moved with greater affection to receive Christ, in Whom is all the hope[20] and merit of those that are to be saved.[21]

For He Himself is our sanctification and redemption,[22] the comfort of those who are but sojourners in this life,[23] and the everlasting possession and enjoyment of saints.

It is, therefore, lamentable that many so little consider the saving mystery[24] that causes joy in heaven and preserves the whole world.

Alas for the blindness and hardness of people's hearts, that do not more deeply consider so inexpressible a gift, but because of its frequent use begin to regard it as nothing.

12. If this most holy sacrament were celebrated in only one place and consecrated by only one priest [see note[25]]in

the whole world, with what great desire do you think people would be attracted to that place, to that priest of God, in order to witness the celebration of the divine mysteries?

But now there are many priests and in many places communion is offered, for the more widely this sacred communion is spread over the world the greater will God's grace and love for us be apparent.

Thanks be to You, O merciful Jesus and eternal Shepherd, that You have consented to refresh us spiritually poor and exiled people with Your precious body and blood,[26] and to invite us to receive these sacred mysteries with words from Your own mouth: "Come to Me, all you who labor and are heavy laden, and I will refresh you" [see note[27]].

1   Matthew 11:28
2   1 King 8:27
3   Exodus 33:11
4   Exodus 25:10-11
5   Deuteronomy 10:1-5
6   1 Kings 6:38
7   1 Kings 8:65-66
8   1 Kings 8:5, 8:63
9   1 Kings 6:19, 8:6
10 Colossians 2:16-17; Hebrews 9:11-12, 10:1
11 2 Samuel 6:14
12 Sacrament—In the Eastern, Roman Catholic, and some
    other Western Christian churches, any of the traditional
    seven rites that were instituted by Jesus and recorded in the
    New Testament, and that are believed to confer sanctifying
    grace. In most other Western Christian churches, sacrament
    refers to the two rites, Baptism and the Eucharist, that
    are believed to have been instituted by Jesus to confer
    sanctifying grace.
13 This paragraph refers to persons officially recognized by the
    Roman Catholic church, especially by canonization, as being
    entitled to public veneration.
14 This concerns the doctrine of transubstantiation. Some
    denominations hold that the bread and wine of the Eucharist
    are transformed into the body and blood of Jesus.
15 Sacrament is often capitalized when referring to the

Eucharist, especially the bread or host.

16 *Sensuality*—Not used as it so much today, but refers to those things of the senses.

17 Hebrews 11:27

18 Romans 8:33, Colossians 3:12-13, 2 Timothy 2:10, James 5:2,

19 John 1:12-13, Romans 5:1, Ephesians 2:8

20 Hebrews 6:19-20

21 Romans 5:10, 10:9-13; Acts 2:47; 1 Corinthians 1:18

22 Romans 3:24, 1 Corinthians 1:30, Ephesians 1:7, Colossians 1:13-14, Hebrews 9:12-15

23 1 Peter 2:11

24 Colossians 1:27

25 Priest: A title given to ordained ministers by some churches. The title is also applicable to the pastors and ministers in any church because they are the ones who perform the spiritual services and ceremonies of the church. In their prayers and intercessions for the members of their congregation and others, the pastors and ministers function much as the priests did in the Old Covenant, in that they speak to God on behalf of the people. When they teach the Word of God (the Scriptures) to their congregations, they function much like the Old Testament prophets, in that they speak to the people on behalf of God.

Aaron and his sons were priests of Jehovah, as recorded throughout the Book of Exodus. Many places in the Book of Hebrews, Jesus Christ is called the High Priest, one after the order of Melchizedek (Hebrews 5:6-11, 6:20), of those who receive Him as their Lord and Savior (Hebrews 2:17, 3:1, 4:14-15, 7:26-27, 8:1-3, 9:11, 9:24-25, 10:19-22).

In Revelation 1:5-6, the beloved apostle John states that Jesus Christ "has made (past tense) us (all the redeemed) kings and priests to His God and Father." Then in Revelation 5:8-10 the twenty-four elders who represent those redeemed by the blood of Christ, repeat the statement in their song to the Lamb. This is again stated by John in Revelation 20:6.

Thus in a very real sense all true Christians are now priests on the earth, both because the Scriptures say so, and because they often minister to God (Acts 13:2) and pray and interceded in the name of Jesus Christ for others here on the earth—in other words, they speak to God on behalf of people, thus fulfilling the main duty of a priest.

26 This is the doctrine of transubstantiation held by certain churches.

27 Matthew 11:28–The verse reads: ""Come to Me, all you who labor and are heavy laden, and I will give you rest.""

## 2

## GOODNESS AND LOVE OF GOD SHOWN IN THIS SACRAMENT

### *The Voice of the Disciple*

With confidence in Your goodness and great mercy, O Lord, I come as one sick to the Healer, as one hungry and thirsty to the Fountain of Life, as one in need to the King of Heaven, a servant to their Lord, a creature to the Creator, a desolate soul to my own tender Comforter.

But why is it granted to me that You should come to me?[1] What am I that You should give Yourself to me?

How dare a sinner appear before You? And how is it that You condescend to come to a sinner?

You know Your servant, and You see that I have nothing good in me for which You should grant me this favor.

I confess, therefore, my unworthiness, I acknowledge Your goodness, I praise Your tender mercy, and give You thanks for Your transcendent love.

For You do this for Your own sake and not because of any merits of mine, so that Your goodness may be better known to me, Your love more abundantly poured down upon me, and your gracious humility better manifested in [and through] me.

Since therefore this is Your pleasure and You have commanded that it should be so, Your graciousness is also pleasing to me. O that my sinfulness does not get in the way!

2. O most sweet and gentle Jesus, what great reverence, thanks, and perpetual praise are due to You for the sacrifice of Your sacred body, whose worthiness no person is able to express.

But on what shall I think at this communion, this approach to my Lord, Whom I am not able to honor properly as I should, and yet Whom I desire devoutly to apprehend?

What thought is better and more profitable to me than to humble myself completely before You and exalt Your infinite goodness above myself?

3. Behold, You are the Holy of holies,[2] and I the scum of sinners!

Behold, You bend Yourself down to me who am not worthy even to look up to You!

Behold, You come to me.! It is Your will to be with me! You invite me to Your banquet!

You are willing to give me the food of angels[3] and heavenly bread to eat, which is none other than Yourself the living bread, Who came down from heaven and gave life to the world.[4]

4. Behold, from where this love proceeds! What gracious condescension shines forth! How great thanks and praises are due to You for these benefits!

O how good and profitable was Your counsel when You ordained it! How sweet and pleasant the banquet when You gave Yourself to be our bread!

O how wonderful is Your work, O Lord, how mighty is Your power, how inexpressible is Your truth!

For You spoke the word and all things were made,[5] and this that You commanded was done.

5. It is a wondrous thing, worthy of all faith, and surpassing human understanding, that You, my Lord God,

true God and man, are represented in a little bread and wine that are consumed by the person who receives them.

You who are the Lord of all things and have need of nothing are pleased to dwell in us.[6]

Preserve my heart and body unblemished, so that with a cheerful and pure conscience I may be able to celebrate often Your  mysteries and receive to my everlasting health those things that you specially ordained and institute for Your own honor and for a never-ending memorial.

6. Rejoice, O my soul, and give thanks to God for having left you so noble a gift and so special a consolation in this valley of tears.

For as often as you call to mind this mystery and receive this spiritual nourishment, so often do you reenact the work of redemption[7] and proclaim all the merits of [the death of] Christ.[8]

For the love of Christ is never diminished and the greatness of His propitiation is never exhausted.[9]

Therefore you should prepare yourself for it by constantly renewing your mind,[10] and ponder with careful consideration this great mystery of your salvation.[11]

When you celebrate or partake of this sacrament, it should be so great, so new, and so joyful, it is as if on this same day Christ first descended into the womb of the Virgin and became flesh, or hung on the Cross on this day and suffered and died for the salvation of humanity.

1   Luke 1:43
2   Exodus 26:33; Hebrews 9:3, 8, 10:19
3   Psalm 78:25
4   John 6:33
5   Genesis 1:1-31, Psalm 148:5, John 1:3, Colossians 1:16
6   John 14:23, Colossians 1:27
7   Galatians 3:13, 1 Peter 1:17-19, Revelation 5:9
8   1 Corinthians 11:26
9   Romans 3:23-26, Hebrews 2:17, 1 John 2:2, 1 John 4:10

10 Romans 12:2
11 Romans 16:25; Ephesians 1:9-10, 3:3-4, 9, 6:19; Colossians
   1:26-27, 2:2, 4:3

## 3

## IT IS SPIRITUALLY BENEFICIAL
## TO RECEIVE COMMUNION OFTEN

### *The Voice of the Disciple*

Behold, O Lord, I come to You that I may be comforted
by Your gift and be delighted at Your holy banquet, which
You, O God, in Your goodness have prepared for the
[spiritually] poor.[1]

Behold, in You is all that I can or should desire—You
are my salvation and my redemption,[2] my hope[3] and my
strength,[4] my honor and glory.[5]

"Rejoice the soul of Your servant, For to You, O Lord,
I lift up my soul."[6]

I desire to receive You now with devotion and reverence.
I long to bring You into my house so that with Zacchaeus[7]
I may be considered worthy to be blessed by You, and be
numbered among the children of Abraham.[8]

My soul longs to receive You, my heart desires to be
united with You.[9]

2. Give Yourself to me and it will be enough, for without
You there is no comfort.

Without You I cannot exist, and without Your visitation
I cannot endure living.

Therefore I must often draw near to You and receive
from You the refreshing of my salvation,[10] lest I grow weak
along the way.[11]

Once when You were preaching to the people, most merciful Jesus, and healing their many diseases, you said, "I will not send them away fasting, lest they faint in the way."[12]

Deal with me in the same manner, You who have given Yourself for the comfort of the faithful.

You are sweet refreshment to the soul, and "whoever eats this bread or drinks this cup of the Lord in an unworthy manner will be guilty of the body and blood of the Lord."[13]

It is indeed necessary for me, who so often falls and sins and so quickly waxes dull and faints, that by frequent prayer and confession[14] and receiving Your grace in this ordinance, I renew, cleanse, and inflame myself, lest by abstaining too long I fall away from my holy purpose.

3. "For the imagination of man's heart is evil from his youth,"[15] and unless some divine remedy helps us we soon fall away to worse things.

Holy communion, therefore, helps to draw us back from evil and strengthens us in good.

For if I am now so often negligent and lukewarm when I receive communion, what would become of me if I did not receive this aid, and did not seek after such great help?

Although everyday I am not fit or prepared to receive communion, I will nevertheless endeavor at appointed times to receive the divine mysteries, and to be partaker of such great grace.

For this is the one chief consolation of the faithful souls, so long as they are absent from You in this mortal body, that being often mindful of their God they should receive their beloved with a devout mind.

4. O the wonderful condescension of Your tender mercy toward us, that You, O Lord God, Creator and Giver of life to all spirits, should condescend to come to the soul of the

[spiritually] poor and replenish its [spiritual] hunger with all Your deity and humanity![16]

O happy minds and blessed souls who are privileged to receive You, their Lord God, with devout affection, and in so receiving You be filled with spiritual joy.

O how great a Lord they entertain! How beloved a guest they harbor! How delightful a companion they welcome! How faithful a friend they gain! How lovely and noble a companion they embrace! Even Him who is to be loved above all that are beloved, and above all things that can be desired.

O most sweet and most beloved, let heaven and earth and all their adornments be silent in Your presence, for whatever beauty and praise they have was received from Your condescending bounty and will never equal the grace and beauty of Your name, whose wisdom is infinite.[17]

1 Psalm 68:10
2 1 Corinthians 1:30, Ephesians 1:7
3 2 Thessalonians 2:16; 1 Timothy 1:1; Titus 1:1-2, 3:7
4 2 Corinthians 12:9, Philippians 4:13
5 Colossians 3:4, 1 Thessalonians 2:12, 2 Thessalonians 2:14, 1 Peter 5:10
6 Psalm 86:4
7 Luke 19:5
8 Luke 19:9, Romans 4:13-16, Galatians 3:5-9
9 Ephesians 3:17
10 Acts 3:19
11 Isaiah 40:29-31, Galatians 6:9, Hebrews 12:3
12 Matthew 15:32
13 1 Corinthians 11:23-32
14 Romans 14:11, James 5:16, 1 John 1:9
15 Genesis 8:21
16 Acts 3:19
17 Psalm 147:5

# 4

## BENEFITS BESTOWED ON THOSE WHO RECEIVE COMMUNION WORTHILY

### *The Voice of the Disciple*

O LORD my God, favor Your servant "with the blessings of goodness"[1] so I can approach Your glorious sacrament worthily and devoutly.

Stir up my heart toward You and deliver me from all dullness. Visit me with Your salvation so I may taste in spirit Your sweetness, which abundantly lies hidden in this sacrament as in a fountain.

Enlighten my eyes to behold this great mystery, and strengthen me with undoubting faith to believe in it.

For it is Your work, not human power[2]—your sacred institution, not human invention.

For none of us by ourselves are able to understand these things, which transcend even the exquisite skill [and knowledge] of angels.

What portion, then, of so high and sacred a mystery will I, an unworthy sinner who is nothing but dust and ashes, be able to search out and understand?

2. O Lord, at Your command I draw near to You in the simplicity of my heart, with a good and firm faith, with hope and reverence—and I truly believe that You are present here in this sacrament, God and man [see note[3]].

It is Your will that I receive You, and that I unite myself to You in love.

Therefore I implore Your mercy and ask for Your special grace, so that I may be wholly dissolved in You and overflow with love for You, and hereafter never allow any external consolation to concern me.

For this most high and precious sacrament is the health of soul and body, and the medicine for all spiritual languor.

By this means my vices are cured, my passions controlled, my temptations overcome or weakened. At the same time greater grace is infused, beginning virtue is increased, faith is confirmed, hope is strengthened, and love is inflamed and enlarged.

3. For You have and often do bestow many benefits in this sacrament upon Your loved ones who receive communion devoutly, O my God, the protector of my soul, the Strengthener of human weakness, and the Giver of all inward comfort.

You also give them great comfort during their many tribulations and lift them up from depths of dejection to hope in Your protection. You inwardly recreate and enlighten them with new grace, so that those who feel full of anxiety and devoid of courage before receiving communion, find themselves changed for the better after being refreshed with heavenly bread and drink.

In the same way You deal with Your elect so that they may truly acknowledge and clearly know how great their own weakness is, and what goodness and grace they obtain from You.

For by themselves they are cold, dull, and lack devotion, but You make them fervent, cheerful, and full of devotion.

For who can humbly approach the fountain of sweetness and not carry away a little sweetness?

Or who can stand by a great fire and not feel a little heat from it?

You are a fountain always full and overflowing,[4] a fire ever burning and never going out![5]

4. Therefore, if I am not permitted to draw out of the full fountain itself, or to drink my full, I will, nevertheless, put my lips to the mouth of this heavenly spring so that from it I may receive at least some small drop to refresh my thirst so I will not be wholly dried up.[6]

And thought I cannot as yet be altogether heavenly or as inflamed as the cherubim and seraphim, yet I will endeavor to apply myself more earnestly to devotion and prepare my heart to obtain even some small spark of divine fire by the humble receiving of this sacrament.

And whatever is lacking in me, O merciful Jesus, most holy Savior, in Your kindness and abundant grace do supply for me, for You have been pleased to call all to You, saying: "Come to Me, all you who labor and are heavy laden, and I will refresh you [give you rest]."[7]

5. I, indeed, labor in the sweat of my brow.[8] I am tormented with grief of heart. I am burdened with sins, troubled with temptations, entangled and oppressed by many evil passions, and there is none to help me, none to deliver and save me but You, O Lord, my God my Savior, to whom I abandon myself and all that is mine, so that You may watch over me and bring me safe to life everlasting.

Receive me for the honor and glory of Your name—You who have given Your body and blood to be [spiritual] food and drink for me.

Grant, O Lord, my God and Savior, that by frequently visiting Your mysteries, the zeal of my devotion may increase.

1   Psalm 21:3
2   Ephesians 2:8-9
3   This is based on the doctrine of transubstantiation.
4   Isaiah 12:3, John 4:10-14
5   Leviticus 6:13
6   Psalm 42:1-2, 63:1
7   Matthew 11:28
8   Genesis 3:19

# 5

## Dignity of the Sacrament and Priestly Work[1]

### *The Voice of the Beloved*

If you had the purity of an angel[2] and the holiness of John the Baptist,[3] you would not be worthy to receive or administer this sacrament.

For it is not within the scope of human merits that a person is able to consecrate and administer the sacrament of Christ,[4] and receive for food the bread of angels.[5]

Grand is the mystery, and great is the dignity of priests to whom is granted that which has not been granted to angels.

For priests alone, rightly ordained in the church [see note[6]] have power to celebrate this sacrament and consecrate the body of Christ.

The priest is indeed the minister of God, using the Word of God by His command and appointment, but God is there as the principal author and invisible worker, to Whom is subject all that He wills, and whom all that He commands obey.[7]

2. You should, therefore, believe God Almighty in this most excellent sacrament instead of your own understanding or any visible sign [see note[8]].

And so you are to approach this holy work with fear and reverence.[9]

"Take heed to yourself and to the doctrine,"[10] and see what ministry it is that has been given to you through the laying on of the bishop's hands [see note[11]].

Behold, you have been made a priest and consecrated to celebrate the Lord's sacraments. See that you perform your office faithfully and devoutly, and that you conduct yourself blamelessly.

You have not lightened your burden, but are now bound by stricter discipline and obligated to a more perfect degree of sanctification.[12]

Priests [pastors, ministers] should be adorned with all virtues and be examples of holy lives to others.

Their manner of living should not be as the popular and ordinary way of the world, but as the angels in heaven or the perfect people on earth.[13]

3. Priests are Christ's ambassadors,[14] and with all supplication and humility beseech God for themselves and for all the people.[15]

They should not cease from prayers[16] and holy sacrifice[17] until they prevail and obtain grace and mercy.[18]

When priests [pastors, ministers] celebrate their office faithfully, they honor God, strengthen the Church,[19] help the living,[20] and make themselves partakers of all good [spiritual] things.[21]

---

1  It should be noted that the author, who was a Roman Catholic monk, wrote many of the passages in Book Four in the Lord's voice because he felt the Lord was speaking to his heart. Naturally, then, the passages confirm the doctrines, practices, and traditions of his church.

2  Matthew 25:31, Luke 9:26

3  Matthew 11:11

4  1 Corinthians 11:26-28

5  Psalm 78:25

6  In certain denominations only the priests ordained in their church are permitted to administer the communion elements.

7  Genesis 1

8  This concerns the doctrine that holds that the bread and wine of the Eucharist are transformed into the body and blood of Jesus, although their appearances remain the same.

9  1 Corinthians 11:28-29, Philippians 2:12-13

10 1 Timothy 4:16

11 The laying on of hands is part of the ordination service in those churches that have bishops and priests. A similar ceremony is performed in many Protestant churches when

ministers are ordained.
12 Romans 15:16; 1 Corinthians 1:2, 6:11; 2 Timothy 2:21;
  Hebrews 6:1, 10:10-14; Jude 1:1
13 2 Corinthians 6:17
14 2 Corinthians 5:20
15 Hebrews 5:3
16 Colossians 1:9, 1 Thessalonians 5:17, 2 Thessalonians 1:11-
  12, 1 Timothy 2:1-2,
17 Hebrews 13:15
18 Hebrews 4:16, James 5:14
19 1 Thessalonians 5:11
20 2 Timothy 4:2
21 Hebrews 3:1, 14; 2 Peter 1:4

# 6

## ASKING FOR GUIDANCE ON
## PREPARING TO RECEIVE COMMUNION

### The Voice of the Disciple

When I consider Your worthiness, O Lord, and my own unworthiness, I tremble exceedingly[1] and am confused within myself.

For if I do not draw near You, I fly from Life,[2] and if I intrude unworthily,[3] I incur Your displeasure.

What, then, shall I do, O my God, my Helper and my Counselor in all necessities?

2. Teach me the right way. Give me some brief [spiritual] exercise [see note[4]] suitable for holy communion.

For it is good for me to know how I should reverently and spiritually prepare my heart for You, so I will profitably receive Your sacrament[5] and properly celebrate so great and divine a sacrifice.[6]

1   Exodus 20:8, Acts 7:32, Philippians 2:12-13
2   John 14:6
3   1 Corinthians 11:27-29
4   As used the text, exercise is an activity that requires spiritual
    and mental exertion, especially when intended to develop or
    maintain spiritual growth.
5   1 Corinthians 11:23-25
6   1 Corinthians 11:26; Hebrews 9:24-26, 10:12, 26

# 7

## SEARCHING OUR OWN CONSCIENCE, AND
## RESOLVING TO CHANGE FOR THE BETTER

### The Voice of the Beloved

Above all things, God's priest should come to celebrate, and to receive this sacrament with great humility of heart, with reverential supplication, with full faith, and with a dutiful regard for God's honor.

Diligently examine your conscience, and to the best of your power purify and cleanse it by true repentance[1] and humble confession,[2] so that there will be nothing in you that will be burdensome to you,[3] or that will breed in you a remorseful conscience[4] and obstruct your free access to the throne of grace.[5]

Be grieved at the memory of your sins, and in particular deplore and bewail your daily transgressions.

And if time permits, confess to God in the secret of your heart all the miserable evils of your undisciplined passions.

2. Lament and grieve because you are still so carnal and worldly, so undisciplined in your passions, so full of sexual desires;

So unwatchful over your outward senses, so often entangled with many useless imaginations;

So much inclined to outward things, so negligent in inward things;

So quickly moved to laughter and immodesty, so little moved to tears and contrition;

So swift to ease and pleasures of the flesh, so dull to strictness of life and zeal;

So curious to hear new things and see what is attractive, so slow to embrace what is humble and low;

So covetous of abundance, so sparing in giving, so tenacious in keeping;

So inconsiderate in speech, so reluctant to keep silent;

So unruly in manners, so troublesome in conduct;

So immoderate about food, so deaf to the Word of God;

So quick to rest, so slow to labor;

So wakeful to hear gossiping tales, so drowsy at the sacred services;

So eager for the services to end, so inclined to be [mentally] wandering and inattentive;

So negligent in prayers, so lukewarm in celebrating holy communion, so dry and heartless in receiving it.

So quickly distracted, so seldom entirely composed;

So quickly moved to anger, so apt to be displeased with another;

So ready to judge, so severe to reprove;

So joyful at prosperity, so weak in adversity;

So often making many good resolutions, and yet bringing them ultimately to such poor results.

3. When you have confessed and deplored these and other faults[6] with sorrow and great displeasure because of

your weakness, firmly resolve to amend your life continually, and to continue to endeavor to advance in holiness.

Then, with complete resignation and with your whole will, offer yourself on the altar of your heart as a perpetual whole burnt offering[7] to the honor of My name, and by faith abandon your body and soul to My care.

Then you may be counted worthy to draw near to celebrate this sacrifice to God, and to receive the sacrament profitably.

4. For there is no offering more worthy, or any greater for washing away sin, than to offer yourself purely and completely to God in preparation for receiving the sacrament.

And when you have done what you are able to do and are truly repentant, as often as you come to Me for forgiveness and grace[8]—"As I live,' says the Lord GOD, 'I have no pleasure in the death of the wicked, but that the wicked turn from his way and live'"[9]—I will no longer remember your sins,[10] but all will be forgiven you.[11]

---

1   Acts 2:38, 3:19, 17:30; Romans 2:4; 2 Corinthians 7:10; 2 Peter 3:9; Revelation 2:5, 16; Revelation 3:3, 19
2   1 John 1:9
3   1 John 5:3
4   Hebrews 9:14, 10:22
5   Hebrews 4:16
6   James 5:16
7   Genesis 22:2, 7-8, Psalm 51:19
8   Hebrews 4:16
9   Ezekiel 33:11
10 Isaiah 43:25, Jeremiah 31:34; Micah 7:19
11 Romans 4:7; Colossians 2:13 1 John 1:9, 2:12

**8**

## CHRIST'S SACRIFICE ON THE CROSS, AND
## OFFERING OURSELVES

### *The Voice of the Beloved*

Of My own free will I offered Myself to God the Father for your sins[1]—My arms were outstretched on the Cross and My body naked, so that nothing remained in Me that was not completely turned into a sacrifice to make propitiation for your sins.[2]

In the same way, you should offer yourself willingly to Me every day in holy communion as a pure and "living sacrifice, holy, acceptable to God, which is your reasonable service,"[3] together with all your strength and affections, and with all the inward devotion that you can.

What more do I require of you than that you abandon yourself entirely to Me?

Whatever You would give Me besides yourself is of no value to Me, for I seek you[4] and not your gifts.

2. Just as it would not be enough for you to have everything but Me, so whatever you give Me cannot please Me if you do not offer yourself.

Offer yourself to Me, and give yourself entirely for God—your offering will be accepted.

Behold, I offered Myself wholly to My Father for you, and gave My whole body and blood for you so I might be entirely yours and you might continue to be Mine.

But if you stay in yourself, and do not offer yourself up freely to My will, your offering will be incomplete and there will not be a perfect union between us.

Therefore a free offering of yourself into the hands of God should go before all your actions, if you desire to obtain liberty and grace.

This is why so few become inwardly free and enlightened, because they are unwilling to renounce themselves entirely.

My Word stands sure: "whoever of you does not forsake all that he has cannot be My disciple."[5] Therefore, if you desire to be My disciple, offer yourself to Me with all your heart.[6]

1  Isaiah 53:5, Hebrews 9:28
2  Romans 3:25; 1 John 2:2, 4:10
3  Romans 12:1
4  Proverbs 23:26
5  Luke 14:33
6  Luke 10:27

# 9

## OFFERING OURSELVES AND ALL THAT WE HAVE TO GOD AND PRAYING FOR EVERYONE

### *The Voice of the Disciple*

O Lord, all things in heaven and on earth are Yours.

I want to offer myself to You as a free-will offering[1] and continue to be Yours forever.

O Lord, in simplicity of heart[2] I offer myself to You this day, in humble submission as a sacrifice of everlasting praise and as Your servant forever.

Receive me with this holy offering of Your precious body, which I make to You this day in the presence of angels invisibly attending,[3] and may this be for my good and the good of all Your people.

2. I offer to You, O Lord, on Your propitiatory altar,[4] all my sins and offenses that I have committed before You and

Your holy angels[5] from the day when I first sinned to this hour,[6] so that You may consume and burn them all with the fire of Your love, blot out all the stains of my sins, cleanse my conscience from all offences,[7] restore to me the grace that I lost by sinning,[8] forgive all my offences,[9] and receive me mercifully with the kiss of peace.[10]

3. What can I do for all my sins but humbly confess and lament them,[11] and unceasingly implore Your mercy?

I implore You to hear me graciously[12] when I stand before You, my God.[13]

All my sins are very displeasing to me, and I will endeavor to never commit them again. I am sorry for them and will be sorry as long as I live. I am resolved to repent[14] and make restitution to the utmost of my power.[15]

Forgive me, O God, forgive me my sins for the sake of Your holy name. Save my soul[16] that You have redeemed[17] by Your most precious blood.[18]

Behold, I have abandoned myself to Your mercy, I submit myself into Your hands.

Deal with me according to Your goodness, not according to my wickedness and iniquity.

4. I offer to You also all that is good in me, though it be very small and imperfect, so that You may change it for the better and sanctify[19] it, make it thankful and acceptable to You, and continually perfect it more and more—also, that You will bring this [spiritually] lazy and unprofitable creature to a good and blessed end.

5. I offer also to You all the holy desires of devout people, the needs of my parents, friends, brothers, sisters, and all who are dear to me, and who have done good either to me or to others for the sake of Your love.[20]

I also commend to You all who desired and asked me to pray for them and all theirs, whether they still live in the flesh or have departed this life [see note[21]].

Grant that they may receive the help of Your grace, the aid of Your consolation, protection from dangers, deliverance from pain, and that, being freed from all evils, they may joyously give abundant thanks to You.

6. I offer up also to You my prayers and intercessions especially for those who have in anything wronged, grieved, or slandered me, or caused me any hurt or injury.[22]

I pray also for all those whom I have at any time distressed, troubled, grieved, or scandalized by words or deeds,[23] knowingly or unknowingly, so that You would grant us all equal forgiveness for our sins and offences against each other.

Take away from our hearts, O Lord, all suspicion, indignation, vindictive anger, contention, and whatever may hurt charity and lessen love for others.[24]

Have mercy, O Lord, have mercy on those who implore Your mercy, give grace to those who need it, and make us such that we may be worthy to enjoy Your grace and go forward to eternal life.[25] Amen.

1   Leviticus 1:3; 19:5; 22:19, 29
2   Acts 2:46; 2 Corinthians 1:12, 11:3
3   Hebrews 1:13-14
4   Romans 3:21-26; Hebrews 2:17; 1 John 2:2, 4:19
5   Revelation 3:5
6   1 Peter 2:24, 3:8; 1 John 2:1, 12
7   Hebrews 9:14, 10:22
8   Ephesians 2:4-9
9   1 John 1:9
10  Romans 5:1, 14:17; Philippians 4:6-7; Colossians 1:20;
      2 Peter 1:2
11  Psalm 32:5
12  1 John 5:14-15

13 Hebrews 4:16

14 Acts 3:19, 2 Peter 3:9

15 Exodus 22:12, Matthew 3:8, Galatians 5:22, Ephesians 5:9

16 Romans 5:9-10, 10:9

17 Galatians 3:12-13

18 1 Peter 1:17-19, Revelation 5:9

19 *Sanctify* – Set apart for sacred use, make holy, purify.

20 Matthew 25:40

21 Based on a doctrine in certain churches that there is a need to pray for the dead to lessen their time of suffering in purgatory or lessen the severity of their judgment. Doctrine may have been derived from 1 Corinthians 15:29.

22 Matthew 9:6, Mark 11:25-26, Luke 6:37

23 Matthew 7:1-5

24 John 13:34

25 Romans 5:20-21, 6:23; Ephesians 2:8-9; 1 Timothy 6:12

# 10
## DO NOT LIGHTLY ABSTAIN FROM COMMUNION

### The Voice of the Beloved

You should often go to the fountain of grace and divine mercy, to the fountain of goodness and all purity, so you may be healed of your sins and passions, and be made stronger and more vigilant against all the temptations and deceptions of the devil.

The enemy knows the exceedingly great profit and restorative aid that comes through holy communion, and so endeavors by all means and ways possible to hinder and keep devout and faithful people away from it.

2. That is why when some people are preparing themselves for holy communion they suffer from the deceptions of Satan worse than before.

That wicked spirit comes among the sons of God [see note[1]] to trouble them with his accustomed malice, to make them overly fearful and perplexed, so he may thereby lessen their affections, or by direct assaults take away their faith, for the purpose of convincing them to either abstain from communion or be lukewarm about receiving it.

But there is no need to pay attention to his crafty and fanciful suggestions, no matter how shameful and hideous—cast them all back upon his own head.

Despise and scorn the miserable wretch, and do not abstain from communion because of his assaults or the turmoil he stirs within you.

3. Often you will also be hindered by too great a concern for obtaining a certain degree of devotion and anxiety over confessing sins.[2]

In that, follow the counsel of the wise[3] and lay aside anxiety and scruple [see note[4]], for it hinders the grace of God and overshadows the devotion of the mind.

Do not stay away from holy communion because of every small trouble or annoyance, but instead proceed at once to confess your sins [to God][5] and cheerfully forgive others for whatever offenses they have committed against you.[6]

And if you have offended anyone, humbly seek pardon and God will readily forgive you.[7]

4. What good is it to delay confessing your sins for a long time or defer holy communion?

Purify your heart thoroughly as soon as possible,[8] spit out the poison quickly, make haste to apply the sovereign remedy, and you will find it better than if you put it off a long time.

If you omit it today for one reason, perhaps tomorrow a stronger one will occur to you, and so you may be kept from communion for a long time and become more and more unfit.

As quickly as you can, shake off this heaviness and laziness, for it is useless to stay uneasy a long time, or continue long with a disturbed conscience, and so withdraw yourself from this divine service because of everyday hindrances.

Yes, it is very hurtful to defer communion long, for it usually brings on a strong spiritual laziness.

5. O how poor and weak is the love and devotion of those who so easily put off holy communion!

How happy and acceptable to God are those who so discipline their lives and keep their conscience so pure,[9] as to be prepared and willing to receive communion even every day, if it were in their power to do so and could be done without drawing the attention of others.[10]

If sometimes you abstain out of humility or for some legitimate reason, you are to be commended—so far as you demonstrate a sense of reverence [when others participate].

But if spiritual laziness has taken hold of you, you must stir yourself up[11] and do everything you can, and the Lord will strength your desire because of the good intention [of the heart] that you show, which is what God chiefly respects.[12]

6. Thus when a legitimately hindrance does occur, you will always have the good will and pious intention to receive communion, and will not lose the fruit of the sacrament.

For any devout person may draw near to Christ in spiritual communion profitably and without restrictions every hour and every day.

Yet on certain days and times appointed [by your church] you should receive the sacrament with affectionate reverence for your redeemer, and seek the honor and glory of Christ rather than your own consolation.[13]

For you communicate mystically and are invisibly refreshed as often as you devoutly call to mind the mystery of the incarnation and the sufferings of Christ, and are [thereby] inflamed with love for Him.

Blessed are those who offer themselves as whole burnt offerings to the Lord[14] as often as they receive holy communion.

Do not be either too slow or too fast in celebrating, but keep the good way that is common among those you are joined with.

You should not be troublesome or tedious to others, and so follow the common way as appointed by our Christian forerunners, and give yourself over to being a profit to others instead of to your own devotion or feelings.

1   Job 1:6, 2:1—Perhaps it should be noted that Revelation 12:7-10 states: "And war broke out in heaven: Michael and his angels fought with the dragon; and the dragon and his angels fought, but they did not prevail, nor was a place found for them in heaven any longer. So the great dragon was cast out, that serpent of old, called the Devil and Satan, who deceives the whole world; he was cast to the earth, and his angels were cast out with him. Then I heard a loud voice saying in heaven, "Now salvation, and strength, and the kingdom of our God, and the power of His Christ have come, for the accuser of our brethren, who accused them before our God day and night, has been cast down."
In conjunction with this, the Book of Hebrews states that Jesus Christ is now our High Priest before God, the Mediator of the New Covenant, and "able to save to the uttermost those who come to God through Him, since He always lives to make intercession for them" (Hebrews 7:25). Not since Jesus was made Lord and Christ (Acts 2:36) has Satan been shown as still able to appear before God to accuse us—they show instead that he has been displaced. Selah

2   James 5:16

3 Proverbs 1:2
4 *Scruple* – An uneasy feeling arising from conscience or principle that tends to hinder action.
5 1 John 1:9
6 Matthew 18:21-22
7 Matthew 5:24, 6:14
8 James 4:8
9 1 Timothy 1:5, 2 Timothy 1:3-5
10 Matthew 6:6, 18
11 2 Timothy 1:6, Hebrews 10:24, 2 Peter 3:1
12 1 Samuel 16:7
13 1 Corinthians 11:23-26
14 Mark 12:33-34

# 11
## Necessity of the Blood of Christ and the Holy Scriptures

### The Voice of the Discpile

O blessed Lord Jesus, how greatly is blessed the devout soul who feasts with You at Your banquet, where there is set no other bread to be eaten but Yourself alone, the only beloved and most to be desired above all desires of the heart!

Truly, it would be a sweet thing for me to pour out tears from the bottom of my heart in Your presence, and like the loving sinner to wash Your feet with my tears[1].

But where is that devotion? Where is that plentiful pouring out of holy tears?

Surely in Your sight and Your holy angels, my entire heart should be inflamed and weep for joy.

For in the sacrament I have You truly present, though hidden in another form [see note[2]].

2. My eyes could not endure seeing You as You are, Your divine brightness—not even the whole world could stand in the splendor of the glory of Your majesty.

In this You have concern for my weakness, and so conceal Yourself in this outward sacramental sign.

I do really possess and adore Him whom the angels adore in heaven—but for the present I see only by faith, while they see by sight without obstruction.

I must be content with the light of the true faith, and walk in it until the day of everlasting brightness dawns and the shadows of figures pass away.

But when that which is perfect shall have come, the use of sacraments shall cease, because the blessed in heavenly glory need no sacramental remedy.[3]

For they rejoice endlessly in the presence of God, behold His glory face to face,[4] are transformed from glory to glory into the image of the incomprehensible Deity [see note[5]], and taste the Word of God made flesh,[6] as He was from the beginning and will be in eternity.

3. Though I am mindful of these wonderful things, even all spiritual solace becomes tedious to me, for so long as I do not openly see the Lord in His glory, everything I hear and see on earth I regard as nothing.

You are my witness, O God, that nothing can comfort me, no creature can give me rest, but only You, my God, Whom I long to contemplate eternally.

But this is not possible while I continue in this mortal life. Therefore I must determine to be highly patient and submit myself to You in all my desire.

For when Your saints, O Lord, who now rejoice with You in the kingdom of heaven lived, they waited in faith and great patience for the coming of Your glory.[7] What they believed, I believe; what they hoped for, I hope for; and where they are now, I trust I will be by Your grace.

In the meantime I will walk in faith, strengthened by the example of the saints.

For my comfort and for the mirror of my life, I will have Your holy Book[8]—and above that, I will have your most holy presence[9] for my unique remedy and refuge.[10]

4. For I perceive that there are two things that are especially necessary for me in this life, without which this miserable life would be unbearable for me.

While I am detained in this prison of this body, I acknowledge that I need two things—food and light.

Therefore, because I am weak and helpless You have given me Your sacred presence to refresh my soul and body,[11] and You have set "Your Word as a lamp to my feet and a light to my path."[12]

Without these two I would not be able to live rightly, for the Word of God is the light of my soul, and You are the bread of [my] life.

These also may be called the two tables, one set on each side in the treasure and jewel-house of the holy Church.[13]

One table is for the showbread, a foretaste of Christ, the true bread.[14] The other table is for the divine law, containing holy doctrine that teaches the true faith[15] and steadfastly leads onward to within the veil, where is the Holy of Holies [Holiest of All, or Most Holy Place[16]].

Thanks to You, O Lord Jesus, Light of everlasting Light, for the table of Your holy teaching that You have prepared for us by Your servants, the prophets and apostles and other teachers.[17]

5. Thanks be to You, O Creator and Redeemer of humanity, Who, to manifest Your love to the whole world prepared a great supper,[18] in which You placed before us to be eaten, not the typical lamb, but Your most sacred body and blood,[19] making glad all the faithful with this sacred banquet and replenishing them to the full with the

cup of salvation [see note[20]], in which are all the delights of paradise—and the holy angels feast with us but with more happiness and sweetness.

6. Oh, how great and honorable is the office of the God's priests, to whom is given the consecration of the sacrament of the Lord of glory in sacred words, whose lips bless Him, whose hands hold Him, whose mouth receives Him, and also administer [Him] to others.

Oh, how clean the hands should be, how pure the mouth, how holy the body, how unspotted the heart, which the Author of purity so often enters.

Nothing but what is holy, no word but what is good and profitable should proceed from the mouth of the priest [pastor, minister] who so often administers the sacrament of Christ.

7. Simple and chaste should be the eyes that are accustomed to beholding the body of Christ, and the hands that are used to handle the Creator of heaven and earth should be pure and lifted up to heaven.

To priests [pastors, ministers] especially it is written in the law, "You shall be holy, for I the LORD your God am holy."[21]

8. Assist us with Your grace, Almighty God, so that we who have received the office of the priesthood[22] may be able to serve You worthily and devoutly, in all purity, and with a good conscience.

And if we cannot live in as great an innocence as we should, grant us to at least lament earnestly the sins that we have committed—and in the spirit of humility and with full purpose of a good will, serve You more earnestly in the future.

1 Luke 7:37-38
2 Doctrine of transubstantiation.
3 1 Corinthians 13:10
4 1 Corinthians 13:12
5 2 Corinthians 3:18—The Scripture reads: "But *we all*, with unveiled face, beholding as in a mirror the glory of the Lord, *are being transformed* into the same image from glory to glory, just as by the Spirit of the Lord." (Italics added to note it's reference to all true Christians and the present tense of "are being transformed.")
6 John 1:1, 14
7 Hebrews 10:35-36, 11:1-40
8 James 1:23-25
9 Hebrews 6:19, 2 Corinthians 2:10
10 Psalm 21:6, 31:20, 51:11
11 John 6:51
12 Psalm 119:105
13 Psalm 23:5
14 Hebrews 9:2
15 Hebrews 5:12, 8:10-11
16 Hebrews 9:3, 12, 25—Although commonly used, the expression "Holy of Holies" is found in only a few Bibles, such as the New American Standard Bible and the New Revised Standard Bible.
17 2 Corinthians 11:3, Galatians 1:6-12, 2 Timothy 2:2, Hebrews 5:12
18 Luke 14:16
19 Based on doctrine of transubstantiation. John 6:53-56
20 Psalm 23:5, Wisdom of Solomon, an Apocryphal book, 16:20-21. The verse reads: "Instead of these things you gave your people food of angels, and without their toil you supplied them from heaven with bread ready to eat, providing every pleasure and suited to every taste. For your sustenance manifested your sweetness toward your children; and the bread, ministering to the desire of the one who took it, was changed to suit everyone's liking."
21 Leviticus 19:2, 20:7, 26; 1 Peter 1:16
22 Revelation 1:6, 5:10, 20:6

# 12

## THOSE WHO ARE ABOUT TO RECEIVE COMMUNION SHOULD PREPARE WITH GREAT CARE

### *The Voice of the Beloved*

I am the Lover of purity, the Giver of all sanctity.[1]

I seek a pure heart and therein is the place of My rest.[2]

Make ready for Me a large room, furnished and prepared, and I will keep the Passover [meal] at your house with My disciples.[3]

If you wish Me to come to you and remain with you, "purge out the old leaven"[4] and make clean the residence of your heart.

Shut out the whole world[5] and all the host of [of your *or* its] sins. Sit "like a sparrow alone on the housetop,"[6] and think over your transgressions with bitterness in your soul.

For everyone who loves prepares the best and loveliest dwelling for their beloved, for in this is revealed the love of the one entertaining their beloved.

2. But understand that no action of yours has enough merit to make this preparation sufficient, even if you spend a whole year preparing yourself and think of nothing else.

It is only by My favor and grace that you are allowed to approach My table—[it is] as if a beggar were invited to a rich person's dinner and had nothing to give in return for the benefits, but to humbly give thanks.

Do what you can and do it diligently, not out of habit or necessity; but with fear, reverence, and affection, receive the body of your beloved Lord God [see note[7]] when He consents to come to you.

I am He that called you, I have commanded that it be done, I will supply what is lacking in you—come and receive Me.

3. When I give the grace of devotion to you, give thanks to your God, for it was not given to you because you are worthy, but because I have had mercy on you.

If you do not have this grace, but instead feel dry, be instantly in prayer, sigh, and knock,[8] and do not give up until you are fit to receive some crumb of saving grace.[9]

You have need of Me, I have no need of you.

And You do not you come to sanctify Me, but I come to sanctify and make you better.

You come to be sanctified by Me and united to Me, to receive new grace, and to be stirred anew to change your life for the better.

Do not neglect this grace, but prepare your heart with all diligence, and receive your beloved into your soul.


4. You should not only prepare yourself devoutly before communion, but be careful afterward to keep yourself in [a state of] devotion.

And the careful guarding of yourself afterward is not less required than devout preparation before.

For carefully guarding yourself afterward is the best preparation for obtaining greater grace.

If you quickly turn yourself to outward consolations, you will become unwilling to remain in a state of devotion.

Beware of much talking,[10] remain in some secret place[11] and enjoy your God—for you have Him whom all the world cannot take from you.

I am He to Whom you should give yourself completely, so that you may now live the rest of your time not in yourself but in Me, free from all anxiety.


1 1 Corinthians 1:30, 2 Thessalonians 2:13, 1 Peter 1:2
2 Psalm 24:4, Matthew 5:8
3 Mark 14:14-15, Luke 22:11-12
4 1 Corinthians 5:7
5 Exodus 24:18, 2 Corinthians 6:17

6 Psalm 102:7
7 Doctrine of transubstantiation.
8 Luke 11:9-10
9 Luke 11:5-8, see also Ephesians 2:8-9
10 Proverbs 10:19
11 Matthew 6:6, 18

# 13

## Seek Union With Christ with Your Whole Heart

### The Voice of the Disciple

How will I obtain the grace, O Lord, to find You alone[1] and by myself, to open my whole heart to You, to enjoy You as my soul desires, to be disturbed by no one, to be moved or regarded by no one, so that You alone may speak to me and I to You, as a beloved speaks to a beloved, and a friend feasts with a friend.[2]

I pray for this, I long for this, that I may be wholly united to You and may withdraw my heart from all created things, and may increasingly learn by means of partaking often of sacred communion to relish heavenly and eternal things.

Ah Lord God, when will I be completely united to You and absorbed by You, and have totally forgotten about myself?

You in me and I in You[3]—grant that we may continue together as one.

2. Truly, You are my Beloved, "chief among ten thousand,"[4] in Whom my soul is thoroughly pleased to dwell all the days of its life.

Truly, You are my peacemaker, in Whom is the greatest peace and true rest, and without Whom there is labor and sorrow and infinite misery.

"Truly, You are a God who hides Yourself,"[5] and Your counsel is not with the wicked, but Your conversation is with the humble and simple of heart.[6]

Oh how sweet is Your spirit, O Lord, Who for the purpose of showing Your sweetness toward Your children consented to feed them with the bread that is full of sweetness, the bread that came down from heaven [see note[7]].

Surely there is no other people so great as to have gods so near to them as You our God are present to all Your faithful ones,[8] to whom You give Yourself to be appropriated and enjoyed for their daily comfort and for the raising up of their hearts to heaven.


3. For what other nation is so highly renowned as the Christian people?

Or what creature under heaven is so beloved as the devout soul into which God Himself enters.

O unspeakable grace! O wondrous condescension! O immeasurable love specially bestowed upon humanity!

But what shall I give to the Lord in return for this grace,[9] for love so unparalleled?

There is nothing I can give that is more acceptable than to offer my heart completely to my God, and to unite it most [to the highest degree] inwardly to Him .

Then all my inward parts will rejoice, when my soul is perfectly united to God.

Then He will say to me: "If you are willing to be with Me, I am willing to be with you."

And I will answer Him: "Consent, O Lord, to remain with me, for I will gladly be with You.

"This is my whole desire, that my heart may be united to You."

1  Proverbs 8:17
2  Exodus 33:11, Song of Songs 8:2—Song of Songs is also
   called Song of Solomon and Canticles.
3  John 15:4
4  Song of Songs 5:10
5  Isaiah 45:15
6  Proverbs 3:34, Isaiah 57:15
7  John 6:31-40, Wisdom of Solomon 16:20-21—Wisdom of
   Solomon is an Apocrypha book. The verses read: "Instead
   of these things you gave your people food of angels, and
   without their toil you supplied them from heaven with bread
   ready to eat, providing every pleasure and suited to every
   taste. For your sustenance manifested your sweetness toward
   your children; and the bread, ministering to the desire of the
   one who took it, was changed to suit everyone's liking."
8  Deuteronomy 4:7
9  Psalm 116:12


# 14
## DESIRE OF THE DEVOUT TO RECEIVE CHRIST

### The Voice of the Disciple

"Oh, how great is Your goodness," O Lord, "which You have laid up for those who fear You."[1]

When I think about some devout persons who approach Your sacrament, O Lord, with the greatest devotion and affection, I am frequently confounded and ashamed within myself that I come with such lukewarmness, yes coldness, to Your altar and the table of sacred communion.

I am sad that I remain so dry and without strong affection toward You, that I am not wholly inflamed in Your presence, O my God, nor so earnestly drawn and affected as many devout persons have been, who out of a fervent desire for holy communion and heart-felt love, could not restrain themselves from tears, but with the mouth of their hearts and bodies alike panted after You[2] from their inmost souls, O God the fountain of life, not being otherwise able to allay or satisfy their hunger except by receiving You with all delight and spiritual eagerness.

2. Oh, the truly ardent faith of those persons!—probable evidence of Your sacred presence.

For they truly know their Lord "in the breaking of bread"[3]—their hearts vehemently burn within them while You, O blessed Jesus, walk with them.

Such affection and devotion, such strong and fervent love, is often far from me.

Be favorable to me, O merciful Jesus, sweet and gracious Lord, and grant that this poor needy creature sometimes at least feel in holy communion a little of your warm affectionate love, so that my faith may grow stronger, my hope in Your goodness increase, and that love [for You], once perfectly inflamed within me after tasting the heavenly manna, may never cease.

3. Your mercy is able to grant me the grace that I long for, and in the day when it pleases You to visit me most graciously with a spirit of fervor.

For although I do not burn with as great a desire as those who are especially devoted to You, by Your grace I long for this great inflamed desire, praying and longing that I may participate with all Your fervent lovers and be numbered among their holy company.

1 Psalm 31:19
2 Psalm 42:1-3
3 Luke 24:32-35

## 15
### GRACE OF DEVOTION OBTAINED BY
### THE HUMILITY OF DENYING OURSELVES

*The Voice of the Beloved*

You should immediately seek the grace of devotion, ask for it earnestly, wait for it patiently and confidently, receive it gratefully, stay humble to keep it, cooperate with it diligently, and when it comes, commit to God the length and manner of its coming.

You should especially humble yourself when you feel little or no inward devotion, but not be overly dejected or immoderately grieved.

God often gives in one short moment what He denied for a long time—sometimes He gives at the end what He deferred granting at the beginning of your prayer.

2. If grace were always given instantly, or came with nothing more than a wish, weak humanity could not endure it well.

Therefore, wait for the grace of devotion with good hope and humble patience.

Nevertheless, when this grace is not given or is taken away for an unknown reason, blame yourself and your sins.

Sometimes it is not a weighty matter that obstructs and hides grace from us, but a small matter—that is, if anything can be called small that hinders such great good.

But whether it is great or small, if you remove it and overcome it perfectly you will have your desire.

3. As soon as you have given yourself to God with your whole heart and do not seek this nor that for your own pleasure or will, but settle yourself wholly in Him, you will find yourself united [to Him] and at peace, for nothing will

provide so sweet a flavor, nothing will be so delightful, as the good pleasure of His will.

Anyone, therefore, who lifts up their intention to God with a simple heart, keeps clear of all immoderate liking or disliking of created things, will be the most fit to receive grace and will be qualified for the gift of true devotion.

For the Lord pours His blessing into the vessel He finds empty [of itself].

And the more perfectly you forsake worldly things, the more completely you die to yourself through contempt of yourself, the more quickly grace will come, the more plentiful it will enter in, and the higher it will lift up your [now] free heart.

4. Then will you [spiritually] see[1] and flow together [see note[2]] and wonder, and your heart will be enlarged within you, for the hand of the Lord is with you and you have put yourself wholly into His hand for all eternity.

Thus you will be blessed[3] when you seek God with your whole heart[4] and do not regard your soul with approval [in vain or vainly].

When you receive holy communion in this way, you obtain the great grace of divine union, because you do not look to your own devotion and comfort, but above all devotion and comfort look to the glory and honor of God.

1   Isaiah 35:5, 42:7, 42:16; John 9:25
2   Isaiah 60:5—Unity or harmony of spirit, soul, and body—
     bringing peace and joy.
3   Psalm 128:4
4   Psalm 119:2

# 16
## Make Our Needs Known to Christ and Seek His Grace

*The Voice of the Disciple*

O most sweet and loving Lord, whom I now desire to receive with all devotion, You know my weaknesses and the necessities that I endure, in how many sins and evils I am involved, and how often I am depressed, tempted, disturbed, and defiled.

I come to You for help, I beg You for consolation and support.

I speak to You Who knows all things, to Whom all my inward thoughts are open, and Who alone can perfectly comfort and help me.

You know what good things I am most in need of, and how poor I am in all virtue.

2. Behold, I stand before You, poor and naked, calling for grace and imploring mercy.

Refresh Your hungry supplicant, inflame my coldness with the fire of Your love, enlighten my blindness with the brightness of Your presence.

Turn all earthly things into bitterness for me, all grievous and contrary things into patience, all low and created things into contempt and oblivion.

Lift my heart up to You in heaven, and do not send me away to wander over the earth.[1]

From now and forever more be only sweet to me, for You alone are my food and drink, my love and joy, my sweetness and all my good.

3. Oh, that with Your presence You would wholly inflame, burn, and conform me to Yourself, that I might be

made one spirit with You[2] by the grace of inward union and by the melting power of [Your] ardent love!

Do not allow me to go away from You hungry and dry, but deal mercifully with me, as [in the same way that] You have often dealt wonderfully with Your saints.

What marvel is it if I should be wholly inflamed by You—and of myself fail and come to nothing—since You are the fire always burning and never dying, love purifying the heart and enlightening the understanding.

1   Genesis 4:12-14
2   1 Corinthians 6:17

## 17

### FERVENT LOVE AND STRONG DESIRE TO RECEIVE CHRIST

### *The Voice of the Disciple*

With deep devotion and ardent love, with all affection and fervor of heart, I desire to receive You, O Lord, as many saints and devout persons, who in their holiness of life were most pleasing to You, and were most fervent in devotion.

O my God, everlasting Love, my entire good, my happiness that can never end, I long to receive You with as earnest an affection, and the most suitable awe and reverence, that any of the saints ever had or could have felt toward You.

2. And though I am unworthy to have all those feelings of devotion, nevertheless I offer You all the affection of my heart, as if I were the only one who had all those most pleasing and ardent longings for You.

Yes, all that a dutiful mind can conceive and desire, I offer and present to You with the deepest reverence and inward affection.

I desire to keep nothing for myself but freely and cheerfully to sacrifice to You myself and all that is mine.

O Lord, my God, my Creator, and my Redeemer, I long to receive You this day with such affection, reverence, praise, and honor, with such gratitude, worthiness, and love, with such faith, hope, and purity as Your most holy mother, the glorious virgin Mary, received and desired You, when she humbly and devoutly answered the angel who declared to her glad tidings of the mystery of the incarnation "Behold the maidservant of the Lord! Let it be to me according to your word."[1]

3. And as Your blessed forerunner, the most excellent among the saints, John the Baptist, rejoicing in Your presence, leaped for joy of the Holy Spirit while he was yet enclosed in his mother's womb,[2] and afterward seeing Jesus walking among men, humbled himself greatly and said with devout affection: "the friend of the bridegroom, who stands and hears him, rejoices greatly because of the bridegroom's voice,"[3]—in like manner I also wish to be inflamed with great and holy desires and to offer myself to You from my whole heart.

Therefore I also offer and present to You the triumphant joys, the ardent affection, the mental ecstasies, the supernatural illuminations and celestial visions of all devout hearts, with all the virtues and praises celebrated and to be celebrated by all creatures in heaven and on earth, for myself, and for all who entrusted themselves to my prayers, that You may be worthily praised and forever glorified.

4. Receive, O Lord my God, my wishes and desires of giving You infinite praise and boundless blessings, which,

in keeping with the measure of Your ineffable greatness, are most justly due You.

I render praises to You, and desire to render [them] every day and every moment. And with all entreaty and loving tenderness, I invite and entreat all heavenly spirits and all Your faithful servants to render with me thanks and praises to You [see note[4]].

5. Let all people, nations, and languages praise You,[5] and magnify Your holy and most delicious name with the highest exultation and ardent devotion.

And when they have obtained their longed-for devotion and joyful union with You, and have departed from Your holy heavenly table, well comforted and marvelously refreshed, O, let them agree to remember my poor soul[6]

1  Luke 1:38
2  Luke 1:44
3  John 3:29
4  Based on a practice in certain churches of praying to cannonized saints and to angels.
5  Psalm 117:1-2, 118:1
6  Based on doctrine in certain churches that cannonized saints in heaven can pray and intercede for those on earth.
   1 Timothy 2:5 reads: "For there is one God and one Mediator between God and men, the Man Christ Jesus," and Hebrews 7:25 reads: "Therefore He is also able to save to the uttermost those who come to God through Him, since He always lives to make intercession for them."

# 18

## DO NOT BE A CURIOUS SEARCHER INTO THIS SACRAMENT, BUT BE A HUMBLE FOLLOWER OF CHRIST AND RECEIVE IT WITH FAITH

You must beware of curious and unprofitable searching into this most profound sacrament, if you do not wish to be plunged into the depths of doubt.

"He that is a searcher of My Majesty, shall be overpowered by the glory of it" [see note[1]]. God is able to do more than mortals can understand.

A dutiful and humble search for truth is allowed, provided we are always ready to be taught, and study to walk according to the sound precepts of the Scriptures.

2. It is a blessed simplicity when a person leaves the difficult way of questions and disputes and goes forward in the plain and firm path of God's commandments.

Many have lost devotion because they sought to search into things too high for them.

Faith is required of you, and a sincere life, not lofty understanding or deep inquiry into the mysteries of God.

If you do not understand things that are beneath you [mentally and spiritually], how can you comprehend what is above you?

Submit yourself to God and humble your understanding to faith, and the light of knowledge will be given you to the degree that is profitable and necessary for you.

3. Some are grievously tempted about faith and the holy sacrament, but this is not imputed to them but rather to the enemy.

Do not be anxious, do not argue with your own thoughts, or answer doubts suggested by the devil, but trust the Word of God, trust His saints and prophets, and the wicked enemy will flee from you.[2]

It is often very profitable to the servant of God to suffer such things.

For the devil does not tempt unbelievers and sinners whom he already securely possesses, but he tempts and troubles faithful and spiritual devout persons in various ways.

4. Go forward, therefore, with simple and undoubting faith, and with humble reverence approach this holy sacrament, and whatever you are not able to understand commit securely to Almighty God.

Goes does not deceive you, you are deceived when you trust too much in yourself.

God walks with the simple, reveals Himself to the humble,[3] gives understanding to the little ones,[4] opens the perception of pure minds,[5] and hides [His] grace from the curious and proud.[6]

Human reason is weak and can be deceived, but true faith cannot be deceived.

5. All reason and natural searching [see note[7]] should follow faith, not go before it, or contradict it.

For in this most holy, most supremely excellent sacrament, faith and love especially take the lead and work in hidden ways.

God, who is eternal and incomprehensible, and of infinite power, does great and unsearchable things in heaven and on earth, and there is no tracing out [visible sign] of His marvelous works.

If all the works of God were such that they could easily be understood by human reason, they could not justly be called marvelous or inexpressible.

1   Our original text referenced Proverbs 25:27, which reads: "... for men to search their own glory is not glory." The text quoted could not be found in any Book of the Bible or the Apocrypha.

2   James 4:6-7

3   Isaiah 57:15, Daniel 10:12, James 4:10

4   Psalm 119:130, Matthew 18:10

5   Psalm 73:1, Matthew 5:8

6   Psalm 101:5, 119:21, 138:6; Luke 1:51; James 4:6; 1 Peter 5:5

7   Searching the natural for answers to spiritual matters.

# STUDY GUIDE

The following questions are designed to help you meditate on the writings of Thomas à Kempis. Some questions are simply factual/memory questions; others are application questions in which you are asked how his writing impacts your own life. There are a few interpretation questions, as well.

This material can be used for both group and individual study related to this Pure Gold classic.

## DEVOTIONAL MEDITATIONS FROM
### *THE IMITATION OF CHRIST*

1.  What comforts the mind? What inspires confidence in God?

2.  What kind of person is truly great?

3.  What causes us to become restless within ourselves?

4.  What kind of person rules most securely?

5.  What causes one to be able to rejoice in the evening?

6.  What will always give you joy?

7.  What kind of person can relate most closely to the suffering of Christ?

8.  What makes every heavy thing light?

9.  Why can we not be satisfied with temporal goods?

10. What will keep you from being frightened by people?

11. With whom does God walk?

12. To whom does God reveal himself?

13. To whom does God give understanding?

## Book One—Advice Useful for a Spiritual Life

### 1. Imitating Christ and Despising All the Worthless Things of the World

a. What should our chief endeavor in life be?

b. What leads to personal holiness?

c. What is the highest wisdom?

d. From what should we remove our hearts?

### 2. Think Humbly of Yourself

a. What will be the result of knowing yourself well?

b. What is the highest and most profitable learning?

### 3. The Doctrine of Truth

a. What should our greatest endeavor be?

b. Who are the truly great?

c. What is truth?

### 4. Wisdom and Forethought in Our Actions

a. With what type of person should you consult?

b. What are some of the results of living a good life?

c. How is wisdom obtained?

### 5. The Reading of the Holy Scriptures

a. For what should we seek in the holy Scriptures?

b. What remains forever?

c. What must we do if we desire to benefit from the Scriptures?

    d.   What is the power of the Word of God?

6. Immoderate Desires

    a.   How is true peace of heart obtained?

    b.   What happens to those who indulge in their sensual desires?

    c.   How do we get our passions under control?

## 7. Fleeing From Fruitless Hope and Pride

    a.   What are some of things that are done by vain people?

    b.   What do the humble enjoy?

## 8. Too Much Familiarity Is to Be Avoided

    a.   With whom should you discuss your personal affairs?

    b.   With what type of people should you keep company?

    c.   Is it true that familiarity breeds contempt?

## 9. Obedience and Subjection

    a.   Where may peace of mind be found?

    b.   What must we give up for the sake of peace?

    c.   What are the benefits of obedience and subjection?

## 10. Avoiding Excess Words

    a. What should we avoid as much as we can?

    b.   Why do we so willingly spend time in conversation with others?

    c.   What causes us to speak too freely in thoughtless ways?

    d.   What helps to promote our spiritual growth?

## 11. Obtaining Peace, and Zealous Desire for Progress in Grace

a. What often prohibits us from enjoying great peace?

b. Why were some of the saints so perfect and given to meditation?

c. Why does God give us opportunities to fight?

## 12. The Benefit of Adversity

a. Why are troubles and crosses good for us?

b. What will keep us from seeking comforts from other people?

## 13. Resisting Temptation

a. In what ways are temptations beneficial to us?

b. Where do evil temptations begin?

c. What do temptations and afflictions prove?

## 14. Avoiding Rash Judgment

a. What should we judge instead of judging others?

b. What enables us to pass beyond the restrictive boundaries of human reason?

## 15. Works Done in Charity

a. What is the difference between external works and works done by love?

b. What do those who have true and perfect love seek?

## 16. Enduring the Faults of Others

a. What do times of adversity reveal about us?

b. What does it mean to "... bear one another's burdens"?

c. What should you do when you encounter faults in others?

## 17. A Community Life

a.   What must you do in order to have peace and harmony with others?

b.   What must you do in order to persevere and grow in grace?

c.   What must you do in order to live a spiritual life?

d.   What factors contribute to making a truly religious person?

e.   In what ways can a sense of community be cultivated?

## 18. Examples of the Holy Saints

a.   In what were the saints poor? In what were they rich?

b.   How did the saints see themselves?

## 19. Spiritual Exercises of Good Religious People

a.   With what should the lives of good, religious people be adorned?

b.   In order to show progress in our spiritual life, what must we be?

c.   Upon what does the purpose of good people depend?

## 20. Love of Solitude and Silence

a.   From what should you withdraw if you want to meditate on good things?

b.   What must the person who intends to achieve the inward and spiritual things of religion do?

c.   With what was the security of the saints always filled?

d.   From what does the security of wicked people arise?

e.   What will you find in the secret place?

f.   What happens to the soul that spends time in silence and stillness?

g.   Why should we love silence and solitude?

## 21. Compunction of Heart

a.   What must you do in order to make progress in godliness?

b.   What causes true freedom and genuine joy?

c.   What makes our miserable bodies complain so easily?

## 22. Consideration of Human Misery

a.   What kind of person is in the best circumstance of all?

b.   For what do the saints of God and all devout followers of Christ long?

c.   What is the time of true blessing in our lives?

d.   What will become of those who begin so early to grow lukewarm?

## 23. Meditation on Death

a.   What will prevent you from having a great fear of death?

b.   What will give you great confidence that you will die happy?

c.   What should you store up for yourself now?

d.   Are you afraid of death?

## 24. Judgment and Punishment of Sinners

a.   What answer will you give to Christ, who knows all you sins?

b.   What is the fuel that feeds the fire of hell?

c.   What will the glutton's punishment be in hell?

d.   What will be exalted above all worldly wisdom in the Day of Judgment?

## 25. Zeal in Improving Your Life

a.   Why did you come to Christ?

b.   What is one thing that draws many away from spiritual progress?

c.   For what is the fervent and diligent person prepared?

## Book Two—Advice About Internal Things

## 1. The Inward Life

a.   Where is the Kingdom of God?

b.   In what does the Kingdom of God consist?

c.   What are the results of trusting sincerely in the wounds and precious scars of the Lord Jesus?

## 2. Humble Submission

a.   Who does God protect and deliver?

b.   To whom does God reveal His secrets?

## 3. A Good Peaceful Person

a.   What will enable you to bring peace to others?

b.   What kind of person is best able to keep one's self in peace?

## 4. A Pure Mind and Simple Intentions

a.   What are the two wings that lift a person up from earthly things?

b.   What does simplicity do?

c.   What does purity do?

d.   What will enable you to enjoy internal liberty?

## 5. Consideration of Ourselves

a.   What will enable you to be moved only by a little by whatever you see outwardly?

b.   What must you do if you desire peace of mind and true unity of purpose?

c.   What kind of soul despises all things that are inferior to God?

## 6. Joy of a Good Conscience

a.   What is the glory of a good person?

b.   What will enable you to always have joy?

c.   What always accompanies the world's glory?

d.   What kinds of people show that they have fully committed themselves to God?

## 7. Loving Jesus Above All Things

a.   What kind of love is deceitful and fickle?

b.   Who will stand firmly forever?

## 8. Friendly Conversations With Jesus

a.   What kind of loss is greater than losing the whole world?

b.   What can the world give you without Jesus?

c.   What kind of person is the richest person in the world?

d.   What does the grace of God enable us to do?

## 9. Wanting All Comfort

a.   What enabled the holy martyr Laurence to overcome the world?

b.   In what can we hope and trust?

c.   Of what might temptation be a sign?

d.   To whom is heavenly comfort promised?

e.   What does divine comfort do for us?

f.   What is the difference between divine and human comfort?

## 10. Gratitude for the Grace of God

 a. Why do you seek rest when you are born to labor?

 b. What kind of person cannot be proud?

 c. Are you thankful for the grace of God in your life?

## 11. How Few Love the Cross of Jesus

 a. What do those who love Jesus for His own sake do?

 b. What kinds of people should be called "mercenary"?

 c. What is the one thing that is most necessary for us?

 d. Have you taken up your cross?

## 12. The King's Highway of the Holy Cross

 a. What are the blessings of the cross in the believer's life?

 b. What kind of person is best able to relate to the suffering of Christ?

 c. Why do you seek any other way than this royal way of the holy cross?

 d. What happens to the spirit of one whose flesh is weakened by affliction?

 e. What will happen in your life when you fully trust in the Lord?

 f. What qualifies us to understand heavenly things?

## BOOK THREE—INTERNAL CONSOLATION

## 1. Christ Speaks Inwardly to the Faithful Soul

 a. What should we let go of?

 b. What should we seek?

   c.   What will enable us to arrive at the true blessedness?

## 2. Truth Speaks Inwardly Without the Sound of Words

   a.   What happens within our soul when the Lord speaks to us?

   b.   What brings about condemnation within us?

## 3. Hear God's Words With Humility—Many Do Not Listen to Them

   a.   What is very necessary for us in times of temptation?

   b.   In what two ways does God customarily visit His elect?

   c.   What enables you to uphold yourself in this difficult life?

## 4. We Should Live in Truth and Humility Before God

   a.   What will happen to the one who walks before God in truth?

   b.   What should please you above all things?

## 5. The Wonderful Effects of Divine Love

   a.   What makes everything light that is heavy?

   b.   What kind of person is able to fly, run, and rejoice?

## 6. Proof of a True Love for Christ

   a.   What is a courageous love able to do?

   b.   What does the enemy strive to do in your life?

   c.   What should always serve as a warning to you?

## 7. Concealing Grace Under the Cover of Humility

   a.   What determines your worth?

   b.   What must those who are still novices and inexperienced in the ways of the Lord do in order to keep from being easily deceived?

## 8. Having a Low Concept of Ourselves Before God

a.   What happens when we abase ourselves and draw back from all self-esteem?

b.   What causes us to be made instantly strong and filled with new joy?

## 9. God Should Be the Ultimate Objective of All Things

a.   What should be our supreme and ultimate objective if we want to be truly blessed?

b.   What truth causes vainglory to be put to flight?

c.   What overcomes all things and enlarges the powers of the soul?

## 10. To Despise the World and Serve God Is a Sweet Life

a.   What must a person do in order to find the sweetest consolations of the Holy Spirit?

b.   What must a person do in order to enter the narrow way and leave off all worldly care?

c.   By what means is a person made truly free and holy?

## 11. Examining and Moderating the Longings and Desires of Our Hearts

a.   What hinders us and weighs us down?

b.   Why is it sometimes desirable to use restraint even in good desires and endeavors?

## 12. Growing in Patience and Striving Against Concupiscence

a.   What should you do to avoid any future punishment (loss of reward)?

b.   What will enable you to overcome old, inbred habits?

## 13. Obeying in Humble Subjection, After the Example of Jesus

a.   What happens to those who withdraw themselves from obedience?

b.   What must you do if you desire to keep your flesh under control?

c.   What is absolutely necessary if you desire to prevail against flesh and blood?

d.   What have you learned from the example of Jesus Christ?

## 14. Consider God's Secret Judgments, so You Will Not Be Lifted Up for Anything Good in You

a.   What happens when we are left to ourselves?

b.   In what is all boastful pride swallowed up?

## 15. How We Should Be Affected by the Things We Desire, and What We Should Say

a.   What should we say in everything?

b.   What points of prayer should we always keep in mind?

## 16. True Comfort Is to Be Sought in God Alone

a.   Why is it impossible for us to be satisfied with temporal goods?

b.   What adjectives describe all human comfort?

## 17. All Our Anxieties Are to Be Placed on God

a.   What keeps a person from being unstable?

b.   What should be the condition of those who desire to walk with God?

c.   How can we learn to be anxious for nothing?

## 18. Temporal Sufferings Must Be Borne Patiently, After the Example of Jesus

a.   What makes this present life profitable?

b.   What enabled the just and elect to enter into the heavenly kingdom?

### 19. Enduring Suffering and Proof of True Patience

a.   What enables us to obtain the victory and win the crown of patience?

b.   What do we refuse when we are unwilling to suffer?

### 20. Acknowledging Infirmities Amid the Difficulties of This Life

a.   What causes one to be often driven backwards and shamed before God?

b.   What three things cause us to love the world?

### 21. We Are to Rest in God Above All Things That Are Good, and Above All His Gifts

a.   What enables your heart to truly rest and be totally content?

b.   What enables us to "fly away" and rest in God?

### 22. Remembering God's Many and Varied Benefits

a.   What kind of person is most fit to receive the greater blessings?

b.   Why should God be praised in everything?

c.   What were some of the chief characteristics of the apostles?

d.   What should be preferred above all things?

### 23. Four Things That Bring Great Inward Peace

a.   What are the four things that bring great inward peace?

b.   What should we pray in order to overcome evil thoughts?

c.   Do you have the peace of God?

## 24. Avoiding Curious Inquiry Into Other People's Lives

a.  Why should we not concern ourselves with the affairs of others?

b.  What are some of the things that distract and darken the heart?

## 25. The Basis of a Constant Peaceful Heart and True Spiritual Progress

a.  What will enable you to enjoy much peace?

b.  In what do spiritual progress and the perfection of a person consist?

## 26. The Excellence of a Free Mind, Which Is Gained Quicker by Humble Prayer Than by Studying

a.  What is the work of a perfect person?

b.  What should we ask God to give us instead of asking for all the comforts of the world?

## 27. It Is Self-love That Is the Most Hindrance to the Highest Good

a.  What hurts you more than anything in the world?

b.  What determines the degree to which things cling more or less to us?

c.  What frees us from the bondage of things?

d.  What will enable you to be free from suffering any harm or loss at all?

## 28. Strength Against the Tongues of Slanderers

a.  What will keep you from being bothered by fleeting words?

b.  Where are true peace and glory to be found?

c.  Where do a restless heart and a distracted mind come from?

## 29. We Should Call Upon God and Bless Him When Tribulation Comes to Us

    a.   What will help us to turn temptation into good?

    b.   What should we say when troubles come our way?

## 30. Seeking Divine Help and Being Confident of Regaining Grace

    a.   What keeps us from receiving heavenly comfort?

    b.   Is anything too difficult for God?

    c.   Why is it useless and unprofitable to be either disturbed or pleased about future things?

## 31. Finding the Creator by Forsaking Everything

    a.   Why are there so few who truly meditate upon spiritual matters?

    b.   From what does the fruit of a good life proceed?

## 32. Self-denial and Renouncing Every Evil Appetite

    a.   What enables us to experience perfect liberty?

    b.   What must we do in order to find everything?

## 33. A Changing Heart and Directing Our Objective Toward God

    a.   Why should we not trust our feelings?

    b.   What are the characteristics of those who are wise and well-instructed in spiritual matters?

## 34. God Is Sweet Above All Things and in All Things to Those Who Love Him

    a.   What can be pleasing to the person who does not delight in God?

    b.   What can be said about those who are truly wise?

    c.   What pleasures are experienced by the person who delights in God?

### 35. There Is No Security From Temptation in This Life

a. What happens to those who are too lazy to fight?

b. Do you think you will always have spiritual consolation when you desire it?

### 36. The Worthless Judgments of People

a. Why should you not fear other people?

b. What harm can the words or abuses of people do to you?

### 37. Pure and Entire Resignation of Ourselves to Obtain Freedom of Heart

a. What must you do in order to find God?

b. What should be the whole endeavor of your life?

### 38. Governing External Things Properly, and Having Recourse to God When in Danger

a. Instead of thinking about temporal things, on what should we be focused?

b. What must you do in order to hear God's answer?

### 39. A Person Should Not Be Anxious in Business Affairs

a. Why should you not be anxious about business affairs?

b. In what does true spiritual progress consist?

### 40. We Have No Good in Ourselves, and Nothing in Which We Can Glory

a. What should we be thinking and saying?

b. In what do we experience true glory and holy exultation?

### 41. Contempt of All Temporal Honor

a. What will keep the contempt of those on Earth from grieving you?

b. What blinds and quickly misleads us?

## 42. Our Peace Is Not to Be Derived From People

a.   What is one thing that will cause you to be in an insecure and entangled condition?

b.   What will keep you from being grieved when friends die or leave you?

c.   What will hinder God's grace from entering your heart?

## 43. Against Useless and Worldly Knowledge

a.   What are some of the benefits of listening well to the Scriptures?

b.   What does the Lord teach us to do?

c.   Why is worldly knowledge useless?

## 44. Not Bringing Trouble to Ourselves From Outward Things

a.   What will enable you to more easily endure being overcome [by others]?

b.   What causes us to ignore the things that are necessary for us?

## 45. Everyone Is Not to Be Believed, for We Tend to Make Mistakes When We Speak

a.   Describe the type of person who does not fail easily.

b.   What did Thomas a Kempis point to as being his instructor?

c.   What things must we avoid in order to keep heavenly grace?

## 46. Trusting in God When Evil Words Are Spoken Against Us

a.   What is the result of paying close attention to the Lord's words?

b.   If everything that could be maliciously invented was said against you, how much would it hurt you if you let it pass and gave it no more consideration than you would a blade of grass?

c.   What should we do when others speak evil about us?

## 47. Endure All Grievous Things for the Sake of Eternal Life

a.   What kinds of things are valueless and fleeting?

b.   Should not all painful trials be endured for the sake of eternal life [in Christ]?

## 48. The Day of Eternity and the Distresses of This Life

a.   When will you enjoy true freedom without any obstacles whatever, without any mental or physical trouble?

b.   What are the causes of unhappiness?

## 49. The Desire for Eternal Life, and the Great Rewards Promised to Those Who Fight Without Wavering

a.   What are two main areas of life in which each of us needs to die to self?

b.   What rewards can you expect in Heaven?

## 50. How Despondent People Should Offer Themselves Into the Hands of God

a.   Why is it good to be humbled by the Lord?

b.   How is a person ever better by being considered great by people?

## 51. When We Lack Strength for Higher [Deeper] Works, We Should Concentrate on Humble Works

a.   What should we sorrow over while we are in the flesh?

b.   What is not worthy to be compared to the glory that shall be revealed in us?

## 52. We Should Not Consider Ourselves Worthy of Consolation, but Rather as Deserving Chastisement

a.  What do we truly deserve?

b.  What do we deserve for our sins but hell and everlasting fire?

c.  What is an acceptable sacrifice to the Lord?

## 53. The Grace of God Is Not With Those Who Cherish Earthly Things

a.  What should we do in order to be truly spiritual?

b.  What is the perfect victory?

c.  What must we do if we desire to walk freely with the Lord?

## 54. The Different Movements of Nature and Grace

a.  What are the attributes of grace?

b.  For what does grace strive?

c.  In what does grace delight?

d.  Contrast nature and grace.

## 55. The Corruption of Nature and the Effectiveness of Divine Grace

a.  What is the mistress of truth and what is the teacher of discipline?

b.  What is stronger than all enemies and wiser than all the wise?

## 56. We Should Deny Ourselves and Imitate Christ by Bearing the Cross

a.  What unites you to God?

b.  What must you do in order to enter into the life of Christ?

## 57. We Should Not Be Overly Depressed When We Sometimes Fail

a.   Why are you grieved by every little thing that is said against you?

b.   What should be sweeter to our mouths than honey and the honeycomb?

## 58. High Matters and God's Secret Judgments Are Not to Be Closely Looked Into

a.   Why are God's judgments to be feared, not discussed?

b.   What were the disciples told when they asked Jesus who would be greatest in the Kingdom of Heaven?

## 59. Our Hope and Trust Are to Be Fixed in God Alone

a.   What is your confidence in this life?

b.   What does God do for you?

### BOOK FOUR—EXHORTATION TO RECEIVE HOLY COMMUNION

## 1. Receive the Emblems of Christ With Reverence

a.   What is Christ's invitation to the weary?

b.   What does this gracious honor and loving invitation mean?

c.   Why are we not more zealous in seeking God's presence?

d.   By what are we attracted to the Lord?

e.   What is the importance of the Sacrament of Holy Communion in the believer's life?

## 2. Goodness and Love of God Shown in This Sacrament

a.   By what means were all things made?

b.   How should we prepare ourselves for Holy Communion?

## 3. It Is Spiritually Beneficial to Receive Communion Often

a.   What does Holy Communion do for us?

b.   What is the one chief consolation of the faithful souls while they are in their mortal bodies?

## 4. Benefits Bestowed on Those Who Receive Communion Worthily

a.   What benefits are bestowed on those who receive communion worthily?

b.   What may increase as a result of frequently visiting the mysteries of Christ?

## 5. Dignity of the Sacrament and Priestly Work

a.   With what should priests [pastors, ministers] be adorned?

b.   What are the results of priests [pastors, ministers] celebrating their office faithfully?

## 6. Asking for Guidance on Preparing to Receive Communion

a.   How should we prepare our hearts to receive Holy Communion?

b.   Do you ask God to teach you His way in all things?

## 7. Searching Our Own Conscience, and Resolving to Change for the Better

a.   How should a priest receive the sacrament?

b.   What is the most worthy of all offerings?

## 8. Christ's Sacrifice on the Cross, and Offering Ourselves

a.   How should we offer ourselves to God?

b.   What does God require of you?

c. Why do so few become inwardly free and enlightened?

d. What must we do if we desire to be the Lord's disciples?

## 9. Offering Ourselves and All That We Have to God and Praying for Everyone

a. What can we do for all our sins but humbly confess and lament them and unceasingly implore God's mercy?

b. What should we offer to God?

## 10. Do Not Lightly Abstain From Communion

a. Why do some people suffer from the deceptions of Satan while they are preparing for Holy Communion?

b. What good is it to delay confessing your sins for a long time or to defer Holy Communion?

c. What negative results take place when one defers Holy Communion?

d. What must you do if spiritual laziness has taken hold of you?

## 11. Necessity of the Blood of Christ and the Holy Scriptures

a. How serious is your devotion to Christ?

b. What two things are especially necessary in life? What is their spiritual application?

## 12. Those Who Are About to Receive Communion Should Prepare With Great Care

a. What is the best preparation for obtaining greater grace?

b. What should you do after receiving Holy Communion?

### 13. Seek Union With Christ With Your Whole Heart

    a.   How do we obtain the grace to find the Lord?

    b.   What should the whole desire of our hearts be?

### 14. Desire of the Devout to Receive Christ

    a.   Do you experience the Lord in the breaking of bread?

    b.   What is God's mercy able to grant to us?

### 15. Grace of Devotion Obtained by the Humility of Denying Ourselves

    a.   What happens when we give ourselves totally to God and do not seek anything for our own pleasure or will?

    b.   Into what kind of vessel does the Lord pour His blessing?

    c.   In what way are you able to partake of the grace of divine union?

### 16. Make Our Needs Known to Christ and Seek His Grace

    a.   In what ways does the Lord enable us to be made one spirit with Him?

    b.   What does God's love do for our hearts and our understanding?

### 17. Fervent Love and Strong Desire to Receive Christ

    a.   What can we learn from the example of John the Baptist?

    b.   What can we learn from the example of the Virgin Mary?

### 18. Do Not Be a Curious Searcher Into This Sacrament, but Be a Humble Follower of Christ and Receive It With Faith

    a.   Why have many lost devotion?

b.  In what way do we receive the light of knowledge to the degree that is profitable and necessary for us?

c.  What is one thing that causes us to be deceived?

d.  What two qualities take the lead and work in hidden ways as a result of receiving the sacrament of Holy Communion?

e.  When is the last time you received communion?

# INDEX

Index listings are by Book.chapter.section—for example, Adversity 1.11.3 is found in Book 1, chapter 11, section 3. If a word is found in the notes, the word *note* appears after the last number—for example, Tonsure 1.17.2.note.

## A

Abstinences 1.18.2

Adversities 1.13.2, 2.2.3, 2.6.1, 2.9.8, 2.11.1, 2.12.4, 2.12.7, 2.12.9-10, 2.12.14, 3.5.8, 3.12.1, 3.30.4, 3.48.3, 3.48.6, 3.57.1

Adversity 1.11.3, 1.13.8, 1.16.4, 2.1.5, 2.12.8, 3.5.3, 3.6.1, 3.7.3, 3.12.1, 3.19.3-4, 3.25.3, 3.30.6, 4.7.2

Affection(s) 3.3.1, 3.4.1, 3.4.4, 3.5.2, 3.5.5, 3.6.2, 3.9.1, 3.24.2, 3.26.1, 3.31.4, 3.39.2, 3.42.1, 3.49.2, 3.49.6, 3.53.2-3, 3.58.3, 3.58.6, 4.1.11, 4.3.4, 4.8.1, 4.10.2, 4.12.2, 4.14.1-2, 4.17.1-3, 4.1.11, 4.3.4, 4.8.1, 4.10.2, 4.12.2, 4.14.1-2, 4.17.1-3

Affectionate(ly) 3.5.7, 3.22.4, 4.1.6, 4.10.6, 4.14.2

Affliction(s) 1.13.8, 1.22.2, 1.23.4, 1.24.5, 2.11.8, 2.12.14, 3.25.3, 3.30.5, 3.35.3, 3.47.3,

Angel(s) 1.19.1, 1.20.6, 2.12.1, 3.10.3, 3.11.6, 3.14.1, 3.43.2, 3.57.3, 4.1.3, 4.1.5, 4.1.8, 4.2.3, 4.4.1, 4.5.1-2, 4.9.1-2, 4.10.2. note, 4.11.1-2, 4.11.5, 4.11.5.note, 4.13.3.note, 4.17.2

Apostle(s) 1.18.2, 3.22.4, 3.53.1, 4.11.4, 4.1.12.note

Appetite(s) 1.19.4, 1.22.4, 3.12.4, 3.47.4

Archangel(s) 3.21.1, 4.1.3

Ark 4.1.3-4,

Ark of God 4.1.7

Ark of the Covenant 4.1.4, 4.1.6

Ark of the Testament 4.1.7

Counsel 1.9.3, 1.13.4, 3.7.2, 3.7.4, 3.11.2, 3.30.1, 3.32.2, 3.38.2, 3.55.5, 3.57.1, 3.59.3, 4.2.4, 4.6.1, 4.10.3, 4.13.2

Courage 3.8.3, 3.14.2, 3.20.1, 3.20.3, 3.46.1, 3.46.3, 3.56.5, 4.4.3,

Courageous(ly) 1.11.4, 1.21.2, 2.3.2, 2.4.3, 2.12.10, 3.5.2-3, 3.5.7, 3.6.1, 3.6.3, 3.11.3, 3.19.4, 3.25.3, 3.30.2, 3.31.5, 3.35.1, 3.47.2, 3.49.4, 3.53.3, 3.56.5, 3.57.1

Covet(ed) 3.26.2, 3.27.1, 3.49.6

Covetous 1.6.1, 1.24.4, 3.32.1, 3.54.4, 4.7.2

Creature(s) 1.3.2, 1.25.9, 2.4.1, 2.5.3, 2.8.5, 2.11.4, 3.1.2, 3.5.1, 3.6.4, 3.12.5, 3.19.3, 3.21.1-2, 3.21.6, 3.23.6, 3.31.1-2, 3.34.2, 3.35.2, 3.40.5, 3.41.2, 3.42.1, 3.48.6, 3.53.3, 3.54.4, 4.1.4-5, 4.2.1, 4.9.4, 4.11.3, 4.13.3, 4.14.2, 4.17.3

Cross(es) 1.12.1, 2.6.1, 2.10.1, 2.11.1, 2.12.1.note, 2.12.1-10, 2.12.15, 3.18.1, 3.47.2, 3.56.2, 3.56.4-5, 4.2.6, 4.8.1

Curiosity 1.5.2, 1.25.2, 3.4.3, 3.58.7, 4.1.8

Curious 3.24.1, 3.32.1, 3.58.1, 4.7.2, 4.18.1, 4.18.4


# D

Daily 1.3.3, 1.11.5, 1.13.5, 1.13.8, 1.18.4, 1.19.1, 1.19.4, 1.23.2, 1.23.8, 2.12.3, 2.12.15, 3.1.1, 3.20.2, 3.37.2, 3.8.54, 4.7.1, 4.13.2

Danger(ous) 1.20.4, 1.23.2, 1.23.6, 3.7.4, 3.8.2, 3.38.2, 3.39.3, 3.59.4, 4.9.5

Dead 1.6.1, 1.11.3, 1.23.8, 2.1.8, 2.9.8, 2.12.6, 3.34.3, 3.44.1, 3.46.2

Defects 1.22.2, 3.33.2

Departed saints 4.1.8

Depressed 1.6.1, 1.11.3, 2.9.5, 2.11.1, 3.4.2, 3.7.3, 4.16.1

Desire(s) 1.1.4, 1.2.1-3, 1.3.2-3, 1.5.2, 1.6.1-2, 1.7.2, 1.8.1, 1.10.1, 1.11.2, 1.14.1-2, 1.15.3, 1.16.3, 1.18.3, 1.18.5, 1.19.4-5, 1.20.5, 1.20.7, 1.21.1-2, 1.22.1-2, 1.22.4, 1.23.4-5, 1.24.3,

### E

Frail(ty) 1.2.4, 1.4.1, 1.22.5-6, 2.1.3, 2.7.1, 3.20.2, 3.45.3, 3.45.6, 3.46.4

Francis, St. 3.50.8

Friend(s) 1.7.2, 1.14.2, 1.18.1, 1.18.3-4, 1.20.5-6, 1.21.3, 1.23.5, 1.23.8, 2.1.5, 2.3.3, 2.7.1, 2.8.3-4, 2.9.2, 2.9.6, 2.12.10, 3.22.4, 3.42.1, 3.45.2, 3.50.4, 3.53.1, 3.54.6, 3.59.3, 4.1.4, 4.3.4, 4.9.5, 4.13.1, 4.17.3

Friendship 2.1.1, 3.24.2, 3.37.2, 3.42.1, 3.58.6

# G

Glory 1.3.6, 1.7.2, 1.15.3, 1.19.7, 2.1.1, 2.2.2, 2.4.1, 2.6.1-2, 2.7.2, 2.8.5, 2.10.4, 2.12.2, 2.12.6, 2.12.10, 2.12.13, 3.3.3, 3.4.2, 3.5.1, 3.7.4, 3.9.2-3, 3.10.5, 3.14.3-4, 3.21.1, 3.21.4, 3.21.6, 3.22.2, 3.22.4-5, 3.26.3, 3.28.2, 3.35.2-3, 3.40.4-6, 3.41.2, 3.48.3, 3.49.1, 3.49.6-7, 3.51.2, 3.54.2, 3.56.5, 3.57.3, 3.58.3, 3.58.8, 3.59.4, 4.1.2, 4.3.1, 4.4.5, 4.10.6, 4.11.2.note, 4.11.2-3, 4.11.6, 4.15.4, 4.18.1, 4.18.1.note

Good work(s) 1.7.3, 1.15.1, 1.24.6, 1.25.2, 2.9.1.note, 3.4.2, 3.55.6

Gospel(s) 1.1.2, 2.8.1.note

Grace 1.1.3, 1.7.1, 1.11.4, 1.13.8, 1.14.3, 1.17.1, 1.18.3-4, 1.19.2, 1.20.3, 1.22.6, 1.25.3, 1.25.10, 2.2.2, 2.3.2, 2.5.1, 2.8.5, 2.9.1, 2.9.5-7, 2.10.2-3, 2.10.5, 2.12.8, 3.3.5-6, 3.6.2, 3.6.5, 3.7.1-3, 3.8.1, 3.9.2-3, 3.10.5, 3.13.1, 3.15.3, 3.18.2, 3.19.4, 3.21.5, 3.23.2, 3.23.5, 3.26.4, 3.27.4, 3.31.1-2, 3.31.5, 3.34.1, 3.37.1-2, 3.38.2, 3.40.1, 3.40.3-4, 3.42.1, 3.45.5-6, 3.46.4, 3.49.1, 3.49.7, 3.50.7, 3.53.1, 3.54.1-8, 3.55.1-6, 3.56.3, 3.57.2, 3.58.3, 3.59.4, 4.1.7, 4.1.9-10, 4.1.12, 4.3.2-4, 4.4.2-4, 4.5.3, 4.7.1, 4.7.4, 4.8.2, 4.9.2, 4.9.5-6, 4.10.1, 4.10.3, 4.11.3, 4.11.8, 4.12.2-4, 4.13.1, 4.13.3, 4.14.3, 4.15.1-4, 4.16.2-3, 4.18.4

Greatness 2.5.3, 3.22.1, 3.34.4, 3.58.7, 3.59.4, 4.2.6, 4.17.4

# H

# Pure Gold Classics

## AN EXPANDING COLLECTION OF THE
## BEST-LOVED CHRISTIAN CLASSICS OF ALL TIME.

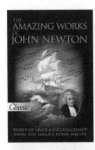

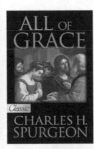
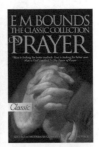

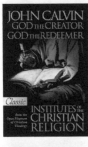

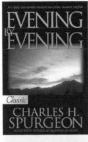

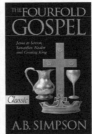

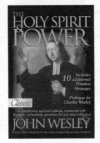

## AVAILABLE AT FINE BOOKSTORES.

### FOR MORE INFORMATION, VISIT WWW.BRIDGELOGOS.COM

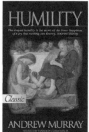

**HUMILITY**

The deepest humility is the secret of the truest happiness, of a joy that nothing can destroy, innermost blessing

*Classic*

**ANDREW MURRAY**

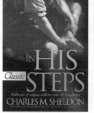

*Classic*

**IN HIS STEPS**

Millions of copies sold in over 45 countries

**CHARLES M. SHELDON**

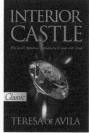

**INTERIOR CASTLE**

The Soul's Spiritual Journey to Union with God

*Classic*

**TERESA OF AVILA**

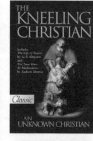

THE **KNEELING CHRISTIAN**

Includes
The Life of Prayer
by A. B. Simpson
and
The True Vine:
31 Meditations
by Andrew Murray

*Classic*

AN **UNKNOWN CHRISTIAN**

**MADAME JEANNE GUYON**

*Classic*

EXPERIENCING UNION WITH GOD THROUGH INNER PRAYER
& THE WAY AND RESULTS OF UNION WITH GOD

**MORNING BY MORNING**

365 daily devotionals revised into plain, modern English

*Classic*

**CHARLES H. SPURGEON**

EDITED BY HAROLD J. CHADWICK

THE **OVERCOMING LIFE**

*Classic*

**D.L. MOODY**

THE **PILGRIM'S PROGRESS**

IN MODERN ENGLISH

John Bunyan's immortal classic is masterfully revised for the 21st century reader

*Classic*

**JOHN BUNYAN**

REVISED AND UPDATED BY L. EDWARD HAZELBAKER

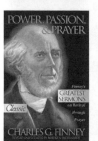

**POWER, PASSION, & PRAYER**

Finney's GREATEST SERMONS on Revival through Prayer

*Classic*

**CHARLES G. FINNEY**

REVISED AND UPDATED BY ROBERT A. INGERSAKER

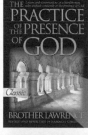

THE **PRACTICE OF THE PRESENCE OF GOD**

Letters and conversations of a humble man who walked constantly in the presence of God

*Classic*

**BROTHER LAWRENCE**

REVISED AND REWRITTEN BY HAROLD J. CHADWICK

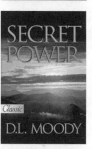

**SECRET POWER**

*Classic*

**D.L. MOODY**

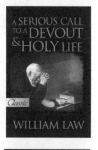

A SERIOUS CALL TO A **DEVOUT & HOLY LIFE**

*Classic*

**WILLIAM LAW**

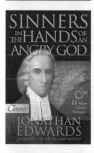

**SINNERS IN THE HANDS OF AN ANGRY GOD**

& 11 More Classic Messages

*Classic*

**JONATHAN EDWARDS**

REVISED AND UPDATED BY MARK ROGSTED

THE **SOVEREIGNTY OF GOD**

*Classic*

**A.W. PINK**

**TABLE TALK**

**MARTIN LUTHER**

*Classic*

The culmination of all that is Martin Luther revealed in conversations with his colleagues and students

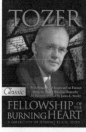

**TOZER**

*Classic*

**FELLOWSHIP OF THE BURNING HEART**

A COLLECTION OF SERMONS BY A.W. TOZER

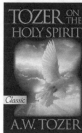

**TOZER ON THE HOLY SPIRIT**

*Classic*

**A.W. TOZER**

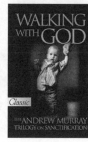

**WALKING WITH GOD**

*Classic*

THE ANDREW MURRAY TRILOGY ON SANCTIFICATION

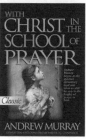

WITH **CHRIST IN THE SCHOOL OF PRAYER**

Andrew Murray begins at the spiritual elementary level and what we don't be able to see in the English of Today

*Classic*

**ANDREW MURRAY**

**WILLIAM WILBERFORCE**

*Classic*

**GREATEST WORKS**

INCLUDES HIS MOST WIDELY PRACTICAL BOOK OF CHRISTIANITY